GREECE & THE GREEK ISLANDS

TOP SIGHTS, AUTHENTIC EXPERIENCES

Simon Richmond, Kate Armstrong, Stuart Butler,
Peter Dragicevich, Anna Kaminski, Hugh McNaughtan,
Kate Morgan, Kevin Raub, Andy Symington, Greg Ward

Contents

Welcome to Greece

Hedonists rejoice! Greece is ancient sun-bleached ruins piercing blue skies, the balmy seas lapping an endless coastline and scatterings of idyllic islands, as well as a culture alive with passionate music, wonderful cuisine and thrill-seeking activities.

Western culture's roots are in Greece. Step into the ring where Olympians first competed. Climb ancient stone steps to Meteora's monasteries, perched atop towering rocks. Contemplate the oracle's insights from the grandeur of Delphi, take in a starlit drama at an ancient outdoor theatre and be stunned by massive marble sculptures dredged up from the Aegean. But then you'll encounter bold modern art, the melancholic throb of *rembetika* (blues songs) and artisans creating new work from traditional techniques.

Greece has endless cultural pursuits and a calendar bursting with festivals, holidays and exhibits. Unique regional produce and cooking styles make travelling here a culinary adventure. Socialising in cafes and restaurants is a way of life.

Days melt from one to the next under wide open skies and a sea speckled with islands fringed with the white-sand, pine-tree shade beaches of your dreams. Wander along cobbled Byzantine footpaths, hike up volcanoes, watch for dolphins and sea turtles, and cycle through lush forests. Meander through olive groves, idyllic villages and petrified forests. Thrill seekers will discover world-class kitesurfing, wreck diving, and rock-climbing locations with dizzying views. Or simply hop on a boat and set sail into the glittering blue beyond.

> *Greece has endless cultural pursuits and a calendar bursting with festivals*

Hora, Mykonos (p230)
GATSI/GETTY IMAGES ©

Pelican, Hora (p230), Mykonos
HELMUT CORNELI / ALAMY STOCK PHOTO ©

Plan Your Trip
Greece's Top 12

IMAGIN.GR PHOTOGRAPHY / SHUTTERSTOCK ©

Athens

The quintessential landmark of Western civilisation

Explore the regal, elegant Acropolis early in the morning or soak up the view from a restaurant terrace; no matter how you experience it, you will be mesmerised by this ancient site's beauty, history and sheer size. The Parthenon (pictured above) is the star attraction, but don't overlook the exquisite Temple of Athena Nike and the Theatre of Dionysos (pictured right). Nearby, the state-of-the-art Acropolis Museum provides a close-up look at the surviving treasures of the site.

1

Crete

In the land of the mighty Minoans

Crete packs the best of Greece into a manageable island scale.
You'll find the magnificent Bronze Age ruins of Knossos (pictured
above) where the Minoans ruled over 4000 years ago. There are
lovely beaches and the dramatic Samaria Gorge (pictured top),
home to soaring birds of prey and a dazzling array of wildflowers in
spring. And there's incredible food and wine, including some of the
world's best virgin olive oil.

VOYAGERIX / SHUTTERSTOCK ©

Meteora

Spectacular stone forest crowned with monasteries

Soaring pillars of rock jut heavenward, a handful complete with monasteries perched on their summits. Built as early as the 14th century, these were home to hermit monks fleeing persecution. The rope ladders that once enabled the monks to reach the top have long been replaced by steps carved into the rock, and six of the 24 monasteries remain open to resident monks, religious pilgrims, rock climbers and tourists alike.

Rhodes

Rhodes' Old Town is a living museum

Wander along the top of the city's walls, meander down twisting, cobbled alleyways with soaring archways and lively squares. In these hidden corners your imagination will take off with flights of medieval fancy. Explore the ancient Knights' Quarter, the old Jewish Quarter or the Hora (Turkish Quarter). Hear traditional live music in tiny tavernas or dine on fresh seafood at atmospheric outdoor restaurants.

Peloponnese

A peninsula well worth exploring

From the evocative ruins of Ancient Olympia to charming Nafplio (pictured right), first capital of Greece after Independence, the Peloponnese is a region of Greece packed with wonderful attractions. The atmosphere at the site of the first Olympics is almost mythical. Nafplio is a good base from which you can strike out for the barren mountain landscape of the Lakonian Mani, broken only by imposing stone towers standing sentinel over the region.

ELOREKO / SHUTTERSTOCK ©

Delphi

Where ancient prophecies were uttered

Early morning is a magical time at Delphi, as the sun's rays pour over the Sanctuary of Athena Pronea. As you gaze out over the Gulf of Corinth, it is easy to understand why the ancient Greeks chose this as the centre of their world. Here stood the Sanctuary of Apollo, home to the renowned oracle. Today, only three columns remain of the magnificent sanctuary, but that's enough to let your imagination soar.

Thessaloniki

Greece's second city has it all going on

Explore the old quarter, a neighbourhood full of colourful, winding streets marked by white-plastered houses, lazy cats and Byzantine churches. Taste-test your way through the city's *zaharoplasteia* (patisseries) for Ottoman-inspired sweets. Drink up with throngs of students at stylish bars and clubs. Tour the galleries of one of the country's most artistically fertile locations and save time for the first-rate museums.

Corfu

A remarkable mix of architecture styles

The story of Corfu is written across the handsome facades of its main town's buildings. Stroll past Byzantine fortresses, neoclassical 19th-century British buildings, Parisian-style arcades, Orthodox church towers and the narrow, sun-dappled streets of the Venetian Old Town. Beyond the town, Corfu is lush green mountains, rolling countryside and dramatic coastlines. And if the architecture and scenery aren't enough, come to enjoy the Italian-influenced food.

9

Kefallonia Island

Paradise for lovers of the great outdoors

Paddle kayaks between white-sand beaches lapped by gentle seas that glow with an unnatural luminosity; explore pretty villages surrounded by vineyards and olive groves; scuba-dive in crystal clear waters blushing with fish and hike up mountains that spiral high into the sky. Kayaking, diving, hiking, sailing, horse-riding. You name it and Kefallonia does it. And best of all it remains remarkably unflustered by tourism.

Karpathos Island

Adrenaline activities, mountaintop villages

One of the most beautiful islands of the Dodecanese, Karpathos offers up wild mountains, blue coves and picturesque villages, such as Olymbos where the women still wear traditional costumes. The island's rugged topography makes it an ideal destination for trekking and mountain climbing while beautiful beaches such as Apella are fine places to try out surfing and windsurfing or simply kick back and relax.

Mykonos & Delos

Party island, plus World Heritage Site

Mykonos is all about hedonism. Mykonos Town (aka Hora) is a gorgeous whitewashed Cycladic maze of cafes, bars and boutiques, the indulgent follow-on from an indolent day lounging on the packed main beaches or by a hip hotel pool. Make sure you spend a day exploring the Unesco World Heritage Site of Delos, mythical birthplace of twins Apollo and Artemis and one of the most important archaeological sites in Greece.

Santorini (Thira)

Cocktail bars over the caldera

The volcanic island's main villages of Fira and Oia (pictured above) are a snow-drift of white Cycladic houses that line the cliff tops and spill like icy cornices down the terraced rock. Come sunset, crowds break into applause as the sun disappears below the horizon. Atmospheric Akrotiri lets you explore the ruins of an ancient Minoan city while across the island are superb restaurants and wineries.

Plan Your Trip
Need to Know

When to Go

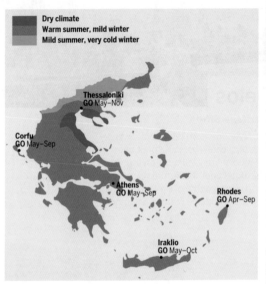

Dry climate
Warm summer, mild winter
Mild summer, very cold winter

Thessaloniki
GO May–Nov

Corfu
GO May–Sep

Athens
GO May–Sep

Rhodes
GO Apr–Sep

Iraklio
GO May–Oct

High Season (Jun–Aug)

○ Sights, tours and transport are running full tilt.

○ Accommodation prices can double.

○ Both crowds and temperatures soar.

Shoulder (Apr & May, Sep & Oct)

○ Accommodation prices can drop by up to 20%.

○ Temperatures are not as blazing.

○ Internal flights and island ferries have reduced schedules.

Low Season (Nov–Mar)

○ Many hotels, sights and restaurants shut down, especially on the islands.

○ Accommodation rates can drop by as much as 50%.

○ Ferry schedules are skeletal.

Currency

euro (€)

Language

Greek

Visas

Generally not required for stays of up to 90 days; however, travellers from some nations may require a visa, so double-check with the Greek embassy.

Money

Debit and credit cards are accepted in cities, but elsewhere it's handy to have cash. Most towns have ATMs, but they may be out of order.

Mobile Phones

Local SIM cards can be used in unlocked phones. Most other phones can be set to roaming. US and Canadian phones need to have a dual- or tri-band system.

Time

Eastern European Time (GMT/UTC plus two hours)

Daily Costs

Budget: Less than €100

- Dorm bed and domatio (Greek B&B): less than €60

- Meal at markets and street stalls: less than €15

Midrange: €100–180

- Double room in midrange hotel: €60–150

- Hearty meal at a local taverna: around €20

- Entrance fee for most sights: less than €15

Top End: More than €180

- Double room in top hotel: from €150

- Excellent dining, some accompanied by Michelin stars: €60–100

- Activity such as diving certification: around €400

- Cocktail: around €12

Useful Websites

Ekathimerini.com (www.ekathimerini.com) English-language edition of daily Greek newspaper *Kathimerini*.

EOT (Greek National Tourist Organisation; www.visitgreece.gr) Concise tourist information.

Greeka (www.greeka.com) Plenty of planning advice, photos and booking services.

Greek Travel Pages (www.gtp.gr) Access to ferry schedules and accommodation.

Lonely Planet (www.lonelyplanet.com/greece) Destination information, hotel bookings, traveller forum and more.

Odysseas (http://odysseus.culture.gr) Portal for info on ancient sites and for booking tickets.

Opening Hours

Use the following as a general guide.

Banks 8.30am to 2.30pm Monday to Thursday, 8am to 2pm Friday

Restaurants 11am to 11pm

Cafes 10am to midnight

Bars 8pm to late

Shops 8am to 2pm Monday, Wednesday and Saturday, 8am to 2pm and 5pm to 9pm Tuesday, Thursday and Friday

Arriving in Greece

Eleftherios Venizelos International Airport (Athens) Express buses (€6, one hour) operate 24 hours between the airport, city centre and Piraeus. Half-hourly metro trains (€10, 50 minutes) run between the city centre and the airport from 5.30am to 11.30pm. Taxis to the city centre cost €38 (€50 at night) and take about 45 minutes.

Nikos Kazantzakis International Airport (Iraklio, Crete) Buses run to the city centre from 6am to midnight (€1.20, every 15 minutes). Taxis to the city centre cost €15.

Getting Around

Air Domestic flights are abundant and significantly cut down travel time. In high season, flights fill up fast so book ahead.

Boat Ferries link the islands to each other and the mainland, including catamarans, well-equipped modern ferries and overnight boats with cabins. Schedules change annually and can be announced as late as May. In high season it's smart to book ahead.

Bus Generally air-conditioned, frequent, and as efficient as traffic allows; good for travel between major cities.

Car & Motorcycle Rentals are reasonably priced and found on all but the tiniest islands. They give you the freedom to explore the islands, but you'll need a good dose of road smarts; some of the islands are becoming over-run with hire vehicles.

For more on **getting around**, see p306 ➡

Plan Your Trip
Hotspots For...

Ancient History

Remnants of ancient Greek civilisation are littered across the country. They range from Athens' Parthenon to the ruins of Ancient Akrotiri on Santorini.

VOLKOVA NATALIA / SHUTTERSTOCK ©

Athens
The Greek capital's top draw is its ancient ruins and blockbuster museums dedicated to the same period.

Ancient Agora
Beautifully preserved ruins in the heart of the city (p46).

Olympia
The flame is still lit here in the Peloponnese town that is the birthplace of the Olympic Games.

Ancient Olympia
World Heritage–listed sanctuary to sporting glory (p132).

Crete
Crete's history spans millennia. Check out Heraklion Archaeological Museum before heading to Knossos.

Knossos
Crete's marquee Minoan site (p176).

Great Outdoors

For lovers of nature and outdoor activities, Greece couldn't be more perfect. There are mountains to climb and hike over and turquoise seas to swim in and sail across.

GEORGIOS TSICHLIS / ALAMY STOCK PHOTO ©

Crete
From pink beaches and magnificent rock gorges to snowy peaks, Crete's range of landscapes is thrilling.

Samaria Gorge
Hikers flock to this spectacular cleft in the earth (p186).

Santorini
Beautiful beaches of red-and-black volcanic sand are easily reached and surprisingly quiet.

Red (Kokkini) Beach
Backed by rust-and-fire coloured cliffs (p211).

Kefallonia
An adventure-seekers' paradise, with lofty mountains, stalagmite-filled caves and water sports.

Mt Ainos
Astounding views from its upper reaches (p171).

Museums

Greece's top museums showcase the ancient world's history and cultural achievements, as well as beautiful modern works of art and craft.

FAZON1 / GETTY IMAGES ©

Athens
The capital is stacked with important museums covering topics from Cycladic to contemporary art.

Acropolis Museum
Sculptures and other finds from the Acropolis (p44).

Delphi
Pleasant village close by the wonderful archaeological site that was centre of the Ancient Greek world.

Archaeological Museum
Mind-blowing galleries of ancient art (p109).

Corfu Town
The neoclassical Palace of St Michael & St George houses one of Greece's top museums.

Corfu Museum of Asian Art
Home to stunning artefacts from across Asia (p150).

Food & Drink

For memorable meals seek out tavernas that produce their own vegetables, wine and oil, where recipes are passed down through generations.

ANITA ISALSKA / LONELY PLANET ©

Thessaloniki
Welcome to Greece's gastronomic capital. There are excellent restaurants all across town.

Modiano Market
Shop for Thessaloniki's culinary bounty (p98).

Crete
Where 'locavore' is not a trend but a way of life. The Cretan diet is among the healthiest in the world.

Iraklio Wine Country
Pair your meal with excellent local wines.

Rhodes
Home to some of the finest restaurants in the Dodecanese, including several irresistible village tavernas.

Marco Polo Cafe
A romantic meal in a fragrant garden courtyard (p260).

Plan Your Trip
Essential Greece

Activities

Greece is graced with blue water, warm winds, undersea life, dramatic cliff faces, flourishing forests and ancient walkways – making it perfect terrain for outdoor activities. If you're a novice kitesurfer or an avid cyclist, if you want to hike deep gorges or ski from lofty heights, opportunities abound.

You'll find diving schools on the islands of Corfu, Mykonos, Rhodes, Santorini and Crete, as well as near Athens. Windsurfing is very popular and you'll find sailboards for hire almost everywhere.

Shopping

Traditional artisans are present in many towns and villages across the country, selling pottery, leather ware, olive-wood carvings, paintings and jewellery. Many use traditional methods to make modern designs. In larger cities, shopping is similar to other European capitals with plenty of international name-brand stores. Even so, traditional farmers markets are a regular feature of towns big and small across the country.

Eating

Whether you're eating seafood at a seaside table or sampling contemporary Greek cuisine under the floodlit Acropolis, dining out in Greece is never just about what you eat; it's about the whole sensory experience. Like many Europeans, the Greeks dine late, with some restaurants not opening for dinner until after 7pm. You will only need reservations in the most popular places and these can usually be made a day in advance.

Key types of places to eat include informal tavernas often specialising in seafood, chargrilled meat or traditional home-style baked dishes; the more formal *estiatorio* serving similar fare to tavernas or international cuisine; and *mezedhopoleio* serving mezedhes (small plates) – an *ouzerie* is similar but serves a round of ouzo with a round of mezedhes.

KARL ALLEN LUGMAYER / SHUTTERSTOCK ©

Drinking & Nightlife

Many venues are equally excellent in the early morning and late at night – so you just might be tempted to while away a whole day in one. *Kafeneio* are one of Greece's oldest traditions, serving coffee, spirits and little else. Older folks sit late into the night at coffee houses with a shot or two of ouzo while younger generations linger at sidewalk cafes sipping cocktails, and fill trendy clubs. Drinking is social in Greece and public drunkenness isn't cool. Heavily touristed towns and cities have bars with drink specials but they mostly draw foreigners.

Entertainment

The music scene is vibrant with local bands playing traditional *rembetika* (blues songs) or spirited numbers on the bouzouki. In summer, you can often catch a play at one

★ Best Restaurants

Marco Polo Cafe (p260)

Peskesi (p192)

Karamanlidika tou Fani (p69)

Lauda (p219)

Mourgá (p100)

of the ancient Greek theatres in Athens or on the Peloponnese, and a calendar over-flowing with festivals and holidays means there's almost always something entertaining going on.

Note that Athens' music scene depends largely on the season: many big halls and theatres close or scale back programming in the summer. Bonus: Greeks consider every musical event an opportunity for a singalong, which can make the most formal concert venue feel friendly (even if you don't know the words).

From left: Grilled sardines, Thessaloniki (p81); Street musicians, Athens (p35)

Plan Your Trip
Month by Month

VERVERIDIS VASILIS / SHUTTERSTOCK ©

January

Most islands go into hibernation during winter. However, there are local religious festivals to enjoy.

🎊 Feast of Agios Vasilios (St Basil)

The first day of January sees a busy church ceremony followed by gifts, singing, dancing and feasting. The *vasilopita* (golden glazed cake for New Year's Eve) is cut; if you're fortunate enough to get the slice containing a coin, you'll supposedly have a lucky year.

🎊 Epiphany (Blessing of the Waters)

The day of Christ's baptism by St John is celebrated throughout Greece on 6 January. Seas, lakes and rivers are all blessed, with the largest ceremony held at Piraeus.

February

If you like a party and can time your visit with Carnival, which starts three weeks before Lent, February is a rewarding time to visit.

🎊 Carnival Season

Minor events from as early as late February lead to a wild weekend of costume parades, floats, feasting and traditional dancing.

March

The islands are sleepy but the weather is warming up, making March a relaxed time to visit.

🎊 Independence Day

The anniversary of the hoisting of the Greek flag by independence supporters at Moni Agias Lavras is celebrated with parades and dancing on 25 March. This

Above: Carnival parade

PACIFIC PRESS AGENCY / ALAMY STOCK PHOTO ©

act of revolt marked the start of the War of Independence.

April

A great month to visit. Reserve accommodation well in advance for Easter weekend. Some businesses shut up shop for the week.

✤ Orthodox Easter

Communities commemorate Jesus' crucifixion with candlelight processions on Good Friday and celebrate his resurrection at midnight on Easter Saturday. Feasting follows on Easter Sunday.

✤ Festival of Agios Georgios (St George)

The feast day of Greece's patron saint is celebrated on 23 April, but if this falls during Lent then it moves to the first Tuesday following Easter. Expect dancing, feasting and a general party atmosphere.

★ Best Festivals

Carnival, February

Orthodox Easter, April or May

Athens & Epidaurus Festival, June to August

August Moon Festival, August

Thessaloniki International Film Festival, November

May

This month is ideal for hiking. Temperatures are relatively mild and wildflowers create a huge splash of colour.

✤ May Day

The first of May is marked by a mass exodus from towns for picnics in the country. Wildflowers are gathered and made into wreaths to decorate houses. It's a day associated with workers' rights, so recent

Above: Orthodox Easter procession, Athens (p35)

years have also seen mass walkouts and strikes.

June

Top national and international performers fill atmospheric stages with dance, music and drama.

☆ Athens & Epidaurus Festival

The most prominent Greek summer festival (p41) features local and international music, dance and drama at the ancient Odeon of Herodes Atticus on the slopes of the Acropolis in Athens and the world-famous Theatre of Epidavros in the Peloponnese. Events run from June to August.

☆ Delphi Festival

With events scheduled for both June and August this cultural festival includes musical and theatrical events in a variety of spaces in and around Delphi and Dorida. See www.delphifestival.gr for details.

August

It's very hot so do a little bit less and relax a little more fully. If you're travelling mid-month, reserve well ahead as Greeks take to the roads and boats in large numbers.

☆ August Moon Festival

Under the year's brightest moon, historical venues in Athens open with free moonlit performances. Watch theatre, dance and music at venues such as the Acropolis or Roman Agora. The festival is also celebrated at other towns and sites around Greece; check locally for details.

☆ Feast of the Dormition

Also called Assumption and celebrated with family reunions on 15 August; the whole population is seemingly on the move on either side of the big day.

☆ XLSIOR

One of the LGBT+ pride season's biggest party events is this week-long festival held on Mykonos at the end of the month. See https://xlsiorfestival.com for the full line-up.

September

The sun is high though less and less blazing, especially on the islands. The crowds begin to thin and some ferry schedules begin to decline mid-month.

☆ Gennisis Tis Panagias

The birthday of the Virgin Mary is celebrated throughout the country on 8 September with religious services and feasting.

October

While most of the islands start to quieten down, the sunny weather often holds in October. City life continues apace.

☆ Ohi Day

A simple 'no' (*ohi* in Greek) was Prime Minister Metaxas' famous response when Mussolini demanded free passage through Greece for his troops on 28 October 1940. The date is now a major national holiday with remembrance services, parades, feasting and dance.

November

Autumn sees temperatures drop. Olive-picking is in full swing in places such as Crete and feta production picks up.

☆ Thessaloniki International Film Festival

Around 150 films are crammed into 11 days of screenings (p95) around the city in mid-November, alongside concerts, exhibitions, talks and theatrical performances.

December

The islands may be quiet but Athens and Thessaloniki are still in full swing. Expect cooler temperatures and a chilly sea.

☆ Christmas

Celebrated on 25 December and traditionally marking the end of a 40-day fast. Expect to see Christmas trees, children carolling and fishing boats decorated with lights. Families gather for a Christmas Day feast including a roasted hog and honey cookies.

Plan Your Trip
Get Inspired

Read

Something Will Happen, You'll See (Christos Ikonomou; 2016) Moving short stories of characters caught in the financial crisis.

Zorba the Greek (Nikos Kazantzakis; 1946) A spiritual bible to many; one man's unquenchable lust for life.

Falling for Icarus: A Journey among the Cretans (Rory MacLean; 2004) A travel writer builds a plane in Icarus.

Greek to Me (Mary Norris; 2019) Passionate Hellenophile and *New Yorker* magazine copy editor on her love of the Greek language and travels in the country.

Watch

Zorba the Greek (1964) British-Greek comedy drama nominated for seven Academy Awards.

Shirley Valentine (1989) Comedy romance set on Mykonos.

Captain Corelli's Mandolin (2001) Lavish retelling of Louis de Bernières' novel, set on Kefallonia during WWII.

Before Midnight (2013) Third in a trilogy following a French-American couple, filmed on the Peloponnese.

The Two Faces of January (2014) Thriller set in Athens and other parts of Greece in the 1960s.

Listen

Rembetika: Songs of the Greek Underground 1925–1947 Classic songs still performed in the country's bars and clubs.

Zorba's Dance (Mikis Theodorakis; 1964) Classic instrumental made famous in the film *Zorba the Greek*, for which Theodorakis wrote the soundtrack.

Tragoudia Apo Ta Ellinika Nisia (Nana Mouskouri & Friends; 2011) The celebrated Greek singer offers contemporary interpretations of classic Greek island songs.

Spasmena Kommatia Tis Kardias (Antonis Remos; 2016) Platinum-selling album by one of Greece's most popular singers.

Above: *Zorba the Greek* (1964)

Plan Your Trip
Five-Day Itineraries

Athens to Thessaloniki

The route between the capital and Greece's vibrant second city is one that is rich in ancient history, tradition-al culture and contemporary aspects of life. You'll pass through spectacular mountainous landscapes and end on Thessaloniki's revamped Waterfront.

Thessaloniki (p81) The White Tower anchors a waterfront that's packed with cocktail bars. There's also Roman remains and a superb gourmet scene.

Meteora (p117) Kalambaka is the gateway to World Heritage–listed Meteora where old monasteries perch atop towering rocks. 🚌 2½ hrs to Thessaloniki

Delphi (p105) At a spectacular cliffside location is the former home of the mysterious Delphic oracle. 🚌 5 hrs to Kalambaka

Athens (p35) Climb the Acropolis, dip into many museums and art galleries, enjoy the nightlife. 🚌 2½ hrs to Delphi

Iraklio (p188) Marvel at the treasures in Heraklion Archaeological Museum, wander the backstreets and the revitalised waterfront of Crete's capital. 🚌 15 mins to Knossos

Hania (p195) Soak up the historical charm of the Venetian harbour, be dazzled by the exhibits in the Hania Archaeological Museum. 🚌 1 hr to Omalos

Exploring Crete

Bookended by two of Crete's great cities, this route is a roller-coaster ride through the natural wonders of mountain and sea and the best of the island's historical treasures as well as its award-winning wine estates.

Samaria Gorge (p186) Hike through one of Europe's longest gorges, ending in the coastal village of Agia Roumeli.

Knossos (p176) Get up early to tour the captivating Minoan ruins of Knossos, spend time sampling vintages in Iraklio Wine Country. 🚌 3 hrs to Hania

FROM LEFT: JEKATARINKA / SHUTTERSTOCK ©; TM_ZML / SHUTTERSTOCK ©

Plan Your Trip
10-Day Itinerary

Corfu to Athens

Start this western Greece itinerary by hopping between the Ionian islands of Corfu and Kefallonia, both great destinations to experience nature and outdoor activities. Then enjoy encounters with ancient history, past sporting glory and varied architecture in key locations around the Peloponnese.

1 Corfu (p145) Spend a couple of days wandering through delightful Corfu Old Town. Try windsurfing, or go cycling in the island's mountainous interior. ✈ 30 mins to Kefallonia

Athens (p35) End your journey in Athens where you can combine visiting iconic ancient sites with indulging in the best of contemporary Greek life.

Kefallonia (p159) Overnight in the picturesque village of Fiskardo. Kayak to isolated golden beaches, sample the island's well-regarded wine. ⚓🚌 3 hrs to Olympia

Ancient Olympia (p132) Tour the evocative ruins of Ancient Olympia; stand in the stadium that hosted the first Olympic Games. 🚌 3 to 4 hrs to Napflio

Napflio (p139) Explore graceful Napflio with its mansions, museums and lively port. Drive around the Lakonian Mani. 🚌 2½ hrs to Athens

Plan Your Trip
Two-Week Itinerary

Greece's Greatest Hits

While it may be very tempting to kick back on a beach for two weeks, Greece's wealth of attractions can also make for an adventurous and action-packed trip that scales cultural highs, takes in contemporary cities *and* samples laid-back island life.

Athens (p35) Visit grand ancient sites and museums. Dive into the markets, contemporary-art scene and award-winning restaurants. ⚓ 5 hrs to Mykonos

Mykonos (p223) Best for fashionable bars and crowd-pleasing beaches. Day-trip to the sacred island of Delos for its fascinating ancient ruins. ⚓ 2 to 3½ hrs to Santorini

Rhodes (p247) Explore Rhodes Town's atmospheric, walled Old Town and enjoy the view from the ancient Acropolis in Lindos. ⚓ 3¾ hrs to Karpathos

Santorini (p203) Watch sunset from the dramatic cliffs of its volcanic caldera. Explore to find ancient ruins and different coloured sand beaches. ⚓ 1¾ hrs to Iraklio

Karpathos (p237) Drive up into the island's craggy mountains to find the time-forgotten village of Olympos.

Hania (p195) Take in the charming harbour and labyrinth of backstreets; trek through the famous Samaria Gorge. ✈ 1 hr to Rhodes

Iraklio (p188) Acclimatise to Crete in its vibrant capital. Explore the nearby magnificent Minoan ruins of Knossos. 🚌 3 hrs to Hania

Plan Your Trip
Family Travel

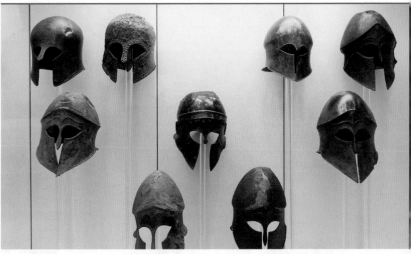

MILAN GONDA / ALAMY STOCK PHOTO ©

Children will be welcomed wherever you go in Greece. Locals generally make a fuss over children, and if you teach your kids some Greek words, they'll feel even more appreciated.

Sights & Activities

The stories behind the objects in Greek museums can captivate a child's imagination – ancient statues hauled up from the depths of the sea or helmets worn by gladiators. Generally more popular than the museums are the many ancient sights where kids can enjoy climbing and exploring.

The beaches are an obvious family attraction. In summer, many of the larger, popular beaches have bodyboards, surfboards, snorkelling gear and windsurfing equipment for rent. Many also offer lessons or trips on boats or giant, rubber, air-filled bananas. While some beaches have steep drop-offs or strong currents, there is generally a calmer side to each island or a shallow, protected bay that locals can direct you to.

Playgrounds are common, while larger cities often have fantastic, modern play or water parks. In many cases, you can admire children's innate ability to overcome language barriers through play while you enjoy a coffee and pastry at the park's attached cafe.

Sleeping & Eating

Many hotels let small children stay for free and will squeeze an extra bed in the room. In all but the smallest hotels, travel cots can often be found, but it's always best to check in advance. Larger hotels and resorts often have package deals for families and these places are generally set up to cater to kids.

Greek cuisine is all about sharing; ordering lots of mezedhes (small dishes) lets your children try the local cuisine and find their favourites. You'll also find lots of kid-friendly options such as pizza and pasta, omelettes, chips, bread, savoury pies and yoghurt.

Tavernas are very family-friendly affairs and the owners will generally be more than

STEFKA PAVLOVA//GETTY IMAGES ©

willing to cater to your children's tastes. Ingredients such as nuts and dairy find their way into lots of dishes, so if your children suffer from any severe allergies, it's best to ask someone to write this down for you clearly in plain Greek to show restaurant staff.

★ Best for Young Explorers

Acropolis (p38)

Rhodes' medieval castles (p256)

Knossos (p176)

Safety

Greece is a safe and easy place to travel with children. Greek children are given a huge amount of freedom and can often be seen playing in village squares and playgrounds late into the night. Nevertheless, it's wise to be extra vigilant with children when travelling, and to ensure they always know where to go and who to approach for help. This is especially true on beaches or in playgrounds where it's easy for children to become disoriented. It's also prudent not to have your children use bags, clothing, towels etc with their name or personal in-

formation (such as national flags) stitched onto them; this kind of information could be used by potential predators to pretend to know you or the child.

Dangers children are far more likely to encounter are heatstroke, water-borne bugs and illness, mosquito bites, and cuts and scrapes from climbing around on ancient ruins and crumbling castles. Most islands have a clinic of some sort, although hours may be irregular so it's handy to carry a first-aid kid with basic medicine and bandages.

From left: Helmets, Olympia Archaeological Museum (p134); Beach near Thessaloniki

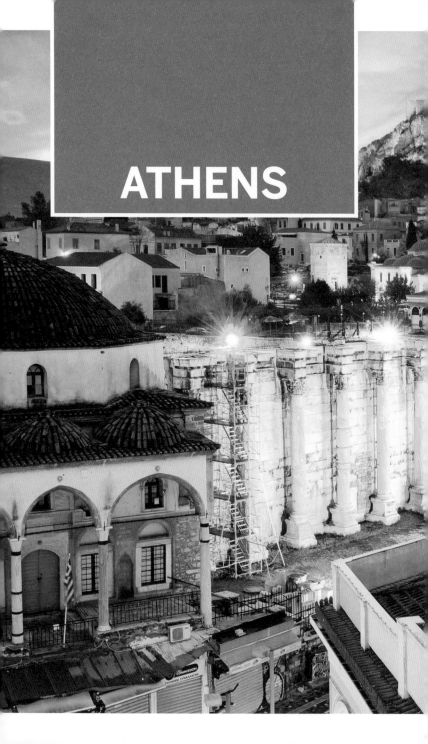

ATHENS

Athens at a Glance...

With equal measures of grunge and grace, Athens is a heady mix of ancient history and contemporary cool. Cultural and social life plays out amid, around and in ancient landmarks. The magnificent Acropolis, visible from almost every part of the city, reminds Greeks daily of their heritage and the city's many transformations. There is crackling energy in galleries, political debates and even on the walls of derelict buildings. This creates a lively urban bustle, but at the end of the day, Athenians build their own villages in the city, especially in open-air restaurants and bars where they linger for hours.

Two Days in Athens

Climb to the **Acropolis** (p38) then wind down through the **Ancient Agora** (p46). Explore Plaka, looping back to the **Acropolis Museum** (p44). On day two, watch the **changing of the guard** at Syntagma Sq before heading to the **Temple of Olympian Zeus** (p60) or the **Panathenaic Stadium** (p63). Spend the afternoon at the **National Archaeological Museum** (p48) then head to the Monastiraki area for dinner and nightlife.

Four Days in Athens

Dip into the **Benaki Museum** (p54), the **Museum of Cycladic Art** (p63) and the **Byzantine & Christian Museum** (p63) before lunch in Kolonaki. Take the *teleferik* (funicular railway) or climb **Lykavittos Hill** (p63) for panoramic views. Bar-hop around Exarhia in the evening. On day four spend the morning exploring the **Varvakios Agora** (p67) and **Kerameikos** (p56), then head in the afternoon to the **Stavros Niarchos Foundation Cultural Center** (p52).

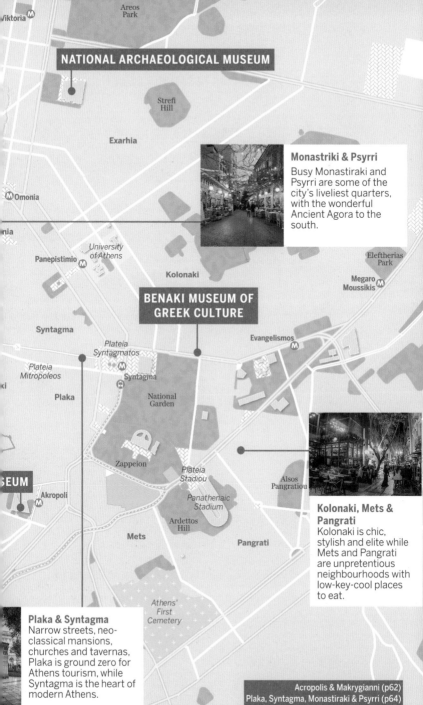

NATIONAL ARCHAEOLOGICAL MUSEUM

Areos Park

Viktoria

Strefi Hill

Exarhia

Omonia

Monastriki & Psyrri
Busy Monastiraki and Psyrri are some of the city's liveliest quarters, with the wonderful Ancient Agora to the south.

University of Athens

Panepistimio

Eleftherias Park

Kolonaki

Megaro Moussikis

BENAKI MUSEUM OF GREEK CULTURE

Syntagma

Plateia Syntagmatos

Evangelismos

Plateia Mitropoleos

Syntagma

Plaka

National Garden

Zappeion

Plateia Stadiou

Alsos Pangratiou

Panathenaic Stadium

Akropoli

Kolonaki, Mets & Pangrati
Kolonaki is chic, stylish and elite while Mets and Pangrati are unpretentious neighbourhoods with low-key-cool places to eat.

Ardettos Hill

EUM

Mets

Pangrati

Athens' First Cemetery

Plaka & Syntagma
Narrow streets, neo-classical mansions, churches and tavernas, Plaka is ground zero for Athens tourism, while Syntagma is the heart of modern Athens.

Acropolis & Makrygianni (p62)
Plaka, Syntagma, Monastiraki & Psyrri (p64)
Kolonaki & Pangrati (p70)

eST STUDIO / SHUTTERSTOCK ©

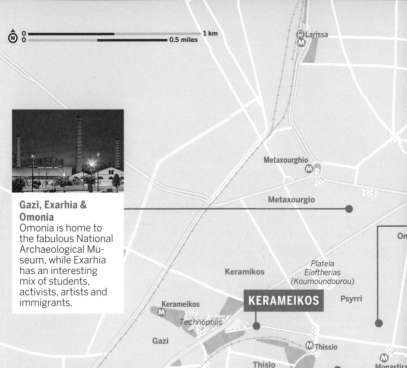

Gazi, Exarhia & Omonia
Omonia is home to the fabulous National Archaeological Museum, while Exarhia has an interesting mix of students, activists, artists and immigrants.

Acropolis Area & Thisio
Athen's crown is the Acropolis. This epic monument soars above the city, and on the hill's southern slopes, a fabulous modern museum holds its treasures.

0 ⟶ 1 km
0 ⟶ 0.5 miles

Ⓡ Larissa
Ⓜ

Metaxourghio
Ⓜ

Metaxourgio

On

Keramikos

Plateia
Eleftherias
(Koumoundourou)

KERAMEIKOS

Psyrri

Kerameikos
Ⓜ

Technopolis

Gazi

Ⓜ Thissio

Thisio

Monastira
Ⓜ

ANCIENT AGORA

Monastir

Hill of the
Nymphs

Areopagus
Hill

ACROPOLIS

Kato
Petralona

Hill of
the Pnyx

ACROPOLIS MU

Ⓜ Petralona

Ano
Petralona

Filopappou
Hill

Makrygiann

Koukaki

Sygrou-Fix

STAVROS NIARCHOS
FOUNDATION
CULTURAL CENTER

(3km)

EVGENY KUZHILEV / SHUTTERSTOCK ©

Arriving in Athens

The airport (p305) is 27km east of Athens. Most ferry, hydrofoil and high-speed catamaran services leave from the massive port at Piraeus, southwest of Athens. Some ferries for the Cyclades arrive at/depart from the small port of Rafina, around 30km east of Athens. The city also has plenty of bus services and some train connections.

Where to Stay

Athens lodging covers the full range, from one- to five-star hotels plus plenty of short-term rental accommodation. In recent years there's been an mini explosion of chic boutique developments, most with only a handful of rooms. To be sure your ideal choice is available, make bookings at least a couple of months ahead; for July and August, ideally aim for four months ahead.

Propylaia (entrance)

DIMITRIOS / SHUTTERSTOCK ©

Acropolis

Crowned by the Parthenon, the most important ancient site in the Western world stands sentinel over Athens, visible from almost everywhere within the city. Its monuments and sanctuaries of white Pentelic marble gleam in the midday sun and gradually take on a honey hue as the sun sinks, while at night they stand brilliantly illuminated above the city.

Great For...

☑ **Don't Miss**

Odeon of Herodes Atticus

Acropolis History

Inspiring as these monuments are, they are but faded remnants of the city of Pericles, who spared no expense – only the best materials, architects, sculptors and artists were good enough for a city dedicated to the cult of Athena. It was a showcase of lavishly coloured buildings and gargantuan statues, some of bronze, others of marble plated with gold and encrusted with precious stones.

The Acropolis was first inhabited in Neolithic times (4000–3000 BC). The earliest monumental buildings were constructed here during the Mycenaean era. People lived on the Acropolis until the late 6th century BC, but in 510 BC the Delphic oracle declared it the sole province of the gods.

After all the buildings on the Acropolis were reduced to ashes by the Persians on

Odeon of Herodes Atticus

❶ Need to Know

Map p62; ☏210 321 4172; http://odysseus.
culture.gr; adult/concession/child €20/10/
free; ⊘8am-8pm May-Sep, reduced hours
in winter, last entry 30min before closing;
ⓂAkropoli

✕ Take a Break

Cafes along Thisio's pedestrian promenade, Apostolou Pavlou, have great
Acropolis views.

★ Top Tip

Buy tickets online at https://etickets.
tap.gr. The combo ticket (€30) covers
the Acropolis and six other sites within
five days.

Visiting the Site

the eve of the Battle of Salamis (480 BC),
Pericles set about his ambitious rebuilding
program. He transformed the Acropolis
into a city of temples, which has come
to be regarded as the zenith of Classical
Greece.

Ravages inflicted during the years of
foreign occupation, pilfering by foreign
archaeologists, inept renovations following
Independence, the footsteps of millions of
visitors, earthquakes and, more recently,
acid rain and pollution have all taken their
toll on the surviving monuments. The
worst blow was in 1687, when the Venetians
attacked the Turks, opening fire on the
Acropolis and causing an explosion in the
Parthenon – where the Turks had been
storing gunpowder – and damaging all the
buildings.

Major restoration programs are ongoing,
and most of the original sculptures and
friezes have been moved to the Acropolis
Museum and replaced with casts. Restoration at the site is ongoing and there are
almost always hordes of tourists here –
visit very early in the morning or last thing
at night to avoid the worst of the crowds.

The site's **main entrance** (Map p62;
Dionysiou Areopagitou; ⓂThissio) is uphill from
the tour bus car park on Dionysiou Areopagitou; stairs here lead first to the Odeon of
Herodes Atticus. Come to this entrance for
the disabled accessible lift. The **southeast
entrance** (Map p62; ⓂAkropoli) is a better
option for individual visitors, as it avoids the
heavy bus traffic and crowds at the main
entrance (and with more than three million
visitors a year we do mean heavy crowds).
Visiting early in the morning also gives

you more time alone before you meet the groups coming the other way.

Site clearance starts 15 minutes before closing. At this time, you must go out via the main (west) entrance. The site closes before sunset, but **Areopagus Hill** (Map p64; MMonastiraki), outside the main gate, is a nice (if sometimes busy) place to watch the light show.

The Parthenon

The Parthenon is the monument that more than any other epitomises the glory of Ancient Greece. It is dedicated to Athena Parthenos, the goddess embodying the power and prestige of the city. One of the largest Doric temples ever completed in Greece, it was designed by Iktinos and Kallicrates to be the pre-eminent monument of the Acropolis and was completed in time for the Great Panathenaic Festival of 438 BC.

The Parthenon's fluted Doric columns achieve perfect form. The eight columns at either end and 17 on each side were ingeniously curved to create an optical illusion: the foundations (like all the 'horizontal' surfaces of the temple) are slightly concave and the columns are slightly convex, making both appear straight. Supervised by Pheidias, the sculptors worked on the architectural detail of the Parthenon, including the pediments, frieze and metopes, which were brightly coloured and gilded.

The temple's pediments (the triangular elements topping the east and west facades) were filled with elaborately carved

Parthenon

three-dimensional sculptures. The west side depicted Athena and Poseidon in their contest for the city's patronage, the east Athena's birth from Zeus' head. See their remnants and the rest of the Acropolis' sculptures and artefacts in the Acropolis Museum.

The Parthenon's metopes, designed by Pheidias, are square carved panels set between channelled triglyphs. The metopes on the eastern side depicted the Olympian gods fighting the giants, and on the western side they showed Theseus leading the Athenian youths into battle against the Amazons. The southern metopes illustrat-

ed the contest of the Lapiths and centaurs at a marriage feast, while the northern ones depicted the sacking of Troy. The internal cella was topped by the Ionic frieze, a continuous sculptured band depicting the Panathenaic Procession.

Odeon of Herodes Atticus

This large amphitheatre was built in AD 161 by wealthy Roman Herodes Atticus in memory of his wife Regilla. It was excavated in 1857–58 and completely restored in the 1950s. The **Athens & Epidaurus Festival** (Hellenic Festival; ☑210 928 2900; www.greek festival.gr; ☺Jun-Aug) holds drama, music and dance performances here in summer, and occasionally there are blockbuster pop concerts and other events.

Express Tour

Most visitors will strive to see the Acropolis in the morning, but if your schedule skews later (and you don't mind a slightly faster pace), you can see the site later in about 90 minutes. Enter from the less busy southeast entrance, but make a beeline up to the Parthenon. Site clearance starts up here about 45 minutes before closing time; then you can start making your way back down along the south slope, a little ahead of the exiting crowds.

What's Nearby?

Also called the Hill of the Muses, **Filopappou Hill** (Map p62; MAkropoli) – along with the hills of the Pnyx and the Nymphs – is a somewhat wild, pine-shaded spot that's good for a stroll, especially at sunset. The hill also gives some of the best vantage points for photographing the Acropolis, and views to the Saronic Gulf.

Free Entry

Check out www.culture.gr for free-admission holidays and changing opening hours.

SIR FRANCIS CANKER PHOTOGRAPHY / GETTY IMAGES ©

The Acropolis

A WALKING TOUR

Cast your imagination back in time, two and a half millennia ago, and envision the majesty of the Acropolis. Its famed and hallowed monument, the Parthenon, dedicated to the goddess Athena, stood proudly over a small city, dwarfing the population with its graceful grandeur. In the Acropolis' heyday in the 5th century BC, pilgrims and priests worshipped at the temples illustrated here (most of which still stand in varying states of restoration). Many were painted brilliant colours and were abundantly adorned with sculptural masterpieces crafted from ivory, gold and semiprecious stones.

As you enter the site today, elevated on the right perches one of the Acropolis' best-restored buildings: the diminutive **①** **Temple of Athena Nike**. Follow the Panathenaic Way through the Propylaia and up the slope towards the Parthenon – icon of the Western world. Its **②** **majestic columns** sweep up to some of what were the finest carvings of their time: wrap-around **③** **pediments, metopes and a frieze**. Stroll around the temple's exterior and take in the spectacular views over Athens and Piraeus below.

As you circle back to the centre of the site, you will encounter those renowned lovely ladies, the **④** **Caryatids** of the Erechtheion. On the Erechtheion's northern face, the oft-forgotten **⑤** **Temple of Poseidon** sits alongside ingenious **⑥** **Themistocles' Wall**. Wander to the Erechtheion's western side to find Athena's gift to the city: **⑦** **the olive tree**.

Themistocles' Wall

Crafty general Themistocles (524–459 BC) hastened to build a protective wall around the Acropolis and in so doing incorporated elements from archaic temples on the site. Look for the column drums built into the wall.

Sanctuary of Pandion

Sanctuary of Zeus Polieus

Erechtheion

Temple of Poseidon

Though he didn't win patronage of the city, Poseidon was worshipped on the northern side of the Erechtheion, which is said to bear the mark of his trident-strike. Imagine the finely decorated coffered porch painted in rich colours, as it was in the past.

ALEXTRAVELERPHOTOGRAPHER / GETTY IMAGES ©

TOP TIP

The Acropolis is a must-see for every visitor to Athens. Avoid the crowds by arriving first thing in the morning or late in the day.

Porch of the Caryatids

Perhaps the most recognisable sculptural elements at the Acropolis are the majestic Caryatids (c 415 BC). Modelled on women from Karyai (modern-day Karyes, in Lakonia), the maidens are thought to have held a libation bowl in one hand, and to be drawing up their dresses with the other.

Parthenon Pediments, Metopes & Frieze

The Parthenon's pediments (the triangular elements topping the east and west facades) were filled with elaborately carved three-dimensional sculptures. The west side depicted Athena and Poseidon in their contest for the city's patronage, the east Athena's birth from Zeus' head. The metopes are square carved panels set between channelled triglyphs. They depicted battle scenes, including the sacking of Troy and the clash between the Lapiths and the Centaurs. The cella was topped by the Ionic frieze, a continuous sculptured band depicting the Panathenaic Procession.

Parthenon

3

2

Chalkotheke

Panathenaic Way

Sanctuary of Artemis Brauronia

Statue of Athena Promachos

Arrephorion

Propylaia

Pinakothiki

1

Entrance

Spring of Klepsydra

Parthenon Columns

The Parthenon's fluted Doric columns achieve perfect form. Their lines were ingeniously curved to create an optical illusion: the foundations (like all the 'horizontal' surfaces of the temple) are slightly concave and the columns are slightly convex, making both appear straight.

Athena's Olive Tree

The flourishing olive tree next to the Erechtheion is meant to be the sacred tree that Athena produced to seize victory in the contest for Athens.

Temple of Athena Nike

Restored, this precious tiny Pentelic marble temple was designed by Kallicrates and built around 425 BC. The cella housed a wooden statue of Athena as Victory (Nike) and the exterior friezes illustrated Athenian battle triumphs.

Parthenon Gallery

SAIKO3P/SHUTTERSTOCK ©

Acropolis Museum

This dazzling museum, showcasing the Acropolis' surviving treasures, covers the Archaic period to the Roman one. The emphasis is on the Acropolis of the 5th century BC, considered the apotheosis of Greece's artistic achievement. The Acropolis itself is always visible through floor-to-ceiling windows.

Great For...

☑ **Don't Miss**

The frieze in the Parthenon Gallery

Ancient Ruins & Ground Floor

Designed by US-based architect Bernard Tschumi with Greek architect Michael Photiadis, the €130-million museum opened in 2009 after decades of planning; it replaced the small museum near the Parthenon.

As you enter the museum, the glass floor reveals the **ruins of an ancient Athenian neighbourhood**. These were uncovered during construction and had to be preserved and integrated into a new building plan. In 2019, the museum opened up a 4000-sq-metre section of these ruins for closer inspection.

The ground floor's **Gallery of the Slopes of Acropolis** emulates the climb up to the sacred hill. Exhibits include painted vases and votive offerings from the sanc-

Horseman statue, Archaic Gallery

Acropolis

Dionysiou Areopagitou

**Acropolis
Museum** 🏛 Ⓜ Akropoli

❶ Need to Know

Map p62; ☎210 900 0900; www.theacrop
olismuseum.gr; Dionysiou Areopagitou 15,
Makrygianni; adult/child €10/free; ⊘8am-
4pm Mon, to 8pm Tue-Thur & Sat-Sun, to 10pm
Fri Apr-Oct, 9am-5pm Mon-Thu, to 10pm Fri, to
8pm Sat & Sun Nov-Mar; ⓂAkropoli

✕ Take a Break

The museum's good-value restaurant
has superb views.

★ Top Tip

To understand the Parthenon's reliefs
see the film that is screened on the
Parthenon Gallery floor.

tuaries where gods were worshipped, plus
more recent objects found in excavations of
the settlement, including two clay statues
of Nike at the entrance.

Archaic Gallery

Bathed in natural light, the 1st-floor **Archaic Gallery** is a veritable forest of statues,
mostly votive offerings to Athena. These
include stunning examples of 6th-century
kore – statues of young women in draped
clothing and elaborate braids, usually carrying a pomegranate, wreath or bird. Most
were recovered from a pit on the Acropolis
where the Athenians buried them after the
Battle of Salamis. The 570 BC statue of a
youth bearing a calf is one of the rare male
statues found. There are also bronze figurines and artefacts from temples predating

the Parthenon (destroyed by the Persians),
including wonderful pedimental sculptures
such as Hercules slaying the Lernaian
Hydra and a lioness devouring a bull. Also
on this floor are five Caryatids, the maiden
columns that held up the Erechtheion (the
sixth is in the British Museum).

Parthenon Gallery

The museum's crowning glory is the top-
floor **Parthenon Gallery**, a glass atrium
housing the temple's 160m-long frieze.
It's mounted as it once was, following
the layout of the building, and you can
stroll along, as though atop the columns,
and examine the fragments at eye level.
Interspersed between the golden-hued
originals are stark-white plaster replicas
of the missing pieces – the so-called Parthenon Marbles hacked off by Lord Elgin in
1801 and now held in the British Museum
in London.

Stoa of Attalos

LKONTA/ALAMY STOCK PHOTO ©

Ancient Agora

Starting in the 6th century BC, this area was Athens' commercial, political and social hub. Socrates expounded his philosophy here, and St Paul preached here. The site today has been cleared of later Ottoman buildings to reveal only classical remains. It's a green respite, with a well-restored temple, a good museum and a Byzantine church.

Great For...

☑ Don't Miss
Well-preserved, iconic Temple of Hephaistos

Stoa of Attalos

In architectural terms, a stoa is a covered portico, but the ancient model, this stoa built by King Attalos II of Pergamum (159–138 BC), was essentially an ancient shopping mall. The majestic two-storey structure, with an open-front ground floor supported by 45 Doric columns, was filled with storefronts. (Today, Greek still uses the word *stoa* for a shopping arcade.) The building, which was restored in the 1950s, holds the site **museum** (☏210 321 0185; http://odysseus.culture.gr; Adrianou 24, Monastiraki; admission included with Ancient Agora ticket; ⊙10am-3.30pm Mon, from 8.30am Tue-Sun; ⓂMonastiraki). Inside, you'll find neat relics that show how the *agora* was used on a daily basis: ancient voting ballots, coins, terracotta figurines and more. Some of the oldest finds date from 4000 BC.

Church of the Holy Apostles

ANAMARIA MEJIA/SHUTTERSTOCK ©

ⓘ Need to Know

Map p64; ☎210 321 0185; http://odys
seus.culture.gr; Adrianou 24, Monastiraki;
adult/student/child €8/4/free; ⏱8am-8pm
Apr-Oct, to 3pm Nov-Mar; Ⓜ Monastiraki

✕ Take a Break

Among the touristy cafes and restaurants on Adrianou, **Kuzina** (☎210 324
0133; www.kuzina.gr; Adrianou 9, Monastiraki;
mains €16-36; ⏱1pm-midnight; Ⓜ Thissio) is
a fine lunch spot.

★ Top Tip

The main (and most reliable) entrance
is on Adrianou; the south entrance is
open only at peak times.

If the crowds get too much, head to the
upper part of the building, which provides
panoramic views over the site.

Temple of Hephaistos

On the opposite (west) end of the *agora*
site stands the best-preserved Doric temple in Greece. Built in 449 BC by Iktinos,
one of the architects of the Parthenon, it
was dedicated to the god of the forge and
surrounded by foundries and metalwork
shops. It has 34 columns and a frieze on
the eastern side depicting nine of the
Twelve Labours of Hercules. In AD 1300
it was converted into the Church of Agios
Georgios, then deconsecrated in 1934. In
1922 and 1923 it was a shelter for refugees
from Asia Minor; iconic photos from that
period show families hanging laundry

among the pillars and white tents erected
along the temple's base.

Stoa Foundations

Northeast of the Temple of Hephaistos
are the foundations of the **Stoa of Zeus
Eleutherios**, one of the places where
Socrates spoke. Further north are the
foundations of the **Stoa of Basileios**, as
well as the **Stoa Poikile**, or 'Painted Stoa',
for its murals of battles of myth and history,
rendered by the leading artists of the day.

Church of the Holy Apostles

This charming little **Byzantine church**,
near the southern site gate, was built in the
11th century to commemorate St Paul's
teaching in the *agora*. It contains several
fine Byzantine frescoes, which were transferred from a demolished church.

Mask of Agamemnon

NEIL SETCHFIELD/LONELY PLANET ©

National Archaeological Museum

Don't miss this museum housing the world's finest collection of Greek antiquities. The enormous 19th-century neoclassical building holds room upon room filled with more than 10,000 examples of sculpture, pottery, jewellery, frescoes and more.

Great For...

☑ **Don't Miss**

Exquisite sculpture *Jockey of Artemision*

Prehistoric Collection & Mycenaen Antiquities

Directly ahead as you enter the museum is the **prehistoric collection**, showcasing some of the most important pieces of Mycenaean, Neolithic and Cycladic art, many in solid gold. The fabulous collection of Mycenaean antiquities (gallery 4) is the museum's tour de force.

A highlight is the great death mask of beaten gold, commonly known as the **Mask of Agamemnon**, the king who, according to legend, attacked Troy in the 12th century BC – but this is hardly certain. Heinrich Schliemann, the archaeologist who set to prove that Homer's epics were true tales, and not just myth, unearthed the mask at Mycenae in 1876. But now some archaeologists have found the surrounding grave

Artemision Bronze

Viktoria Ⓜ

Areos Park

Leof Alexandras

3is Septemvriou

28 Oktovriou

National Archaeological Museum ⓐ

❶ Need to Know

📞21321 44800; www.namuseum.gr; Patision 44, Exarhia; adult/child €12/free Apr-Oct; €6/free Nov-Mar; ⊙8am-8pm Wed-Mon, 12.30pm-8pm Tue mid-Apr–Oct, reduced hours Nov–Mar; 🚌2, 3, 4, 5 or 11 to Polytechneio, ⓂViktoria

✕ Take a Break

The self-service museum cafe has seating in a lovely open-air internal courtyard with a garden and sculptures.

★ Top Tip

A joint ticket is available for €15 (€8 for students), valid for three days here and at the Epigraphical Museum, Byzantine & Christian Museum and the Numismatic Museum.

items date from centuries earlier. And one researcher even asserts that Schliemann, a master of self-promotion, forged it completely.

Cycladic Collection

Gallery 6 contains some of the superbly minimalist marble figurines of the 3rd and 2nd millennia BC that inspired artists such as Picasso. One splendid example measures 1.52m and dates from 2600 to 2300 BC.

Sounion Kouros

The galleries to the left of the entrance house the oldest and most significant pieces of the sculpture collection.

Galleries 7 to 13 exhibit fine examples of Archaic *kouroi* (male statues) from the 7th century BC to 480 BC. The best by far is the colossal 600 BC **Sounion Kouros** (room 8), which stood before the Temple of Poseidon at Cape Sounion. Its style marks a transition point in art history, starting with the rigid lines of older Egyptian carving but also showing some of the lifelike qualities – including the smile – that the Greeks would come to develop in later centuries.

Artemision Bronze

Gallery 15 is dominated by the incredibly precise, just-larger-than-life 460 BC bronze **statue** of Zeus or Poseidon (no one really knows which), excavated from the sea off

Evia in 1928. The muscled figure has an iconic bearded face and holds his arms outstretched, his right arm raised to throw what was once a lightning bolt (if Zeus) or trident (if Poseidon).

Varvakeion Athena

In gallery 20, admire the details on the **statue of Athena**, made in 200 AD: the helmet topped with a sphinx and griffins, a Gorgon shield and the hand holding a small figure of winged Nike (missing its head). Now imagine it all more than 10 times larger and covered in gold – that was the legendary, now-lost colossal figure of Athena (11.5m tall) that the master sculptor Pheidias erected in front of the Parthenon in the 5th century BC. This daintier version is thought to be the best extant replica of that colossus.

Jockey of Artemision

In gallery 21 is a find from the shipwreck off Evia excavated in 1928. This delicately rendered **bronze horse and rider** dates from the 2nd century BC; only a few parts were found at first, and it was finally re-assembled in 1972. Opposite the horse are several lesser-known but equally exquisite works, such as the **statue of Aphrodite** showing the demure nude goddess struggling to hold her draped gown over herself.

Jockey of Artemision

Antikythera Shipwreck

Precious treasures discovered in 1900 by sponge divers off the island of Antikythera (gallery 28) include the striking bronze **Antikythera Youth**, forged in the 4th century BC. His hand once held some spherical object, now lost.

More mysterious is the **Antikythera Mechanism** (gallery 38), an elaborate clockwork device, now in fragments, apparently for calculating astronomical positions as well as dates of eclipses and the Olympic Games, among other events. Who made it, and when, is still unknown.

The exquisite **Vaphio gold cups**, with scenes of men taming wild bulls, are regarded as among the finest surviving examples of Mycenaean art.

SVINEYARD/SHUTTERSTOCK ©

Akrotiri Frescoes

Upstairs, room 48 is devoted to the spectacular and incredibly old **Minoan frescoes** from a prehistoric settlement on Santorini (Thira). They were preserved by being buried by a volcanic eruption in the late 16th century BC. The frescoes include *Boxing Children* and *Spring,* depicting red lilies and a pair of swallows kissing in mid air. The **Thira Gallery** also has videos showing the 1926 eruption and the Akrotiri excavation.

Pottery Collection

The superb pottery collection (galleries 49 to 56) traces the development of ceramics from the Bronze Age through the Proto-geometric and Geometric periods, to the famous **Attic black-figured pottery** (6th century BC), and **red-figured pottery** (late 5th to early 4th centuries BC). Other uniquely Athenian vessels are the **Attic White Lekythoi**, slender vases depicting scenes at tombs.

Panathenaic Amphorae

In the centre of gallery 56 are ceramic vases presented to the winners of the Panathenaic Games. Each one contained oil from the sacred olive trees of Athens; victors might have received up to 140 of them.

The vases are painted with scenes from the relevant sport (wrestling, in this case) on one side and an armed Athena *promachos* (leading warrior) on the other.

Egyptian Collection

Rooms 40 and 41 present the best of the museum's significant Egyptian collection, the only one in Greece.

Centre exterior

GIANNIS KATSAROS/ALAMY STOCK PHOTO © / ARCHITECT RENZO PIANO BUILDING WORKSHOP

Stavros Niarchos Foundation Cultural Center

Sitting beneath an artifical slope overlooking Faliron Bay, this stunning Renzo Piano building is home to the Greek National Opera and the National Library. The centre includes a beautiful, sustainably designed park and hosts an impressive range of mainly free events and exhibitions.

Great For...

☑ **Don't Miss**

Stavros Niarchos Park

National Library of Greece

In 2018, the **National Library** (📞216 809 1000; www.nlg.gr; Pisistratou 172, Kallithea; ⊙public areas 6am-midnight, exhibition floor 9am-10pm, library 9am-5pm Mon-Fri; 🚌550 to Onasseio, 10 to Epaminonda) **FREE** shifted more than 720,000 items from its collection to this stunning new building that forms one of the two main halves of the Cultural Center. A soaring 'book castle' envelops the main entrance; free temporary exhibitions are scattered across the library's four floors. Anyone can register to borrow or read books from the general collection but for access to the academic and special collections (including many precious manuscripts) you must have a scholarly purpose. The Cultural Center offers free guided tours of the library.

National Library of Greece

Stavros Niarchos Foundation Cultural Center

Saronic Gulf

❶ Need to Know

SNFCC; (📞216 809 1001; www.snfcc.org; Leoforos Syngrou 364, Kallithea; 🚌550 to Onasseio, 10 to Epaminonda; **FREE**

✖ Take a Break

There are several kiosks in the park but the best cafe with seating and table service is **Canal Cafe** (📞210 943 0688; www.canalcafe.gr; Evripidou 6, Kallithea; ⊙9am-10pm, until 11pm Fri & Sat; 🚌550 to Onasseio, 10 to Epaminonda).

★ Top Tip

The lighthouse lookout atop the Cultural Center provides panoramic views of the park, city and seaside.

Greek National Opera

The Cultural Center also provides state-of-the-art digs for the **Greek National Opera** (Ethniki Lyriki Skini; 📞210 366 2100; www.nationalopera.gr; Leoforos Syngrou 364, Kallithea; tickets €10-90; 📞; 🚌550 to Onasseio, 10 to Epaminonda). The season, which includes classic works, quirkier new ones and big international coproductions, runs from November to June. Performances are top quality, tickets prices are very reasonable, and the main 1400-seater auditorium is a stunning space with superb sight lines throughout and subtitle panels built into the back of each seat. The Greek National Ballet, Orchestra and Choirs also perform here. The complex includes the **Alternative Stage**, a flexible space that accommodates up to 450 people for more experimental and intimate productions.

Stavros Niarchos Park

Athens is short on green spaces, so this 21-hectare seaside **park** (📞216 809 1000; www.snfcc.org; Leoforos Syngrou 364, Kallithea; ⊙6am-midnight Apr-Oct, to 8pm Nov-Mar; 🚌550 to Onasseio, 10 to Epaminonda) **FREE** is a blessing. Covering a man-made slope that incorporates the roof of the Cultural Center, the park has been sustainably designed with paths cutting through plantings of lavender, olive trees and other Mediterranean flora. There are kids' play areas, an outdoor gym and much more. A variety of free activities are laid on, but you can also simply sit in a chair, soak up the sunshine and enjoy the cooling sea breezes.

Folk costumes

PETER EASTLAND/ALAMY STOCK PHOTO ©

Benaki Museum of Greek Culture

After decades of collecting, in 1930 Antonis Benakis turned the family's house into a museum. Now three storeys and many rooms larger, the museum presents all facets of Greek culture through the ages, with just the right amount of everything, and all of it beautiful.

Great For...

☑ **Don't Miss**

The dazzling confection of the Kozani Rooms

Flint Flakes

The ground floor is organised chronologically, up through to the Byzantine era. The 1st floor covers regional history and traditions. The 2nd floor covers dance, agriculture and the establishment of the Greek state.

In room 1, **shards of flint** chipped into tool shapes date from 50,000–40,000 BC, in the Middle Paleolithic period – maybe the oldest human-made thing you'll ever see.

Cretan School of Painters

In gallery 12, the last room on the ground floor, are **masterpieces** from Venetian-held Crete (15th–16th centuries). These include works by Domenikos Theotokopoulos (later known as **El Greco**, 1541–1614), and several by Theodoros Poulakis (1622–1692). The

ADAM EASTLAND/ALAMY STOCK PHOTO ©

❶ Need to Know

Map p70; ☏ 210 367 1000; www.benaki.org;
Koumbari 1, cnr Leoforos Vasilissis Sofias,
Kolonaki; adult/student/child €9/7/free,
6pm-midnight Thu free; ⊙10am-6pm Mon,
Wed, Fri & Sat, to midnight Thu, to 4pm Sun;
Ⓜ Syntagma, Evangelismos)

✕ Take a Break

The Benaki's **cafe** (☏ 210 367 1000; mains
€10-24; ⊙10am-6pm Mon, Wed, Fri & Sat,
to midnight Thu, to 4pm Sun) is renowned
for great food and has a lovely outdoor
terrace.

★ Top Tip

Visit on Thursday: admission is free
from 6pm and the museum is open till
midnight.

Cretan School developed techniques still
used in icons today: sharp outlines, a
geometric depiction of fabrics, and subtly
highlighted skin tones.

Kozani Rooms

On the 1st floor, the rooms dedicated to the
wealth of 18th- and 19th-century Epiros,
themselves quite dazzling, lead into **two
reception halls** that have been relocated
from mansions in neighbouring Kozani,
Macedonia. They are confections of carved
and painted wood and stained glass.

Folk Costumes

Also on the 1st floor is room upon room of
the finest and most intricately fashioned
Greek traditional clothing, showing the
diversity of the islands and the various

regions of the mainland, including the Peloponnese, Epiros, Macedonia and Thrace.
The spacious displays are interspersed
with other priceless objects, such as carved
marble door frames and jewel-encrusted
Ottoman crowns.

Other Branches

A €25 pass is valid for one visit to each of
the Benaki museums – including the mod-
ern/contemporary **Benaki Museum at 138
Pireos St** (☏ 210 345 3111; www.benaki.org;
Pireos 138, Rouf; adult/concession from €6/3;
⊙10am-6pm Thu & Sun, to 10pm Fri & Sat, closed
Aug; Ⓜ Kerameikos) and the **Museum of
Islamic Art** (Map p64; ☏ 210 325 1311; www.be-
naki.org; Agion Asomaton 22, Keramikos; adult/
student/child €9/7/free; ⊙10am-6pm Thu-Sun;
Ⓜ Thissio), plus six other smaller sites – over
three months.

Street of Tombs

Kerameikos

This lush, tranquil site, uncovered in 1861 during the construction of Pireos St, is named for the potters who settled it around 3000 BC, then on the clay-rich banks of the Iridanos River. But it's better known as a cemetery, used through the 6th century AD; the vividly carved grave markers give a sense of ancient life.

Great For...

☑ **Don't Miss**

Archaeological Museum of Kerameikos

The Grounds

Once inside, on a small knoll, you'll find a **plan of the site**. A path leads down to the right to the remains of the city wall built by Themistocles in 479 BC, and rebuilt by Konon in 394 BC, and around the grounds. The wall is broken by the foundations of two gates; tiny signs mark each one.

Sacred Gate

This **gate**, of which only foundations remain, was where pilgrims from Eleusis entered the city during the annual Eleusian procession. The gate marked the end of the **Sacred Way**, aka Iera Odos, which is now a wide city street that still follows a straight route west to modern Elefsina.

Archaeological Museum of Kerameikos

SAIKO3P/SHUTTERSTOCK ©

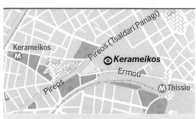

❶ Need to Know

Map p64; ☑210 346 3552; http://odys seus.culture.gr; Ermou 148, Kerameikos; adult/ child incl museum €8/free; ☺8am-8pm, reduced hours in low season; Ⓜ Thissio

✕ Take a Break

Il Rantanplan (2 Rantanplan; Map p64; ☑210 325 0052; https://2-rantanplan. business.site; Agion Asomaton 3, Kerameikos; ☺9.30am-1am; Ⓜ Thissio) is a pleasant spot for a coffee or another drink.

★ Top Tip

Admission to the site and the museum is included in the Acropolis combo ticket.

Dipylon Gate

The once-massive **Dipylon Gate** was the city's main entrance and where the Panath-enaic Procession began. It was also where the city's prostitutes gathered to offer their services to travellers. From a platform outside the gate, Pericles gave his famous speech extolling the virtues of Athens and honouring those who died in the first year of the Peloponnesian Wars. Between the Sacred and Dipylon Gates are the founda-tions of the **Pompeion**, used as a dressing room for participants in the Panathenaic Procession.

Street of Tombs

Leading off the Sacred Way to the left as you head away from the city is this **avenue**

reserved for the graves of Athens' elite, while ordinary citizens were buried in the bordering areas. Some surviving *stelae* (grave markers) are now in the on-site museum and the National Archaeological Museum (p49). What you see here are mostly replicas, but look for poignant details such as a *stela* showing a little girl with her pet dog.

Archaeological Museum of Kerameikos

The small but excellent **museum** (incl entry to Kerameikos) contains remarkable *stelae* and sculptures from the site, such as the amazing 4th-century-BC **marble bull** from the plot of Dionysos of Kollytos, as well as funerary offerings and ancient toys. Outside, don't miss the lifelike stone mountain dog.

Central Athens

The key ancient sites of Athens make for an action-packed but manageable walk through central Athens, If you only have one day to see the sights, follow this itinerary.

Start Temple of Olympian Zeus

Distance 2.4km

Duration 3½ hours

7 The **Ancient Agora** (p46) also has a top-notch museum in the colonnaded Stoa of Attalos.

PSYRRI

Ⓜ Thissio

Plateia Monastirakiou

Monastiraki Ⓜ

FINISH

Adrianou

Peikilis

Areos

Theorias

6 The highlight of the **Roman Agora** (p61) is the 1st century BC Tower of the Winds.

4 The magnificent **Odeon of Herodes Atticus** (p41) built in AD 161 is still in use today.

Filopappou Hill

Take a Break...
Dioskouri (p68) near the Ancient Agora is good for drinks and traditional Greek snacks.

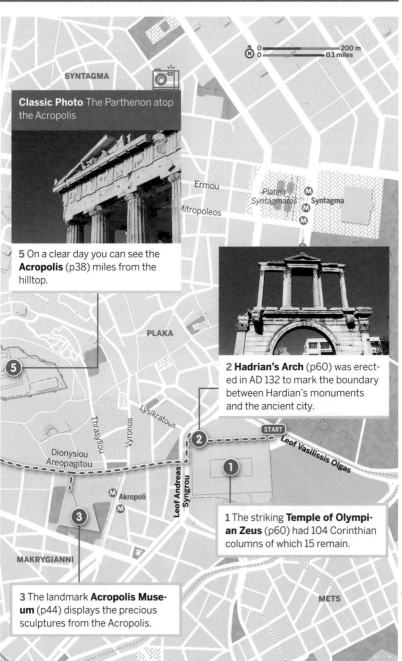

Classic Photo The Parthenon atop the Acropolis

Ermou

Mitropoleos

Plateia Syntagmatos Ⓜ Syntagma
Ⓜ

5 On a clear day you can see the **Acropolis** (p38) miles from the hilltop.

PLAKA

2 Hadrian's Arch (p60) was erected in AD 132 to mark the boundary between Hardian's monuments and the ancient city.

Ⓜ

Lysikratous

Thrasyllou

Vyronos

Dionysiou Areopagitou

START

Leof Vasilissis Olgas

Leof Andreas Syngrou

Ⓜ Akropoli
Ⓜ

1 The striking **Temple of Olympian Zeus** (p60) had 104 Corinthian columns of which 15 remain.

MAKRYGIANNI

METS

3 The landmark **Acropolis Museum** (p44) displays the precious sculptures from the Acropolis.

200 m
0.1 miles

⊙ SIGHTS

◉ Syntagma & Plaka

Temple of Olympian Zeus   Temple

(Olympieio; Map p62; ☑210 922 6330; http://od-ysseus.culture.gr; Leoforos Vasilissis Olgas, Plaka; adult/student/child €6/3/free; ☺8am-3pm Oct-Apr, to 8pm May-Sep; Ⓜ Akropoli, Syntagma) A can't-miss on two counts: it's a marvellous temple, once the largest in Greece, and it's smack in the centre of Athens. Of the temple's 104 original Corinthian columns (17m high with a base diameter of 1.7m), only 15 remain – the fallen column was blown down in a gale in 1852.

Hadrian's Arch   Monument

(Map p62; cnr Leoforos Vasilissis Olgas & Leoforos Vasilissis Amalias, Plaka; Ⓜ Akropoli, Syntagma) FREE The Roman emperor Hadrian had a great affection for Athens. Although he did his fair share of spiriting its Classical artwork to Rome, he also embellished the city with many temples and infrastructure improvements. As thanks, the people of Athens erected this lofty monument of Pentelic marble in 131 AD. It now stands on the edge of one of Athens' busiest avenues.

National Garden   Gardens

(Map p70; ☑210 721 5019; www.cityofathens.gr; ☺7am-dusk; Ⓜ Syntagma) FREE The former royal gardens, designed by Queen Amalia in 1838, is a pleasantly unkempt park that makes a welcome shady refuge from summer heat and traffic. Tucked among the trees are a cafe, a playground, turtle and duck ponds, and a tiny (if slightly dispiriting) zoo. The main entrance is on Leoforos Vasilissis Sofias, south of Parliament; you can also enter from Irodou Attikou to the east, or from the adjacent **Zappeion** (Map p70; Leoforos Vasilissis Amalias; Ⓜ Syntagma) FREE to the south.

Museum of Greek Popular Instruments   Museum

(Map p64; ☑210 325 4119; Diogenous 1-3, Plaka; ☺10am-2pm Tue & Thu-Sun, noon-6pm Wed; Ⓜ Monastiraki) FREE A single avid ethno-musicologist collected almost 1200 folk instruments; the best are on display in three floors of this house-turned-museum. Headphones let visitors listen to the *gaïda*

Temple of Olympian Zeus

ANDERS BLOMQVIST/LONELY PLANET ©

(Greek goatskin bagpipes) and the wood planks that priests on Mt Athos use to call prayer times, among other distinctly Greek sounds. Musical performances are held in the lovely garden in summer.

Anafiotika   Area

(Map p64; Stratonos, Plaka; ⓂMonastiraki, Akropoli) Clinging to the north slope of the Acropolis (p38), the tiny Anafiotika district is a beautiful, architecturally distinct subdistrict of Plaka. In the mid-1800s, King Otto hired builders from Anafi to build a new palace. In their homes here, they mimicked their island's architecture, all whitewashed cubes, bedecked with bougainvillea and geraniums. The area now is a clutch of about 40 homes, linked by footpaths just wide enough for people and stray cats.

◎ Monastiraki & Psyrri

Roman Agora   Historic Site

(Map p64; ☑210 324 5220; http://odysseus.culture.gr; Dioskouron, Monastiraki; adult/student/child €6/3/free; ⊙8am-3pm Mon-Fri, to 5pm Sat & Sun, mosque from 10am; ⓂMonastiraki) This was the city's market area under Roman rule, and it occupied a much larger area than the current site borders. You can see a lot from outside the fence, but it's worth going in for a closer look at the well-preserved **Gate of Athena Archegetis**, the propylaeum (entrance gate) to the market, as well as an Ottoman mosque and the ingenious and beautiful **Tower of the Winds**, on the east side of the site.

Museum of Greek Folk Art   Museum

(Map p64; ☑210 322 9031; www.mnep.gr; Adrianou & Areos, Monastiraki; ⓂMonastiraki) This museum has been closed since 2015, when it began its transition to this new site at Adrianou. Once it reopens in 2020, it will display secular and religious folk art, mainly from the 18th and 19th centuries. Exhibits will include embroidery, pottery, weaving and puppets, and a reconstructed traditional village house with paintings by Theophilos. Greek traditional costumes will also be on display.

🏛 Parliament & the Presidential Guard

Designed by Bavarian architect Friedrich von Gärtner, Greece's **Parliament** (Map p70; www.hellenicparliament.gr; Plateia Syntagmatos, Syntagma; ⊙tours 3pm Mon & Fri Jun, Jul & Sep; ⓂSyntagma) FREE was originally the royal palace. From its balcony, the *syntagma* (constitution) was declared on 3 September 1843, and in 1935 the palace became the seat of parliament. For history and politics geeks, the building is open by guided tour a few months of the year; book at least five days ahead.

In front of Parliament, the traditionally costumed *evzones* (presidential guards) stand by the tomb and change every hour on the hour. On Sunday at 11am, a whole platoon marches down Vasilissis Sofias to the tomb, accompanied by a band. The *evzones* uniform of the *fustanella* (white skirt) and pompom shoes is based on the attire worn by the klephts, the mountain fighters of the War of Independence.

You can also see *evzones* outside the **Presidential Guard** (Map p70; 10 Irodou Attikou, Syntagma; ⓂSyntagma) and nearby Presidential Palace. It's interesting to see them here, alone and away from tourist cameras, going through their ritual pomp even in the dead of night.

Guards outside the Greek Parliament
BANEDEKI/SHUTTERSTOCK ©

Church of Agios Eleftherios   Church

(Little Metropolis; Map p64; Plateia Mitropoleos, Monastiraki; ⓂMonastiraki) This 12th-century church, dedicated to both Agios Eleftherios and Panagia Gorgoepikoos (Virgin Swift to Hear), is Athens' religious history in one tiny building. The cruciform-style marble church was erected on the ruins of an ancient temple and its exterior is a mix of medieval beasts and ancient gods in bas-relief, and columns appropriated from older structures. It was once the city's cathedral, but now stands in the shadows of the much larger **new cathedral** (Map p64; ☏210 322 1308; http://iaath.

gr; Plateia Mitropoleos, Monastiraki; ⏰7am-7pm; Ⓜ Monastiraki).

⊙ Gazi, Keramikos & Exarhia

Industrial Gas Museum
Notable Building

(Technopolis; Map p64; ☏210 347 5535; https://gasmuseum.gr; Pireos 100, Gazi; adult/child €1/free; ⏰10am-8pm Tue, Wed, Fri & Sat, to 9pm Thu & Sun mid-Oct–mid-Apr, to 6pm Tue, Wed, Fri & Sat, to 9pm Thu & Sun mid–Apr-mid-Oct;

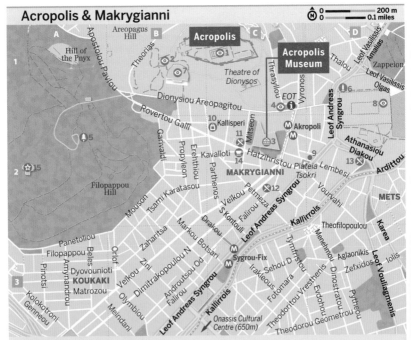

Acropolis & Makrygianni

⊙ Sights
1 Acropolis	C1
2 Acropolis Main Entrance	B1
3 Acropolis Museum	C2
4 Acropolis Southeast Entrance	C1
5 Filopappou Hill	A2
6 Hadrian's Arch	D1
7 Odeon of Herodes Atticus	B1
8 Temple of Olympian Zeus	D1

⊛ Activities, Courses & Tours
9 Solebike	D2

⊕ Shopping
10 Athena Design Workshop	C2

⊗ Eating
11 Ellevoro	C2
12 Mani Mani	C2
13 Veganaki	D2

⊖ Drinking & Nightlife
14 Little Tree Book Cafe	C2

⊛ Entertainment
15 Dora Stratou Dance Theatre	A2

Ⓜ Kerameikos) It's fascinating to follow the walking route that runs through the old gasworks in Gazi, in operation from 1862 until 1984. The preserved complex of furnaces and industrial buildings from the mid-19th century appear like giant art installations. Photos and interactive elements provide an idea of what the works were like when in operation. Make sure you go up the watchtower of the New Watergas building for a panoramic city view.

◎ Kolonaki, Mets & Pangrati

Byzantine & Christian Museum   Museum

(Map p70; ☑ 213 213 9500; www.byzantinemuseum.gr; Leoforos Vasilissis Sofias 22, Kolonaki; adult/student/child €8/4/free; ☺ 12.30-8pm Tue, from 8am Wed-Sun Apr-Oct, reduced hours Nov-Mar; Ⓜ Evangelismos) This outstanding museum, based in the 1848 Villa Ilissia, offers exhibition halls, most of them underground, crammed with religious art. The exhibits go chronologically, charting the gradual and fascinating shift from ancient traditions to Christian ones, and the flourishing of a distinctive Byzantine style. Of course there are icons, but also delicate frescoes (some salvaged from a church and installed on floating panels) and more personal remnants of daily life.

Museum of Cycladic Art   Museum

(Map p70; ☑ 210 722 8321; https://cycladic.gr; Neofytou Douka 4, Kolonaki; adult/child €7/free, Mon €3.50, special exhibits €10; ☺ 10am-5pm Mon, Wed, Fri & Sat, to 8pm Thu, 11am-5pm Sun; Ⓜ Evangelismos) The 1st floor of this exceptional private museum is dedicated to the iconic minimalist marble Cycladic figurines, dating from 3000 BC to 2000 BC. They inspired many 20th-century artists, such as Picasso and Modigliani, with their simplicity and purity of form. Most are surprisingly small, considering their outsize influence, though one is almost human size. The rest of the museum features Greek and Cypriot art dating from 2000 BC to the 4th century AD.

Lykavittos Hill   Landmark

(Map p70; www.lycabettushill.com; Ⓜ Evangelismos) The 277m summit of Lykavittos – 'Hill of Wolves', from ancient times, when it was wilder than it is now – gives the finest panoramas of the city and the Attic basin, *nefos* (pollution haze) permitting. Perched on the summit is the little **Chapel of Agios Georgios**, floodlit like a beacon over the city at night. Walk up the path from the top of Loukianou in Kolonaki, or take the 10-minute funicular railway (p78) from the top of Ploutarhou.

Basil & Elise Goulandris Foundation   Museum

(Map p70; ☑ 210 725 2895; https://goulandris.gr; Eratosthenous 13, Pangrati; Ⓜ Akropoli) Opened in October 2019, this new museum showcases the collection of modern and contemporary artworks belonging to shipping magnate Basil Goulandris and his wife Elise. Alongside pieces from top European artists including Cézanne, Van Gogh, Picasso and Giacometti are works from pioneering Greek painters such as Parthenis, Vasiliou, Hadjikyriakos-Ghikas, Tsarouchis and Moralis.

Panathenaic Stadium   Historic Site

(Kallimarmaro; Map p70; ☑ 210 752 2985; www.panathenaicstadium.gr; Leoforos Vasileos Konstantinou, Pangrati; adult/student/child €5/2.50/free; ☺ 8am-7pm Mar-Oct, to 5pm Nov-Feb; 🚌 2, 4, 10, 11 to Stadio, Ⓜ Akropoli, 🚋 Zappeio) With its serried rows of white Pentelic marble seats built into a ravine next to Ardettos Hill, this ancient-turned-modern stadium is a draw both for lovers of classical architecture and sports fans who can imagine the roar of the crowds from millennia past. A ticket gets you an audio tour, admission to a tiny exhibit on the modern Olympics (mainly eye-candy games posters) and the opportunity to take your photo on a winners' pedestal.

Numismatic Museum   Museum

(Map p70; ☑ 210 363 2057; www.nummus.gr; Panepistimiou 12, Kolonaki; adult/student €6/3; ☺ 8.30am-3.30pm Tue-Sun; Ⓜ Panepistimio,

Plaka, Syntagma, Monastiraki & Psyrri

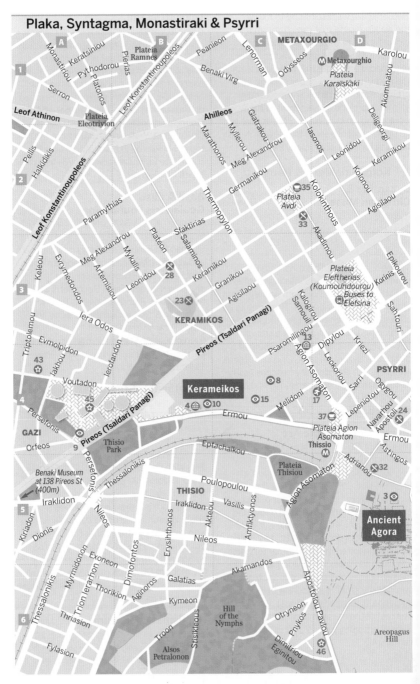

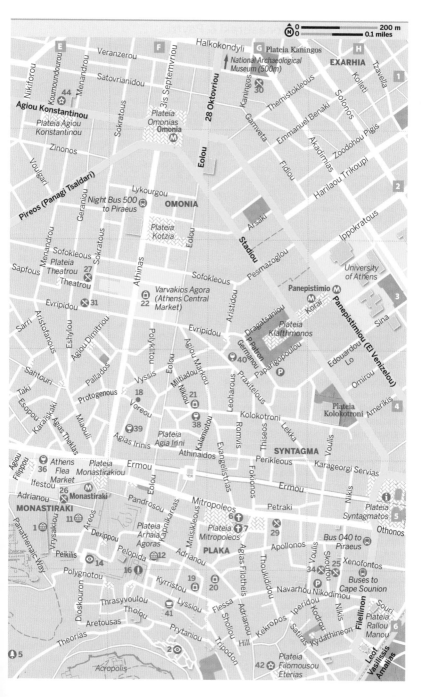

N 0 —— 200 m
0 —— 0.1 miles

Halkokondyli

G Plateia Kaningos

National Archaeological
Museum (500m)

EXARHIA

Veranzerou

Satovrianidou

3ís Septemvriou

28 Oktovriou

Themistokleous

Solonos

Kolleti

Tzavela

1

Nikiforou

Koumoundourou

Menandrou

44

Agiou Konstantinou

Plateia Agiou
Konstantinou

Plateia
Omonias
Omonia Ⓜ

Kaningos

30

Emmanuel Benaki

Akadimias

Zoodohou Pigis

Harilaou Trikoupi

Gamveta

Fidiou

Zinonos

Voulgari

Eolou

Arsaki

H

Ippokratous

2

Pireos (Panagi Tsaldari)

Geraniou

Lykourgou

OMONIA

Night Bus 500 🚏
to Piraeus

Plateia
Kotzia

Eolou

Stadiou

Pesmazoglou

University
of Athens

Menandrou

Sofokleous

Sokratous

Athinas

Sofokleous

Aristidou

Panepistimio Ⓜ

Ⓜ

Panepistimiou (El Venizelou)

Sina

Plateia
Theatrou **27**

Theatrou

Sapfous

Evripidou **31** 🍴

Varvakios Agora
(Athens Central
Market) **22** 🔒

Evripidou

Dragatsaniou
Dp.Patron
Germanou
Papirigopoulou

Plateia
Klafthmonos

Korai

Panepistimiou

Edouardou
Lo

Omirou

Sarri

Aristofanous

Eshylou

Agiou Dimitriou

Polyklitou

40 🔒

P

Sahtouri

Palladas

Miltiadou

Nikiou

Vyssis

Praxitelous

Plateia
Kolokotroni

Amerikis

4

Taki

Esopou

Protogenous

18 ●
Voreou

21 🔒

Leoharous

Kolokotroni

Lekka

Karaiskaki

Agias Theklas

Miaouli

39 🍴

38 🍴

Plateia
Agia Irini

Kalamiotou

Romvis

Thiseos

Voulis

Agiou
Filippou

Athens **36** 🍴
Flea
Market

Plateia
Monastirakiou

Ermou

Athinaidos

Evangelistrias

Perikleous

SYNTAGMA

Karageorgi Servias

Ifestou

26 Ⓜ **Monastiraki**

Eolou

Foknos

Ermou

Nikis

i

Plateia
Syntagmatos

5

Adrianou

MONASTIRAKI

Pandrosou

Mitropoleos

Petraki

Othonos

Panathenaic Way

1 🏛

11 🏛

Areos

Vrysakiou

Dexippou

Pelopida

Plateia
Arhaia
Agoras

Mnisikleous

6 🔒

Plateia
Mitropoleos **7** 🔒

29 🍴

Bus 040 to 🚏
Piraeus

Peikilis

14 🍴

16 🔒 **i**

12 🏛

PLAKA

Adrianou

Agias Filotheis

Apollonos

Thoukididou

34 🍴

Skoufou

Xenofontos

25 🍴

Buses to
Cape Sounion

Polygnotou

Dioskouron

Kyrristou

19 🔒

20 🔒

Flessa

Adrianou

Navarhou Nikodimou

P

Nikis

Filellinon

Thrasyvoulou

Tholou

41 🍴

Lyssiou

Sholiou

Kekropos

Iperidou

Kodrou

Satiras

Souri

Aretousas

Prytaniou

Tripodon

Hill

Kydathineon

Plateia
Rallou
Manou

6

Theorias

2 🔒

Leof Vasilissis Amalias

🚏 **5**

Acropolis

Plateia
Filomousou
Eterias **42** ✦

Plaka, Syntagma, Monastiraki & Psyrri

Syntagma) The collection of coins here, dating from ancient through to modern times, is excellent, but of more general interest is the dazzling 1881 mansion in which it's housed. Built by architect Ernst Ziller, it was the home of Heinrich Schliemann, the archaeologist who excavated Troy; fittingly, its mosaic floors and painted walls and ceilings are covered in classical motifs.

❸ ACTIVITIES & TOURS

This Is My Athens (http://myathens.thisis athens.org) An excellent city-run program that pairs you with a volunteer local to show you around for two hours. You must book online 72 hours ahead.

Alternative Athens
Tours

(☑211 012 6544; www.alternativeathens.com; tours from €40) As the name promises, this well-run company offers walking tours with less-typical slants, covering various corners of the city. There's an excellent three-hour street-art tour and another visiting Athenian designers, as well as an LGBTQ bar and club crawl, food tours and even day trips out of town.

Athens Walking Tours
Tours

(☑6945859662, 210 884 7269; www.athenswalk ingtours.gr) Runs a full range of guided tours around and outside the city. It's especially notable for its cooking class (€77) in a Thisio taverna, which cuts no corners and even shows you how to roll out your own filo for *spanakopita* (spinach pie).

Roll in Athens
Cycling

(Map p64; ☑6974231611; www.rollinathens. tours; Voreou 10, Monastiraki; half-day tours €40; Ⓜ Monastiraki) This small company does only two tours, and does them very well: a city highlights tour, around all the main central sights, and – highly recommended – an excursion out of the centre to the sea, a pleasant way to expand your understanding of Athens. Bikes are well maintained, and the guides are great.

Hammam Spa

(Map p64; ☎210 323 1073; www.hammam.gr; Melidoni 1, cnr Agion Asomaton, Keramikos; 1hr €25, bath-scrub combos from €45; ⊗11am-10pm Mon-Fri, 10am-10pm Sat & Sun; MThissio) The marble-lined steam room may be a bit small, but thanks to the attention to detail throughout, this Turkish-style place is the best of the three major bathhouses in central Athens. Amenities include proper-size water bowls, and hot tea and Turkish delight in the lounge afterwards. For the full effect, reserve ahead for a full-body scrub.

🅐 SHOPPING

Varvakios Agora Market

(Athens Central Market; Map p64; Athinas, btwn Sofokleous & Evripidou, Psyrri; ⊗7am-6pm Mon-Sat; MPanepistimio, Omonia) A wonderful sight in its own right, this huge old wrought-iron market hall is dedicated to fish and meat, especially row upon row of lamb carcasses, hanging in just-barely-EU-compliant glass cases. Tavernas within the market, many open 24/7, are an Athenian institution for hangover-busting *patsas* (tripe soup).

Athena Design Workshop Fashion & Accessories

(Map p62; ☎210 924 5713; www.athenadesign workshop.com; Parthenonos 30, Makrygianni; ⊗11.30am-7pm Mon-Fri, until 5pm Sat; MAkropoli) You can often find Krina Vronti busy woodblock printing her appealing graphic designs on T-shirts, cushion covers and paper at this combined studio and shop. The images are often inspired by ancient and classical themes but are given a contemporary twist.

Forget Me Not Gifts & Souvenirs

(Map p64; ☎210 325 3740; www.forgetmenot athens.gr; Adrianou 100, Plaka; ⊗10am-9pm Apr & May, until 10pm Jun, Sep & Oct, until 11pm Jul & Aug, until 8pm Nov-Mar; MSyntagma, Monastiraki) This impeccable small store (two shops,

one upstairs and one down around the corner) stocks super-cool gear, from fashion to housewares and gifts, all by contemporary Greek designers. Great for gift shopping – who doesn't want a set of cheerful 'evil eye' coasters or some Hermes-winged beach sandals?

Shedia Arts & Crafts

(Map p64; ☎213 023 1220; www.shediart.gr; Nikiou 2, Monastiraki; MMonastiraki) Meaning 'raft', *Shedia* is Greece's version of street-vendor magazines such as the *Big Issue*. Unsold copies are now being upcycled into an appealing range of homewares and accessories including papier-mâché lampshades and bowls, and dainty earrings and necklaces. The space beneath their editorial offices has been reimagined as a shop and stylish cafe-bar.

Mastiha Shop Food

(Map p70; ☎210 363 2750; www.mastihashop. com; Panepistimiou 6, Kolonaki; ⊗9am-8pm Mon & Wed, to 9pm Tue, Thu & Fri, to 5pm Sat; MSyntagma) Mastic (*mastiha* in Greek), the medicinal resin from rare trees only found on the island of Chios, is the key ingredient in everything in this store, from natural skin products to a liqueur that's divine when served chilled.

Alexis Papachatzis Jewellery

(Map p64; ☎210 325 4064; www.alexisp.gr; Erehtheos 6, Plaka; ⊗10am-4pm Mon, Wed & Fri, to 7pm Tue, Thu & Sat; MMonastiraki, Syntagma) This charming jewellery store is a delight before you even enter: turn the handle on the window display and watch as gears and pulleys animate the scene. Papachatzis' designs have a storybook quality: small figures, clouds and animals rendered in sterling silver and enamel.

Zacharias Fashion & Accessories

(Map p70; www.zacharias.es; Zoodohou Pigis 55, Exarhia; ⊗10am-5pm Mon-Sat; MOmonia) A Greek-Spanish duo specialising in silk-screen designs inspired by classical motifs. Especially nice are their leather notebooks, wallets and more, where black ink on the natural hide echoes the colours of ancient pottery. Some of their work shows up in museum shops, but this storefront and workspace has the best selection.

🍴 EATING

Acropolis, Filoppapou Hill & Thisio

Veganaki   Vegan €
(Map p62; 📞210 924 4322; www.facebook.com/ VeganakiGR; Athanasiou Diakou 38, Kynosargous; mains €3.50-6.50; ⓧ8.30am-11.30pm; 🍴; MAkropoli) A fine addition to Athens' vegan dining options, this convivial spot may occupy a spot overlooking a busy road, but inside all is calm as customers enjoy falafel wraps and plates, sandwiches and traditional Greek pies, some of which are also gluten free. Also served here, a great cup of fair trade organic coffee.

Ellevoro   Greek €€
(Map p62; 📞210 924 6256; www.facebook.com/ ellevoro; Rovertou Galli 2, Makrygianni; mains €17-28; ⓧ2pm-midnight Mon-Sat, 1-9pm Sun; 🛜; MAkropoli) Three generations of a family work at this romantic homestyle restaurant that's decorated with wood beams, lacy white tablecloths, twinkling candles and chandeliers. Traditional Greek dishes – such as fava beans with smoked eel, and slow oven-baked lamb *kleftiko* – are superbly prepared and presented. A nice touch is the welcoming amuse bouche of a small cup of soup.

Mani Mani   Greek €€
(Map p62; 📞210 921 8180; www.manimani.com. gr; Falirou 10, Makrygianni; mains €12-23; ⓧ2-11pm; MAkropoli) Head upstairs to the relaxing, elegant dining rooms of this delightful modern restaurant, which specialises in herb-filled cuisine from the Mani region in the Peloponnese. Standouts include the ravioli with Swiss chard, the tangy sausage with orange, and the chicken stuffed with mushrooms and pecorino cheese.

Syntagma & Plaka

Avocado   Vegetarian €
(Map p64; 📞210 323 7878; www.avocado athens.com; Nikis 30, Plaka; mains €9-14; ⓧnoon-11pm Mon-Fri, 11am-11pm Sat, noon-7pm Sun; 🛜🍴; MSyntagma) This popular cafe offers a full array of vegan, gluten-free and organic treats with an international spin. Next to an organic market, and with a tiny front patio, here you can enjoy everything from sandwiches to quinoa with aubergine, or mixed-veg coconut curry. Juices and mango lassis are all made on the spot.

Ergon House Agora   Greek €€
(Map p64; 📞210 010 9090; https://house.ergon foods.com; Mitropoleos 23, Syntagma; mains €8-11.50; ⓧ7.30am-midnight; 🛜; MSyntagma) A superb addition to Athens' culinary landscape is this deli, cafe and restaurant occupying a gorgeously designed atrium space flooded with light. There are separate areas for a greengrocer, fishmonger, butcher and bakery, plus shelves packed with top-quality Greek products sourced from small-scale producers around the country. You'll dine well here and, most likely, leave laden down with goodies.

Sushimou   Japanese €€€
(Map p64; 📞211 407 8457; www.sushimou. gr; Skoufou 6, Syntagma; set menu €50-60; ⓧ6.30-10.30pm; 🛜; MSyntagma) Sushi in Athens doesn't get any better than this. Tell Antonis Drakoularakos, the Tokyo-trained chef who holds court behind the counter, your budget and he'll prepare a feast of local seafood sliced up as sashimi (raw fish) and nigiri (atop vinegared rice). It's a tiny place so book ahead at least a month to be sure of a spot.

Monastiraki & Psyrri

Dioskouri   Mezedhes €
(Map p64; 📞210 325 3333 www.dioskouriathens. gr; Adrianou 37-39, Monastriki; mezedhes €3-8; ⓧ8.30am-1am) This landmark cafe restaurant sprawls over the road, overlooking the railway line. On the cafe side, tables sit under a huge shade tree that gives the place a

Kleftiko (slow-cooked lamb) with vegetables

traditional village feel. For coffee, ouzo and snacks, it's popular with students – and of course tourists, thanks to its location on this pedestrian street.

Diporto Agoras — Taverna €

(Map p64; ☑210 321 1463; Sokratous 9 & Theatrou, Psyrri; plates €5-7; ☺7am-7pm Mon-Sat, closed 1-25 Aug; ⓂOmonia, Monastiraki) This charming old taverna is an Athens gem. There's no signage – look for two sets of doors leading to a rustic cellar. There's no printed menu either, just a few dishes that haven't changed in years. Order the house speciality *revythia* (chickpea stew) and follow up with grilled fish, paired with wine from one of the giant barrels lining the wall.

Karamanlidika tou Fani — Greek €€

(Map p64; ☑210 325 4184; www.karaman lidika.gr; Sokratous 1, Psyrri; dishes €6-15; ☺11am-midnight; ⓂMonastiraki) At this modern-day *pastomageireio* (combo tavern-deli) tables are set alongside the deli cases, and staff offer complimentary tasty morsels while you're looking at the menu. Beyond the Greek cheeses and cured meats, there's good seafood, such as

marinated anchovies, as well as rarer wines and craft beers. Service is excellent, as is the warm welcome, often from Fani herself.

Atlantikos — Seafood €€

(Map p64; ☑213 033 0850; Avliton 7, Psyrri; mains €6-13; ☺1pm-midnight; ⓂMonastiraki, Thissio) Tucked down a little lane, this small, hip fish restaurant is easy to miss – look for happy people chatting over heaps of shrimp shells. The atmosphere is simple and casual, with low prices to match – but there's excellent-quality seafood, whether it's fried or grilled.

ⓧ Gazi, Keramikos & Metaxourgio

Elvis — Greek €

(Map p64; ☑210 345 5836; Plateon 29, Keramikos; skewers €1.70; ☺noon-3am, to 5am Fri & Sat; ⓂKerameikos or Thissio) This souvlaki joint is mobbed, and not just because the counter staff slide you a shot of booze while you're waiting. The meat quality is high, the prices are right and the music is great. Every skewer comes with good chewy bread and fried potatoes.

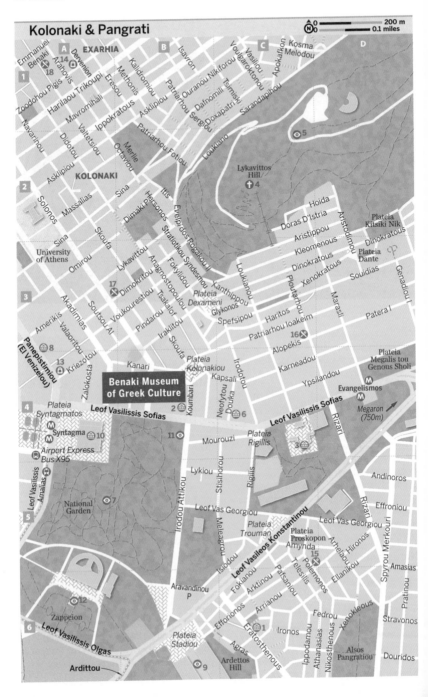

Kolonaki & Pangrati

N 0   200 m
0   0.1 miles

EXARHIA

KOLONAKI

University
of Athens

Lykavittos
Hill

Plateia
Kitsiki Nik

Plateia
Dante

Plateia
Dexameni

Plateia
Megalis tou
Genous Sholi

Plateia
Kolonakiou

Benaki Museum
of Greek Culture

Panepistimiou
(El Venizelou)

Leof Vasilissis Sofias

Leof Vasilissis Sofias

Evangelismos

Megaron
(750m)

Plateia
Syntagmatos

Syntagma

Airport Express
Bus X95

Plateia
Rigillis

Leof Vasilissis
Amalias

National
Garden

Leof Vas Georgiou

Leof Vas Georgiou

Plateia
Trouman

Plateia
Proskopon
Amynda

Leof Vasileos Konstantinou

Zappeion

Leof Vasilissis Olgas

Plateia
Stadiou

Ardettos
Hill

Alsos
Pangratiou

Ardittou

Kolonaki & Pangrati

Seychelles
Greek €€

(Map p64; ☑210 118 3478; www.seycheles.gr; Keramikou 49, Metaxourgio; mains €8.50-14.50; ☺2pm-12.30am Sun-Thu, until 1am Fri & Sat; MMetaxourghiou) Gutsy fresh food, an open kitchen, friendly service, a handwritten daily menu and rock on the soundtrack: Seychelles may be the Platonic ideal of a restaurant. Dishes can look simple – meaty pan-fried mushrooms with just a sliver of sheep's cheese, say, or greens with fish roe – but the flavours are excellent. Go early or book ahead; it's deservedly popular.

Athiri
Greek €€

(Map p64; ☑210 346 2983; www.athirirest aurant.gr; Plateon 15, Keramikos; mains €17-20; ☺7-11.30pm Tue-Sat, plus 1-5pm Sun Oct-May; MThissio) Athiri's lovely garden courtyard is a verdant surprise in this pocket of Kera-mikos. The small but innovative menu plays on Greek regional classics, with seasonal specialities. This might include Santorini *fava* (split-pea dip) and hearty beef stew with *myzithra* (sheep's-milk cheese), and handmade pasta from Karpathos.

⊗ Omonia & Exarhia

Ama Lachei stis Nefelis
Greek €

(☑210 384 5978; https://restaurant-47828. business.site; Kalidromiou 69, Exarhia; mezedhes €5.50-11.50; ☺1pm-12.30am Thu-Sun, from 6pm Tue & Wed; ☒2, 5, 9, 11 to Polytechneio) This modern *mezedhopoleio* (restaurant specialising in mezedhes) is a minor hike up Exarhia's hill, but you're rewarded with a lovely setting – an old school building,

with tables outside in the vine-shaded play-ground – and super-savoury small plates that go well with drinks. Think pickled oc-topus, meatballs flavoured with cinnamon and cloves, and lamb kebabs.

I Kriti
Cretan €€

(Map p64; ☑210 382 6998; Veranzerou 5, Omonia; mains €6-12; ☺noon-midnight Mon-Sat; 🛜; MOmonia) There is no shortage of Cretan restaurants in Athens, but this is the one that Cretans recommend, especially for rare seasonal treats such as stewed snails, bittersweet pickled *volvi* (wild bulbs), and tender baby goat with nuts and garlic. It oc-cupies several storefronts inside the arcade; on weekends it's a good idea to reserve.

Yiantes
Taverna €€

(Map p70; ☑210 330 1369; www.yiantes.gr; Valtet-siou 44, Exarhia; mains €9-15; ☺1pm-midnight; 🍴; MOmonia) This lovely restaurant with a central courtyard garden is upmarket for Ex-arhia, but the food is superb and made with largely organic produce. Expect interesting seasonal greens such as *almirikia* (sea beans), perfectly grilled fish or delicious mussels and calamari with saffron.

⊗ Kolonaki, Mets & Pangrati

Oikeio
Mediterranean €€

(Map p70; ☑210 725 9216; www.facebook.com/ oikeio; Ploutarhou 15, Kolonaki; mains €10-12; ☺12.30pm-midnight Mon-Thu, to 1am Fri & Sat, to 6pm Sun; MEvangelismos) With excellent homestyle cooking, this modern taverna lives up to its name (meaning 'homey'). It's decorated like a cosy bistro, and tables on the footpath allow people-watching without the usual Kolonaki bill. Pastas, salads and international fare are tasty, but try the daily *mayirefta* (ready-cooked meals), such as the excellent stuffed zucchini. Book ahead on weekends.

Mavro Provato — Mezedhes €€

(Black Sheep; Map p70; ☎210 722 3466; www.tomauroprovato.gr; Arrianou 31-33, Pangrati; dishes €6-17.50; ⊗1pm-1am Mon-Sat, to 7pm Sun; MEvangelismos) Book ahead for this wildly popular modern *mezedhopoleio* in Pangrati, where tables line the footpath and delicious small (well, small for Greece) plates are paired with regional Greek wines.

Philos Athens — International €€

(Map p70; ☎210 361 9163; www.facebook.com/philos.athens; Solonos 32, Kolonaki; mains €8-16; ⊗9am-5pm Mon-Fri, from 10am Sat & Sun; MPanepistimio, Syntagma) Distressed walls, a beautiful old tiled floor and a cascade of paper cranes dangling from the tall ceiling set the shabby-chic tone for this delightful cafe. It's a lovely spot to browse style magazines while grazing on breakfast or lunch dishes such as macrobiotic bowls or bolognese ragu over pasta.

Spondi — Mediterranean €€€

(☎210 756 4021; www.spondi.gr; Pyrronos 5, Pangrati; mains €48-60; set menus from €79; ⊗8-11.45pm; ☐209 to Plateia Varnava, ☐2, 4 or 11 to Plateia Plastira) Athenians frequently vote two-Michelin-starred Spondi the city's best restaurant, and its Mediterranean haute cuisine, with a strong French influence, is indeed excellent. It's a lovely dining experience, in a relaxed setting in a charming old house with a bougainvillea-draped garden. Book ahead.

🍸 DRINKING & NIGHTLIFE

The Clumsies — Bar

(Map p64; ☎210 323 2682; www.theclumsies.gr; Praxitelous 30, Syntagma; ⊗10am-2am Sun-Thu, to 4am Fri & Sat; MSyntagma) Look for the red neon in the hallway of this discreet bar that fills your coffee and creative cocktail needs. Founded by three award-winning bartenders, it's very serious about its drinks, but the

Six d.o.g.s.

atmosphere is definitely fun, and full of slick, handsome types on the weekends. From 6pm to 10pm you can order their degustation of four cocktails for €20.

Noel   Bar
(Map p64; ☑211 215 9534; https://noelbar.gr; Kolokotroni 59b, Monastiraki; ⏱10am-2am Sun-Thu, to 4am Fri & Sat; ⓂMonastiraki) One of the best of Athens' breed of maximalist-designed cafe-bars, Noel's slogan is 'where it's always Christmas' – meaning the candlelit cocktail-party kind of Christmas, no Santa suits required. Under softly glimmering chandeliers, smartly suited bartenders serve some of the most creative cocktails in town. Music is a mix of 1980s, '90s and jazz.

Six d.o.g.s.   Bar
(Map p64; ☑210 321 0510; https://sixdogs. gr; Avramiotou 6-8, Monastiraki; ⏱10am-late; ⓂMonastiraki) The core of this super-creative events space is a rustic, multi-level back garden, a great place for quiet daytime chats over coffee or a relaxed drink. From there, you can head in to one of several adjoining buildings to see a band, art show or other generally cool happening.

Couleur Locale   Bar
(Map p64; ☑216 700 4917; www.couleur localeathens.com; Normanou 3, Monastiraki; ⏱10am-2am Sun-Thu, to 3am Fri & Sat; ⓂMonastiraki) Look for the entrance to this rooftop bar down a narrow pedestrian lane, then inside the arcade. From there, an elevator goes to the 3rd floor and its lively all-day bar-restaurant. It's a go-to spot for Athenians who love a chill coffee or a louder evening, all in view of their beloved Acropolis.

Little Tree Book Cafe   Cafe
(Map p62; ☑210 924 3762; www.facebook.com/ littletreebooksandcoffee; Kavalloti 2, Makrygianni; ⏱8am-11pm Tue-Thu, until 11.30pm Fri, 9am-11.30pm Sat & Sun; ⓂAkropoli) This friendly social hub is much beloved by neighbourhood residents, who go for books (they stock a small selection of translated Greek authors here), but also excellent coffee, cocktails and snacks.

⚢ LGBT+ Travellers

Athens' LGBT+ scene is lively and increasingly becoming an international drawcard. **Athens Pride** (☑697 418 7383; www.athenspride.eu), held in early June, is an annual event; there's a march and a concert on Syntagma. For nightlife, Gazi is Athens' LGBT+ hub. For more information check out http://athens-real.com and www.athensinfoguide.com.

Pride parade outside Greek Parliament
KOSTAS KOUTSAFTIKIS/SHUTTERSTOCK ©

Blue Parrot   Cafe
(Map p64; ☑211 012 1099; Leonidou 31, Metaxourgio; ⏱9am-2am Sun-Thu, until 3am Fri & Sat; ⓂMetaxourghiou) Lashes of hanging greenery and a laid-back vibe, both inside and outside, make the Blue Parrot one of the area's most pleasant spots to hang out over a drink.

Yiasemi   Cafe
(Map p64; ☑213 041 7937; www.yiasemi.gr; Mnisikleous 23, Plaka; ⏱10am-3am; ⓂMonastiraki) Proof that Plaka is still very much a Greek neighbourhood despite the tourists, Yiasemi attracts a good mix of young Athenians, who set up for hours in the big armchairs or out on the scenic steps. It's better by day (especially for the great veg breakfast buffet) and on weeknights, when it's not overwhelmed by the scene at nearby restaurants.

✪ ENTERTAINMENT

For comprehensive events listings, with links to online ticket-sales points, try the following:

www.thisisathens.org Athens tourism site.

www.athensculturenet.com English listings of events and performances

www.viva.gr Major ticket vendor, including for the Athens & Epidaurus Festival.

www.ticketservices.gr Event ticket sales.

Megaron   Performing Arts

(Athens Concert Hall; ☑210 728 2333; www.me garon.gr; Kokkali 1, cnr Leoforos Vasilissis Sofias, Ilissia; tickets from €7; ☉box office 10am-6pm Mon-Fri, to 2pm Sat, later on performance days; ⓂMegaro Mousikis) The city's premier performance hall presents an impressive program of entertainments, including classical concerts, opera, theatre and dance shows, featuring world-class international and Greek performers. There's often some sort of art exhibition on here, and between June and September concerts are also staged outdoors in the complex's back garden.

Onassis Cultural Centre   Arts Centre

(☑info & tickets 210 900 5800; www.sgt.gr; Leoforos Syngrou 107-109, Neos Kosmos; ☎; 🚌10 or 550 to Panteio, ⓂSygrou-Fix) Housed in an eye-catching piece of architecture that livens up the dull urbanity of Leoforos Syngrou, this visual- and performing-arts centre is well worth a visit. Cloaked in a striped cage of white marble, the building glows at night when it hosts big-name productions, installations and lectures. Check the schedule for free events.

Cine Paris   Cinema

(Map p64; ☑210 322 2071; www.cineparis.gr; Kydathineon 22, Plaka; adult/child €8/6; ☉May-Oct; ⓂSyntagma) The Paris was established in the 1920s and it's still a magical place to see a movie. On a rooftop in Plaka, it offers great views of the Acropolis from some seats.

Thission   Cinema

(Map p64; ☑210 342 0864; www.cine-thisio.gr; Apostolou Pavlou 7, Thisio; tickets €6-8; ☉May-Oct; ⓂThissio) Across from the Acropolis, this is a lovely old-style outdoor cinema in a garden setting. Sit towards the back if you want to catch a glimpse of the glowing

edifice. Tickets are the lower price if you attend Monday to Wednesday shows.

National Theatre   Theatre

(Map p64; ☑210 528 8100; www.n-t.gr; Agiou Konstantinou 22-24, Omonia; ⓂOmonia) One of the city's finest neoclassical buildings hosts contemporary theatre and ancient plays. The organisation also supports performances in other venues around town and, in summer, in ancient theatres across Greece. Happily for tourists, some of the productions are subtitled in English, and tickets are reasonably priced.

Dora Stratou Dance Theatre   Dance

(Map p62; ☑210 921 4650; www.grdance.org; Filopappou Hill, Thisio; adult/child €15/5; ☉performances 9.30pm Wed-Fri, 8.15pm Sat & Sun late May-Sep; ⓂPetralona, Akropoli) Every summer this company of 75 singers and dancers performs Greek folk dances, showing off the rich variety of regional costume and musical traditions. Performances are held at its open-air theatre on the western side of Filopappou Hill. It also runs folk-dancing workshops.

Gazarte   Live Music

(Map p64; ☑210 346 0347; www.gazarte.gr; Voutadon 32-34, Gazi; tickets from €10; ⓂKerameikos) At this respected arts complex, you'll find largely mainstream music and a trendy 30-something crowd. A ground-level theatre hosts live performances and there's also a rooftop bar and restaurant.

❶ INFORMATION

DANGERS & ANNOYANCES

Since the financial crisis, crime has risen in Athens. But this is a rise from almost zero, and violent street crime remains relatively rare. Nonetheless, travellers should be alert. Stay aware of your surroundings at night, especially in streets southwest of Omonia and parts of Metaxourgio, where sex workers and drug users gather.

LEFT LUGGAGE

There is reasonably priced (from €3.50 for six hours) storage at the airport (p305), and most hotels store luggage free for guests, although many simply pile bags in a hallway. Additionally, in the centre of Athens you'll find:

Athens Lockers (☑213 035 4760; www. athenslockers.com; Athinas 2, Monastiraki; €4-11; ☺8am-9pm May-Oct, to 8pm Apr-Nov; ⓂMonastiraki)

LeaveYourLuggage.gr (☑211 410 8440; www. leaveyourluggage.gr; Voulis 36, Plaka; €4-11; ☺8am-9pm May-Oct, to 8pm Nov-Apr; ☎; ⓂSyntagma)

MEDICAL SERVICES

Check pharmacy windows for details of the nearest duty pharmacy, or call ☑1434 (Greek only). There's a 24-hour pharmacy at the airport.

SOS Doctors (☑210 821 2222, 1016; www.sos iatroi.gr; ☺24hr) Pay service with English-speaking doctors who make house (or hotel) calls.

MONEY

Major banks have branches around Syntagma. ATMs are plentiful enough in commercial districts, but harder to find in more residential areas.

National Bank of Greece (☑210 334 0500; cnr Karageorgi Servias & Stadiou, Syntagma; ⓂSyn-

tagma) Has a 24-hour automated exchange machine.

Onexchange (www.onexchange.gr) Currency and money transfers. Branches include **Syntagma** (☑210 331 2462; Karageorgi Servias 2; ☺9am-9pm; ⓂSyntagma) and **Monastiraki** (☑210 322 2657; Areos 1; ☺9am-9pm; ⓂMonastiraki).

TOURIST INFORMATION

Athens City Information Kiosk (Map p64; www. thisisathens.org; Plateia Syntagmatos, Syntagma; ☺9am-6pm; ⓂSyntagma) Dishes out leaflets and advice.

Athens City Information Kiosk Airport (☑210 353 0390; www.athensconventionbureau.gr/ en/content/info-kiosk-athens-international-air port; Eleftherios Venizelos International Airport; ☺8am-8pm; ⓂAirport) Maps, transport information and all Athens info.

Athens Contemporary Art Map (http://athens artmap.net) Download a PDF of art spaces and events; alternatively, pick up a paper copy at galleries and cafes around town.

EOT (Greek National Tourism Organisation; Map p62; ☑210 331 0347, 210 331 0716; www.visit

National Theatre

greece.gr; Dionysiou Areopagitou 18-20, Makry-gianni; ⊗8am-8pm Mon-Fri, 10am-4pm Sat & Sun May-Sep, 9am-7pm Mon-Fri Oct-Apr; MAkropoli) Free Athens map, current site hours and bus and train information. Also has desk at the **airport** (⊗9am-5pm Mon-Fri, 10am-4pm Sat).

ⓘ GETTING THERE & AWAY

AIR

Athens' airport (p305), at Spata, 27km east of Athens, is a manageable single terminal with all the modern conveniences.

BOAT

PIRAEUS

Most ferry, hydrofoil and high-speed catamaran services to the islands leave from the massive port at **Piraeus** (☎210 455 0000, €0.89 per 1min 14541; www.olp.gr), southwest of Athens. Purchase tickets online at **Greek Ferries** (☎281 052 9000; www.greekferries.gr), over the phone or at booths on the quay next to each ferry. Travel agencies selling tickets also surround each port; there is no surcharge.

RAFINA

Some services for the Cyclades arrive at/depart from the small port of Rafina, around 30km east of Athens and the airport. To reach Athens from Rafina, take a KTEL bus (€2.60, one hour, approx half-hourly 6am to 10.45pm), which arrives at the **Mavromateon Terminal** (☎210 880 8000, 210 822 5148; www.ktelattikis.gr; cnr Leoforos Alexandras & 28 Oktovriou-Patision, Pedion Areos; 🚌2, 4, 5 or 11 to OTE, MVictoria), north of Athens centre.

BUS

Athens has two main intercity bus stations – **Kifissos Terminal A** (☎210 515 0025; Drakontos 76, Peristeri; MAgios Antonios), about 4km northwest of Omonia, for buses to/from the Peloponnese, the Ionian Islands and destinations in western Greece; and Liossion Terminal B, 3.5km north of Omonia, for buses to central and northern Greece, such as Trikala (for Meteora) and Delphi – plus a small bay for buses bound for south and east Attica.

Pick up timetables at the tourist office (p75), or see the relevant KTEL operator's website; find a master list of KTEL companies at www.ktelbus. com. **KTEL Attikis** (☎210 880 8000; http://ktelattikis.gr) covers the Attica peninsula; **KTEL Argolida** (☎275 202 7423; www.ktelargolida.gr) serves Epidavros, with dedicated buses during the summer festival season.

Advance tickets for services from Kifissos Terminal A can be purchased at the **ticket office** (☎210 523 3810; Sokratous 59, Omonia; ⊗7am-5.15pm Mon-Fri; MOmonia) near Omonia.

For international buses (from Bulgaria, Turkey etc), there is no single station; some come to Kifissos, while others stop between Plateia Karaïskaki and Plateia Omonias. **Tourist Service** (www.tourist-service.com) is one operator from Piraeus and Athens to Bulgaria.

CAR & MOTORCYCLE

Attiki Odos (Attiki Rd), Ethniki Odos (National Rd) and various ring roads facilitate getting in and out of Athens.

The airport has all major car-hire companies, and the north end of Leoforos Syngrou, near the Temple of Olympian Zeus (p60), is dotted with firms. Expect to pay €45 per day, less for three or more days.

TRAIN

Intercity (IC) trains to central and northern Greece depart from the central **Larisis train station** (Stathmos Larisis; ☎14511 , €1 per 1min 6am-11pm; www.trainose.gr; MLarissa), about 1km northwest of Plateia Omonias.

For the Peloponnese, take the **suburban rail** (Proastiakos; ☎14511; www.trainose.gr) to Kiato and change for a bus there.

ⓘ GETTING AROUND

Central Athens is compact and good for strolling, with narrow streets and a lovely pedestrian promenade. From Gazi in the west to the Byzantine & Christian Museum in the east, for example, takes only about 45 minutes – so you may find you rarely need a transit pass. In summer, however, take the punishing sun into consideration.

GETTING TO/FROM THE AIRPORT

BUS

Express buses operate 24 hours between the airport and key points in the city. At the airport, buy tickets (€6; not valid for other forms of public transport) at the booth near the stop.

Plateia Syntagmatos Bus **X95** (Map p70; tickets €6; ⊙24hr), one to 1½ hours, every 20 to 30 minutes. The Syntagma stop is on Othonos St.

Kifissos Terminal A and **Liossion Terminal B** **bus stations** Bus X93, one hour (terminal B) to 1½ hours (terminal A), every 20 to 30 minutes (60 minutes at night).

Piraeus Bus X96, 1½ hours, every 20 minutes. To Plateia Karaïskaki.

METRO

Metro line 3 goes from the airport to the city centre. Trains run every 30 minutes, leaving the airport between 6.30am and 11.30pm, on the hour and half-hour. Coming from the centre, trains leave Monastiraki between 5.40am and 11pm; some terminate early at Doukissis Plakentias, so disembark and wait for the airport train (displayed on the train and platform screen).

Tickets from the airport are priced separately from the rest of the metro. The cost is €10 per adult or €18 return (return valid seven days). A €22 pass, good for three days, includes round-trip airport service and all other transit in the centre.

SUBURBAN RAIL

Suburban rail (one hour) is an option to the centre, if you're headed near Larisis train station (after a change at Ano Liosia) or a stop on metro line 1 (change at Neratziotissa). It's the same price as the metro. Trains to Athens run every 15 minutes from 5.10am to 11.30pm; to the airport, from 6am to midnight.

Suburban rail also goes from the airport to Piraeus (change trains at Neratziotissa) and Kiato in the Peloponnese (via Corinth).

TAXI

From the airport to the centre, fares are flat day/night €38/54 rates; tolls are included. The ride takes 30 to 45 minutes. For Piraeus (one hour), expect day/night €50/60.

 **Tickets & Passes**

The transit system uses the unified Ath.ena Ticket, a reloadable paper card available from ticket offices and machines in the metro. You can load it with a set amount of money or buy a number of rides (€1.40 each; discount when you buy five or 10) or a 24-hour/five-day travel pass for €4.50/9.

Children under six travel free; people under 18 or over 65 are technically eligible to pay half fare, but you must buy the Ath.ena Ticket from a person at a ticket office. If you're staying a while, you may want the sturdier plastic Ath.ena Card, also available at ticket offices; you must load at least €4.50 to start.

Swipe the card at metro turnstiles or, on buses and trams, validate the ticket in the machine as you board, and keep it with you in case of spot-checks. One swipe is good for 90 minutes, including any transfers or return trips.

Ath.ena Ticket

To the airport, drivers will usually propose a flat fare of €40 from the centre. You can insist on the meter, but with all the legitimate add-ons – tolls, airport fee, luggage fees – it usually works out the same.

To prebook a taxi, contact **Welcome Pickups** (www.welcomepickups.com), which charges at the same flat rate as regular taxis.

BICYCLE

Even experienced cyclists might find Athens' roads a challenge, with no cycle lanes, often reckless drivers and loads of hills – but some hardy locals do ride. A bike route runs from Thisio to the coast. A few outfits offer bicycle hire, such as **Funky Ride** (☑211 710 9366; www.funkyride.gr; Dimitrakopoulou 1, Makrygianni; 3hr/day €7/15; ☺10.30am-3.30pm & 5.30-8.30pm Mon-Fri, 10.30am-4pm Sat; MAkropoli). **Solebike** (Map p62; ☑210 921 5620; www.solebike.eu; Lembesi 11, Makrygianni; 2hr/1 day €28/36; ☺9.30am-2.30pm & 4.30-8.30pm Mon-Fri, 9.30am-4.30pm Sat Apr-Oct, shorter hours Nov-Mar; MAkropoli) runs bike tours.

BUS & TROLLEYBUS

Local express buses, regular buses and electric trolleybuses operate every 15 minutes from 5am to midnight. In lieu of maps, use Google Maps for directions or the trip planner on the website of the bus company, **OASA** (Athens Urban Transport Organisation; ☑11185; www.oasa.gr; ☺call centre 6.30am-10.30pm Mon-Fri, from 7.30am Sat & Sun) – click 'Telematics'. The most useful lines for tourists are trolleybuses 2, 5, 11 and 15, which run north from Syntagma past the National Archaeological Museum (p48). For all buses, board at any door; swipe your ticket on validation machines.

CAR & MOTORCYCLE

Athens' notorious traffic congestion, confusing signage, impatient drivers and narrow one-way streets make for occasionally nightmarish driving.

Contrary to what you see, parking is actually illegal alongside kerbs marked with yellow lines, on footpaths and in pedestrian malls. Paid parking areas require tickets available from kiosks.

METRO

The metro works well and posted maps have clear icons and English labels. Trains operate from 5.30am to 12.30am, every four minutes during peak periods and every 10 minutes offpeak. On Friday and Saturday, lines 2 and 3 run till 2.30am. Get information at www.stasy.gr. All stations have wheelchair access.

Line 1 (Green) The oldest line, Kifisia–Piraeus, known as the Ilektriko, is slower than the others and above ground. After hours, a **night bus** (Map p64; 500, Piraeus–Kifisia) follows the route, stopping outside the metro stations.

Line 2 (Red) Runs from Agios Antonios in the northwest to Agios Dimitrios in the southeast.

Line 3 (Blue) Runs northeast from Egaleo to Doukissis Plakentias, with airport trains continuing on from there. Transfer for line 1 at Monastiraki; for line 2 at Syntagma.

TAXI

Athens' taxis are excellent value and can be the key for efficient travel on some routes. But it can be tricky getting one, especially during rush hour. Thrust your arm out vigorously...you may still have to shout your destination to the driver to see if he or she is interested. Make sure the meter is on. It can be much easier to use the mobile app **Beat** (www.thebeat.co/gr) or **Taxiplon** (☑210 277 3600, 18222; www.taxiplon.gr) – you can pay in cash. Or call a taxi from dispatchers such as **Athina 1** (☑210 921 0417, 210 921 2800; www.athens1.gr), **Enotita** (☑6980666720, 18388, 210 649 5099; www.athensradiotaxi enotita.gr) or **Parthenon** (☑210 532 3300; www.radiotaxi-parthenon.gr). For day trips, **Athens Tour Taxi** (☑6932295395; www.athenstourtaxi.com) comes recommended.

If a taxi picks you up while already carrying passengers, the fare is not shared: each person pays the fare on the meter minus any diversions to drop others (note what it's at when you get in). Short trips around central Athens cost about €5; there are surcharges for luggage and pickups at transport hubs. Nights and holidays, the fare is about 60% higher.

TRAIN

Suburban rail (p76) is fast, but not commonly used by visitors – though it goes to the airport and as far as Piraeus and the northern Peloponnese. The airport–Kiato line (€14, 1½ hours) connects to the metro at Doukissis Plakentias and Neratziotissa. Two other lines cross the metro at Larisis station.

A short **funicular railway** (Teleferik; ☑210 721 0701; www.lycabettushill.com; Aristippou 1, Kolonaki; one way/return €5/7.50; ☺8.30-2.30am) runs up Lykavittos Hill.

Where to Stay

Athens' range of lodging is comprehensive. In recent years there's been a mini-explosion of chic, small boutique developments. Make bookings at least a couple of months ahead; for July and August, ideally aim for four months ahead.

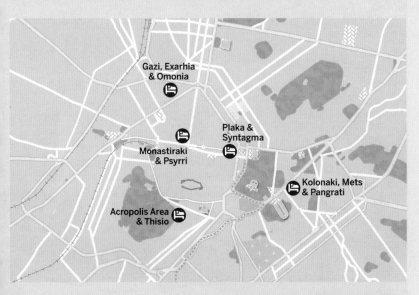

Neighbourhood	For	Against
Plaka & Syntagma	Close to Acropolis. Rooms in Syntagma tend to be larger with more amenities.	A bit loud in summer and definitely tourist central.
Monastiraki & Psyrri	Convenient to good nightlife and easy metro access from airport.	Noise from bars can be an issue.
Kolonaki, Mets & Pangrati	Upmarket, convenient to museums. Plenty of good restaurants and cafes.	Hotels here tend to be expensive.
Acropolis area & Thisio	Makrygianni, Koukaki (both popular with tourists) and Thisio are quieter, pleasant residential areas.	While handy areas for walking to the Acropolis. Thisio has limited hotel options.
Gazi, Exarhia & Omonia	Athens' hipster fringes, with good bars and crumbling, graffiti-covered mansions. Omonia offers new and renovated hotels.	Visible drug use, prostitution, some distance from central sights.

THESSALONIKI

Thessaloniki at a Glance...

Thessaloniki is easy to fall in love with – it has beauty, chaos, history and culture, a remarkable cuisine and wonderful, vast sea views. This is Greece's second city, which, like the rest of the country, has suffered the hit of the economic crisis, but the streets remain full of life and vibrancy. The city's neighbourhoods are little worlds unto themselves while old and new cohabit wonderfully. The revamped waterfront area is a marvellous addition to the city and is great for walking and cycling. After dark, the city reverberates with music and nightlife.

Two Days in Thessaloniki

Hang out for a day by the iconic **White Tower** (p91) and revamped **New Waterfront** (p90). Get a dose of local history and culture at the **Museum of Byzantine Culture** (p90) and **Archaeological Museum** (p90). On day two stick by the water to explore Ladadika and the old Jewish neighbourhood, stopping by the **Macedonian Museum of Contemporary Art** (p96) and **Modiano Market** (p98).

Four Days in Thessaloniki

Take in the splendid views from the city's old **Kastra** (p97) and Byzantine Walls. Drop by the Unesco-listed **Monastery of Vlatadon** (p98) as well as the Roman ruins the **Rotunda of Galerius** (p91) and **Arch of Galerius** (p94). On day four do some more deep diving into Thessaloniki's gourmet scene.

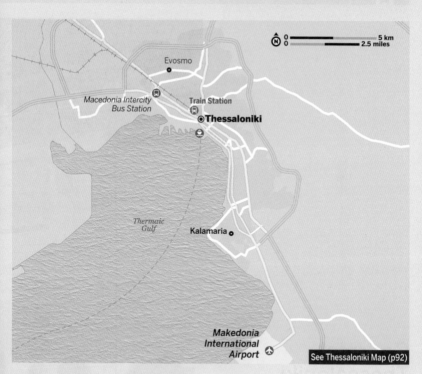

Evosmo

Macedonia Intercity
Bus Station

Train Station

Thessaloniki

*Thermaic
Gulf*

Kalamaria

*Makedonia
International
Airport*

See Thessaloniki Map (p92)

Arriving in Thessaloniki

Thessaloniki is northern Greece's transport hub and gateway to the Balkans. Major European airlines and budget airlines fly to the city's **Makedonia International Airport** (p305). Ferries from Thessaloniki port are limited and change annually. There are also international and domestic bus and train connections to the city.

Where to Stay

Thessaloniki has a diverse range of places to stay, across all of its neighbourhoods, and some trendy boutique hotels have opened up in recent years. Ano Poli is the quietest area, but count on a serious uphill hike to your chambers. The waterfront places have the best views, but can be noisy with Leoforos Nikis nightlife.

Outdoor eating

Gourmet Thessaloniki

Thessaloniki may be Greece's second city, but when it comes to the pleasures of the table it yields to none. Taking the bounty of the Thermaic Gulf and its fertile hinterland and ennobling it through the Greek, Turkish, Jewish and Slavic culinary traditions absorbed down the centuries, it is nothing less than one of the Mediterranean's great foodie destinations.

Great For...

ℹ Need to Know

Some of Thessaloniki's better kitchens open at the unusual daytime hour of 1pm, or even 2pm.

★ Top Tip

Thessaloniki's version of fish and chips – juicy salt cod, fried potato disks and garlicky *skordalia* (dip) – is best served at Tou Aristou (p100), a family joint frying near the port for more than 70 years.

Seafood

With its broad seafront and deep-rooted maritime traditions, Thessaloniki stands as a playground of piscine pleasures, even in a country as devoted to seafood as Greece. While the bounty of the deep features on nearly all Salonican menus, some places naturally stand out from the crowd. For expertly grilled dentex and red mullet, raw anchovies, or whatever is best at the market that morning, seek out Mourgá (p100), in the backstreets east of the Roman Forum.

Vegetables

Thessaloniki's broad, fertile hinterland produces some of the country's sweetest and most flavoursome veggies. *Horta*, the wild mountain greens thought to be one of

the secrets of Greek longevity, are raised to a higher plane by the simple addition of gorgeous, grassy olive oil, zinging-fresh goat curd and popping-sweet tomatoes at **Sempriko** (☑2310 557 513; Fragkon 2; mains €9-15; ⊗noon-11pm; ☎), beneath the western edge of the Byzantine walls. **I Nea Follia** (☑2310 960 383; cnr Aristomenous & Charitos; mains €7.50-12; ⊗2pm-midnight Sep-Jun; ☎☑), hidden amongst the apartment blocks and busy streets northeast of the Forum, performs a similar trick with another staple, puree of (dried) fava beans, serving it with astringent sea fennel, char-grilled octopus and (of course) more superb olive oil. **Full tou Meze** (☑2310 524 700; www.fullmeze.gr; Katouni 3; mezedhes €4-6, mains €7-9; ⊗1pm-midnight; ☎), in portside Ladadika, is another place where fava puree, here strewn with tart caperberries, is

Trigona pastries

given the expert treatment accorded to all vegetables.

Tavernas & Ouzeris

Tavernas (informal restaurants serving food to go with alcohol) and *ouzeris* (near cousins where the tipples of choice are ouzo and *tsipouro*, distilled from grape must) are naturally abundant in Thessaloniki. Some of the best are to be found in the twisting, hilly streets of Ano Poli, the delightfully scenic Upper Town that escaped devastation in the fire of 1917. The

> **☑ Don't Miss**
>
> Bit Bazaar, just west of the Roman Forum, is worth seeking out for top-notch mezedhes (small plates) in a gregarious, open-air setting.

BOAZ ROTTEM/ALAMY STOCK PHOTO ©

oldest, sitting beneath dusty blooms at a neighbourhood crossroad, is Tsinari (p100), while **Igglis** (☎2313 011 967; Irodotou 32; mains €7; ☉1pm-midnight; ☎), a top-notch taverna in the eastern lee of the Byzantine walls, has also pleased locals for more than 100 years.

Markets & Bazaars

Thessaloniki's markets are a joy. Taking up prime real estate near Plateia Aristotelou (as befits their position in Salonican society) they're the lifeblood of the city's dining scene, laying out the freshest vegetables, shiniest seafood and choicest smallgoods and cheeses for the delectation of its citizens. The largest, Modiano (p98), opened on the site of a Jewish neighbourhood razed by the fire of 1917. Bazaars, a legacy of Thessaloniki's deep-rooted Turkish population, now often house jostling collections of restaurants and tavernas.

Sweet Things

Salonicans, who need no encouragement when it comes to devising sweet sensations to cap off their meals or fuel them between lunch and dinner, learnt a thing or two from Turkish pastry cooks. Ottoman and Arab treats such as baklava, *halva* and *basbousa* (a syrup-drenched semolina cake known locally as *revani*) can now be found alongside Greek classics such as *rizogalo* (rice pudding) at ubiquitous sweet shops such as long-standing **Chatzis** (☎2310 279 058; http://chatzis.gr; Venizelou 50; sweets €1.40-4; ☉8am-1am; ☎).

> **✗ Take a Break**
>
> Sample the classic Thessaloniki sweet treat the *trigona*, a custard-filled pastry triangle, at its place-of-origin: **Trigona Elenidis** (☎2310 257 510; www.elenidis. gr; cnr Dimitriou Gounari & Tsimiski; trigones €2.50; ☉9am-11pm).

Thessaloniki City Walk

Start this city stroll around 9am, as many churches close by noon. Avoid Mondays, when most sites are closed.

Start Eptapyrgion
Distance 4km
Duration 3 hours

5 The burly 7th-century **Church of Agios Dimitriou** (p91), occupying its own square, shelters relics of St Dimitrios.

Kassandrou

Agiou Nikolaou

Olymbiados

Agiou Dimitriou

5

Agnostou Stratiotou

Olympou

Filippou

Take a Break...
Mourgá (p100) is everything that's delightful about Greek food.

Egnatia

Mitropoleos

Plateia Fanarioton

Tsimiski

Leof Nikis

7 The waterfront **White Tower** (p91) was once a notorious prison, but now harbours a multimedia museum.

FINISH **7**

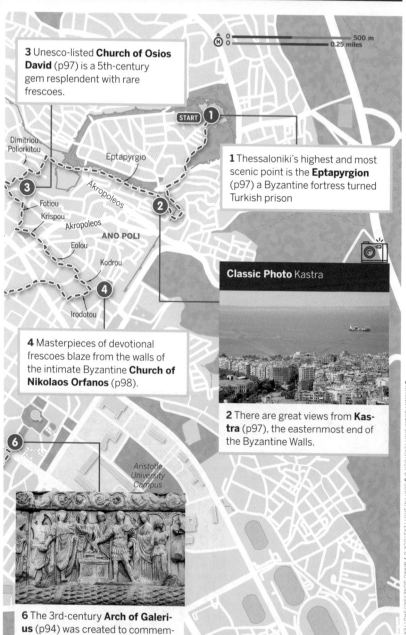

3 Unesco-listed **Church of Osios David** (p97) is a 5th-century gem resplendent with rare frescoes.

Dimitriou Poliorkitou

Eptapyrgio

Akropoleos

Fotiou

Krispou

Akropoleos

ANO POLI

Eolou

Kodrou

Irodotou

START

1 Thessaloniki's highest and most scenic point is the **Eptapyrgion** (p97) a Byzantine fortress turned Turkish prison

Classic Photo Kastra

2 There are great views from **Kastra** (p97), the easternmost end of the Byzantine Walls.

4 Masterpieces of devotional frescoes blaze from the walls of the intimate Byzantine **Church of Nikolaos Orfanos** (p98).

Aristotle University Campus

6 The 3rd-century **Arch of Galerius** (p94) was created to commemorate Galerius' victory over the Persian army.

500 m
0.25 miles

2 ATHINA PSOMA/SHUTTERSTOCK © 6 CORTYN/SHUTTERSTOCK © 7 MIRKO GONESVKI/SHUTTERSTOCK ©

⊙ SIGHTS
⊙ White Tower & Waterfront

Archaeological Museum · Museum
(☎2313 310 201; www.amth.gr; Manoli Andron-ikou 6; adult/concession €8/4, 1st Sun of month Nov-Mar free; ⊗8am-8pm Apr-Oct, 9am-4pm Nov-Mar) Macedonia's prehistory, Hellenistic and Roman periods are charted in this wonderful museum, home to many of the region's major archaeological discoveries. Highlights include goldwork from various hoards and graves, and the **Derveni Krater** (330–320 BC), a huge, ornate Hellenistic bronze-and-tin vase marked by intricate relief carvings of Dionysos, along with mythical figures, animals and ivy vines. The **Derveni Papyrus**, Greece's oldest surviving papyrus piece (320–250 BC), is recognised by Unesco as Europe's oldest 'book'.

Museum of Byzantine Culture · Museum
(☎2313 306 400; www.mbp.gr; Leoforos Stratou 2; adult/concession Apr-Oct €8/4, all tickets Nov-Mar €4; ⊗8am-8pm Apr-Oct, 9am-4pm Nov-Mar) This fascinating museum has treasures to please Byzantine buffs, plus simple explanations to introduce this long-lived empire and its culture to beginners. More than 3000 Byzantine objects, including mosaics, intriguing tomb paintings, icons, jewellery and glassware, are showcased with characterful asides about daily life. You'll be confidently discerning early-Christian from late-Byzantine icons in no time. Temporary exhibitions might focus on anything from satirical maps to the work of Cretan writer and mystic Nikos Kazantzakis.

New Waterfront · Waterfront
(Nea Paralia) Thessaloniki's New Waterfront is evidence that architecture can improve urban life through intelligent redesign of the space in which it is lived. Recipient of numerous awards for its architects Prodromos Nikiforidis and Bernard Cuomo, this 3.5km walkway extends from the White Tower to the Thessaloniki Concert Hall. Completed in 2013, it has been embraced by Thessalonikans with absolute delight as the perfect place to promenade, roller-blade, bike, play, eat ice cream or just enjoy peripatetic conversation.

Arch of Galerius (p94)

PIT STOCK/SHUTTERSTOCK ©

White Tower   Tower

(Lefkos Pyrgos; 2310 267 832; www.lpth.gr; Leoforos Nikis; adult/concession €4/2; 8am-8pm Apr-Oct, 9am-4pm Nov-Mar) Thessaloniki's iconic landmark, the 34m-high White Tower has a harrowing history as a prison and place of execution. Built by the Ottomans in the 15th century, it was here in 1826 that Sultan Mahmud II massacred the garrison of rebellious janissaries (forcibly Islamicised elite troops). One story goes that the structure was known as the Tower of Blood until a prisoner painted the tower white in exchange for his liberty in 1883, when it was renamed Lefkos Pyrgos (White Tower).

Thessaloniki
Concert Hall   Architecture

(Megaro Mousikis/M1 & M2; 2310 895 800; www.tch.gr; 25 Martiou, cnr Paralia; box office 10am-6pm Mon-Sat & 2hr before every event) **FREE** Japanese architect Arata Isozaki created the M2, one of two waterfront buildings that house Thessaloniki's highbrow music scene. It's a strikingly contemporary structure with impeccably simple geometry, using glass, stone and steel, and making the most of the city's sea views and natural light. The neighbouring M1 is a red-brick structure; yet the two work oddly together, the M1 solid and dense and the M2 transparent and light. International and domestic artists perform here. Check the website for details.

⊙ Egnatia & Central

Following the path of the 2nd-century-BC Roman road between the Adriatic and Byzantium, Egnatia is still Thessaloniki's main drag, and much of the city is divided as above and below Egnatia. Three major Roman monuments of early-4th-century emperor Galerius spill across Egnatia at Plateia Navarinou: the ruined Palace of Galerius, the Arch of Galerius and the now-renovated Rotunda to its north. This central Thessaloniki neighbourhood also has some of the city's most fascinating churches.

🎟 Combo Ticket

The combined ticket to the Museum of Byzantine Culture, Archaeological Museum, White Tower, Roman Forum and Galerian Complex-Arched Hall, will save history buffs plenty. Valid for three days and obtainable from any of the museums involved, it's just €15/8 for adults/concession holders.

White Tower
ANITA ISALSKA/LONELY PLANET ©

Church of Agios Dimitrios   Church

(2310 270 008; www.inad.gr; Agiou Dimitriou 97; 6am-10pm, crypt 8am-2pm Wed-Mon) This enormous 7th-century basilica honours Thessaloniki's patron saint. A Roman soldier, Dimitrios was killed around AD 306 at this former Roman bath site by order of Emperor Galerius, infamous persecutor of Christians. The martyrdom site is now a **crypt**; Dimitrios' remains occupy a silver reliquary inside. The Ottomans made Agios Dimitrios a mosque, and plastered over frescoes that were again revealed after the 1913 Greek reconquest. While the city's fire of 1917 was very damaging, five 8th-century mosaics survive.

Rotunda of Galerius   Historic Building

(2310 204 868; Plateia Agiou Georgiou; €2; 8am-9.30pm Mon & Wed-Fri, 9am-4.30pm Sat & Sun) **FREE** In AD 306 Roman emperor Galerius built this harmonious 30m-high dome, comparable to Rome's Pantheon and possibly intended as his mausoleum. Marking the momentous arrival of Christianity as the religion of Empire, the Rotunda

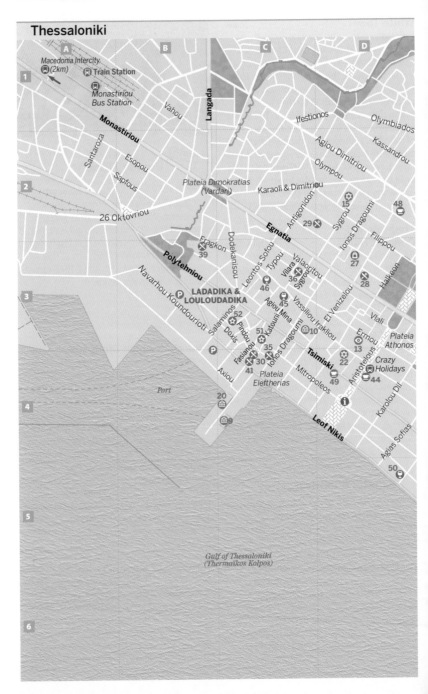

Thessaloniki

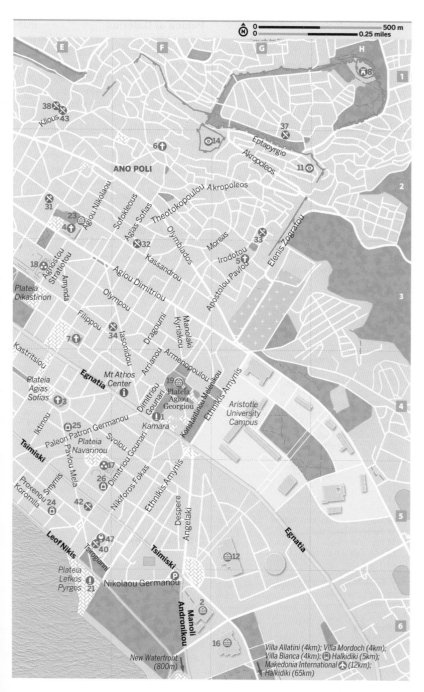

0   500 m
0   0.25 miles

ANO POLI

38 Klious 43

31

23
4

18 Agnostou Stratiotou
Amynda

Plateia Dikastirion

7

Kastritsiou

Plateia Agias Sofias 3

Iktinou

Tsimiski

Proxenou Koromila

Smyrnis

42

Leof Nikis

47
40
Tsirogianni

Plateia Lefkos Pyrgos 21

Nikolaou Germanou

New Waterfront (800m)

Agiou Nikolaou
Sofokleous
Agias Sofias
Theotokopoulou Akropoleos

32
Kassandrou

Olymbados

Agiou Dimitriou

Olympou

Filippou

34 Iasonidou

Dragoumi

Egnatia

Mt Athos Center

Dimitriou Gounari

Paleon Patron Germanou

Plateia Pavlou Mela

Svolou

17
26 Dimitriou Gounari

Nikiforos Fokas

Ethnikis Amynis

Despere

Angelaki

Tsimiski

Manoli Andronikou

12

2

16

6
14

Eptapyrgio
Akropoleos

37

11

Akropoleos

Moreas

Irodotou

5
Apostolou Pavlou

33

Elenis Zografou

Manolaki Kyriakou

Armenopoulou

19
Plateia Agiou Georgiou

1
Kamara

Konstantinou Melenikou

Ethnikis Amynis

Aristotle University Campus

Ethnikis Amynis

Egnatia

8

Villa Allatini (4km); Villa Mordoch (4km); Villa Bianca (4km); Halkidiki (5km); Makedonia International (12km); Halkidiki (65km)

25

became Thessaloniki's first church (Agios Georgios; observe dragon-slaying St George above the door). The Ottomans in turn made it a mosque (hence the restored minaret), but since the Greek reconquest of 1912 it has served both sacred and secular purposes.

Arch of Galerius   Monument

(Egnatia) **FREE** South of the Rotunda on Egnatia, the Arch of Galerius (AD 303) celebrates the eponymous emperor's victory over the Persians in martial scenes carved into the marble panels that face its masonry core. Known locally as Kamara, this landmark is also the city's main meeting spot. The Arch originally had four main and four supporting pillars, with eight gates and arches, and a dome – only two of the central arches and one supporting arch can be seen today.

Palace of Galerius   Ruins

(http://galeriuspalace.culture.gr; Plateia Navarinou; ☺8am-3pm Tue-Sun) **FREE** Sprawling in splendid incongruity amidst the souvenir shops and crêperies of Plateia Navarinou, the ruins of this 3rd- to 4th-century palace remain impressive in scope. You can descend into it, or just peer over the handrail to see the surviving mosaics, columns, walls and infrastructure. What most brings the site to life is the Arched Hall, where exhibits, videos and digital re-creations convey something of the nature and scope of not just the palace, but the nearby triumphal arch and rotunda.

Roman Forum   Ruins

(Ancient Agora; ☏2310 221 260; btwn Olimpou, Fillippou, Makedonikis Aminis & Agnostou Stratiotou; adult/concession €4/2; ☺8.30am-4pm Wed-Mon) **FREE** As immaculately laid

Thessaloniki

out as you'd expect of the Romans, this rectangular site was the centre of public and commercial Thessaloniki from the 1st to the 4th centuries. Understandably much reduced, you'll nonetheless be able to make out streets, shops, baths, cloisters, an amphitheatre, fountains and more. Underground is the small but very-worthwhile museum, which adds considerably to the understanding of the site you'll take away.

Church of the Panagia Achiropiitos   Church

(Agias Sofias 56; ☺8am-noon & 5-7pm) This basilica-style 5th-century Byzantine church, built over Roman baths and one of the oldest in Greece, has notable mosaics and frescoes. The name, meaning 'made without hands', refers to a miraculous 12th-century appearance of an icon of the Virgin. The first of Thessaloniki's churches to be transformed into a mosque under Ottoman rule, its transition is marked by a marble column on the western side bearing the inscription 'Sultan Murad Conquered Thessaloniki in 833', recounting Murad II's victory in 1430.

Church of Agia Sofia   Church

(Plateia Agias Sofias; ☺7am-1pm & 6-7.30pm) Candlelight on gold chandeliers pierces the gloom in this stunning 8th-century church, modelled on its İstanbul namesake. Among many striking 8th- and 9th-century mosaics is an image of the Ascension of Christ in the central dome, while the 11th-century frescoes are masterpieces of Byzantine devotional art. Built over a previous 3rd-century church, it's notable for the cross-basilica style associated with middle-Byzantine architecture. The narthex and south aisle were used as a burial place for dignitaries from the 10th century.

Yeni Hammam   Historic Building

(☏2313 059 024; Agiou Nikolaou 3; ☺bar 7am-3pm) An atmospheric 16th-century structure, this former Turkish bath has great acoustics. Today it houses a bar that's gone to great lengths to turn the lovely old historic space into something colourful, vibrant, and fitting for nights of music and celebration.

✻ Festive Thessaloniki

Festivals in Thessaloniki are youth-focused, vibrant and often provocative. Book accommodation far in advance if your visit coincides with **Reworks International Music Festival** (www.reworks. gr; 3-day pass €50; ☺Sep). The two film festivals – **Thessaloniki Documentary Festival** (☏2310 378 400; www.filmfestival. gr; 10-screening tickets €25; ☺Mar) and the **Thessaloniki International Film Festival** (☏2310 378 400; www.filmfestival. gr; 10-screening ticket €40; ☺Nov) – are also worth attending if you're in town for their eclectic programming and promotion of local talent.

Thessaloniki International Film Festival

◉ Ladadika & Port

Former bazaar neighbourhood Ladadika has Thessaloniki's most concentrated dining and social scene, and is bordered to the east by the former Jewish neighbourhood along Mitropoleos. Opposite, the old port area's bulky pier supports three hip museums and is a favourite evening haunt for students.

Thessaloniki Museum of Photography   Museum

(☏2310 566 716; www.thmphoto.gr; Warehouse A, Port of Thessaloniki; adult/concession €2/1; ☺11am-7pm Tue-Thu, Sat & Sun, to 10pm Fri) This 1910 port warehouse presents thought-provoking exhibitions of historic and contemporary photography in Greece's

es **PhotoBiennale** (☏2310 566 716; www.
photobiennale-greece.gr; ⊗Apr-Oct even years),
an international photography festival every
even-numbered year.

Macedonian Museum of
Contemporary Art   Museum

(MOMus; ☏2310 240 002; www.mmca.gr;
Egnatia 154, TIF-Helexpo; ⊗10am-6pm Tue-Sun)
FREE One of the most respected modern-
art institutions in Greece, MOMus grew
from an initial bequest of 30 modern
masterpieces in 1979, and now exhibits
over 2000 examples of painting, sculpture, photography and other visual art.
While Greek artists such as Opi Zouni and
Angelos Skourtis are given plenty of attention, there are many treasures from other
countries and schools. A rich program of
temporary shows augments the perma-
nent collection.

Experimental Center
for the Arts   Museum

(☏2310 593 270; www.cact.gr; Warehouse B1,
Port of Thessaloniki; adult/concession €4/2;
⊗10am-6pm Tue, Wed & Fri-Sun, to 10pm Thu)
The wonderful programming at this old
harbour space features fine art, video,
installations, photography and all other
forms of expression. Exhibitions range from
reflections on radical humanist John Berger
to the economic crisis, gender and identity
issues, Greek art since 1960, and many
more fascinating themes.

Jewish Museum
of Thessaloniki   Museum

(☏2310 250 406; www.jmth.gr; Agiou Mina 13;
⊗9am-2pm Mon-Fri plus 5-8pm Wed, 10am-2pm
Sun) **FREE** This touching museum is housed
in one of the few Jewish buildings to survive
the great fire of 1917, the former office of
Jewish newspaper *L'Independent*. The
museum traces the city's Jewish heritage
through the 15th-century Sephardic immi-
grations and its peak period of creativity
in the 16th century, before the community was brutally annihilated during the
Holocaust.

📖 **Jewish Thessaloniki**

Thessaloniki's Jewish community
swelled following the arrival of exiled
Sephardic Jews from Spain in the 15th
century. The city enjoyed a golden age
of Jewish industry and culture, including
crafts such as weaving and silk dyeing,
in the 16th century.

The flourishing Jewish community
was brutally cut down in 1943 when
43,850 Jews were deported to their
deaths at Auschwitz. The history is
movingly conveyed at the city's Jewish
Museum.

In the city centre, find Thessaloniki's
principal synagogue, **Monastirioton**
(☏2310 275 701; www.jmth.gr; Sygrou 35;
⊗9am-2pm Mon-Fri plus 5-8pm Wed, 10am-
2pm Sun), used as a Red Cross centre
during the WWII Nazi occupation and
therefore spared. Services are held at
the newer **Yad Lazikaron** (www.jct.gr;
Vassiliou Irakliou 26).

Find other traces of this rich history
at 19th- and 20th-century former
Jewish mansions **Villa Allatini** (Leoforos
Vasilissis Olgas 198), **Villa Bianca**
(Municipal Art Gallery; ☏2310 427 555;
Themistokli Sofouli 3; ⊗10am-5pm Tue-Fri,
11am-3pm Sat) **FREE** – now the Centre for
Contemporary Art – and **Villa Mordoch**
(Leoforos Vasilissis Olgas 162), a 15-minute
bus ride along Leoforos Vasilissis Olgas.

Monastirioton

only dedicated photography museum.
Temporary exhibitions rotate every four
months or so, and the museum organis-

Ano Poli

The labyrinthine, steep streets of Ano Poli, Thessaloniki's upper town, have magnificent ruins, lesser-visited churches, and a wonderful atmosphere. Only Ano Poli (then, the Turkish Quarter) largely survived the city-wide devastation of the 1917 fire – although the fire originated here, the wind swept the flames towards the sea.

Church of Osios David   Church
(Epimenidou 17; ⊘10am-5pm Wed-Sun) This serene little 5th-century church, once the *katholikon* (major church) of the Monastery of Saviour Christ of Latomos, is one of the most significant early-Christian sites in Thessaloniki. It contains rare 12th-century frescoes and an even-more extraordinary 5th-century mosaic of Christ and the prophets Ezekiel and Habakkuk. Utterly glorious, it was covered up by the Turks during the church's time as a mosque, and only rediscovered in 1920.

Eptapyrgion   Fortress
(Yedi Kule; ☏2313 310 400; ⊘8am-5.45pm Mon-Fri, to 3.45pm Sat & Sun) `FREE` A former Byzantine fortress repurposed as a prison by the Ottomans and only decommissioned in 1989, the Eptapyrgion (Seven Towers) is a grim reminder of Thessaloniki's penal past, recounted in the Greek blues songs known as *rembetika*. Reached by a steep walk to the heights of Ano Poli, it's perfectly preserved, allowing access to some towers (of which there are actually 10), communal blocks and isolation cells, and displaying historical information and scattered artworks. The views from the Byzantine walls are the best in the city.

Kastra   Historic Site
`FREE` The *kastra* (castle) encloses Byzantine churches and timber-framed houses with overhanging upper storeys. Enjoy panoramic views from the tower by the eastern edge of the **Byzantine Walls**, built to survive sieges in the late 4th century BC. Emperor Theodosius fortified the walls; in places they were 10m high and 5m thick. They stood until the 19th century when the Ottomans demolished large stretches. Enjoy the views of the sunset over the city, along with students and locals.

Byzantine Walls

Modiano Market

The city's largest indoor **market** (btwn Ermou & Vassiliou Irakliou; ⊘8.30am-2.30pm Mon, Wed & Fri, 8.30am-1.30pm & 5.30-8.30pm Tue, Thu & Sat) sits on the ashes of former Jewish neighbourhood Kadi, which burned down in the 1917 fire. The architect Eli Modiano designed the market, which opened in 1930 and has carried his name ever since. Covered by a glass roof, there are several shops and tavernas here, and it's a charming place to wander around. There are abundant food vendors and delis in the markets and streets surrounding Modiano.

Modiano Market stalls
PETER EASTLAND/ALAMY STOCK PHOTO ©

Monastery of Vlatadon   Monastery
(Eptapyrgio 64; ⊘7.30am-8pm) **FREE** Believed to have been founded around 1351 on the place where Paul preached in Thessaloniki, this secluded monastery blends fascinating history with some of the best views of the city. Listed by Unesco, it is thought to have been significant for Hesychasm, a controversial movement whose foremost 14th-century proponent, St Gregory Palamas, is depicted in a fresco here. You can explore the grounds, the ancient church, a museum of icons, and an aviary filled with peacocks.

Church of Nikolaos Orfanos   Church
(Apostolou Pavlou; ⊘hours vary) This early-14th-century church, one of the most beautiful in a city heavy with stunning examples, has superb (though age-darkened) frescoes, many dating to the church's

earliest days. The 'orphan' in the church's name remains a mystery: it may be a nod to an anonymous benefactor or be linked to a former orphanage nearby.

⊙ TOURS

Thessaloniki Walking Tours   Walking
(☎6798186900; www.thessalonikiwalkingtours. com) Started by a Thessaloniki journalist, who enlisted architect, archaeologist and historian friends to work as guides, this is a great opportunity to go on specialised walks with expert locals. There are themed tours, such as a sailing tour exploring the city's bay as well as specific buildings, or a music tour that takes you around famous *rembetika* bars. Call for details.

🛍 SHOPPING

Ergon Agora   Food
(☎2310 288 008; www.ergonproducts.gr; Pavlou Mela 42; ⊘9am-1am) Fresh fish and meat, cheeses, top-notch fruit and vegetables, bread, oils, honey, vinegars – you name it, it's all to be found in this high-end 'closed market'. If you're overwhelmed by all you might create, you can simply put yourself in the hands of the central kitchen, which pumps out mainly Greek food from 10am to midnight.

From Thessaloniki   Arts & Crafts
(☎2310 272 298; www.fromthessaloniki.gr; Dimitriou Gounari 21; ⊘10.30am-8.30pm Mon-Sat) Architect Evangelia and set designer Athanasia, two wonderfully creative and warm women, started this little shop that makes and sells the most original and beautiful souvenirs in town. Choose from painted tiles, Greek god and goddess pillows, T-shirts, tote bags, mugs, jewellery, notebooks – all original and locally produced, and all useful objects that you can enjoy for years.

R2 Rebelou 2   Arts & Crafts
(Art Store Cafe; ☎2310 265 999; Rempelou 2; ⊘9am-1am) It's difficult to categorise this place – it includes a workshop, a shop,

an exhibition space and a cafe-bar. Run by agriculturist Christos and the graphic designer Nikos, who is also a marvellous carpenter, the pair find old furniture and decoration and turn them into something new and original.

Bientôt   Wine

(☎2310 253 781; Morgentaou 5; ⊗11am-4pm Mon, Wed & Sat, 11am-3pm & 5-9pm Tue, Thu & Fri) This passionate little wine shop is the ideal place to learn more about the varied, expanding and ever-refining world of Greek wine. The staff, who cultivate close relationships with producers working with indigenous Greek grape varieties, are happy to talk visitors through prebooked tastings.

✖ EATING

Omikron   Greek €

(☎2310 532 774; Oplopiou 3; mains €7-15; ⊗noon-midnight Tue-Sat; 🛜) Beneath walls strikingly decorated with mash-ups of classical paintings (think Botticelli's Venus emerging from a piece of aerosol art), this charming little place dishes up heart-

warming plates such as homemade pasta with mushrooms and pureed fava beans with chilli oil. Bounteous seasonal salads, expertly grilled meat and super-fresh seafood complete the picture.

Pizza Poselli   Pizza €

(☎2314 019 687; Vilara 2; pizza slices €2.30; ⊗noon-5am Sun-Thu, to 6am Fri & Sat) Many locals will agree that this is the best pizza place in town. Simple decor, with chic touches in the way of elegant wooden tables and vintage lamps, Poselli has mozzarella and truffle-oil pizzas, margheritas and the classic standards done to perfection. It also does a roaring trade in pizza by the slice for the Valaoritou bar crowd.

Rediviva Cucina Povera   Greek €

(☎2313 067 400; Papadopoulou 70; mains €5-8; ⊗1pm-midnight; 🛜) This earthy Ano Poli restaurant sources many of its ingredients locally and from its own back garden. Using what's in season, it serves a diverse range of Greek dishes with particular emphasis on the food of Crete and Lesvos. Try the Cretan herb *pita* (pie), sun-dried fish and

Monastery of Vlatadon

fantastic salads, then perhaps buy a jar of their marmalade to take away.

Tou Aristou   Fish & Chips €
(2310 542 906; www.mpakaliaros.gr; Katouni 3; fish & chips €9; 10.30am-7.30pm) This close to the port, it makes sense to try Thessaloniki's take on fish and chips, prepared here since 1940. Thick cuts of salt cod are expertly fried in oil that changes daily, then served with golden-fried potato discs (chips, really) and garlic sauce. Delicious.

To Etsi   Greek €
(2310 222 469; Nikoforos Fokas 2; grills €2.80-4; 1pm-2am Sun & Mon, to 3am Tue-Thu, to 4am Fri & Sat) This bawdily decorated, iconic eatery near the White Tower is a local institution offering refreshingly light souvlaki and *soutzoukakia* (meat rissoles in tomato sauce) with vegetable dips, in Cypriot-style pitta bread.

Giannoula   Greek €
(2310 263 928; Kassandrou 50; mains €5-6; noon-11pm Mon-Sat Sep-Jun) This is grandmother's cooking in a very literal way. Simple Greek classics from grills to salads to cheese-stuffed meats have been served with the same simple expertise for decades in this tiny checked-tablecloth taverna above the Roman Forum. Kyria Giannoula's sons run the taverna now, but her cooking wisdom has been well preserved.

Tsinari   Greek €
(2310 284 028; Papadopoulou 72; mains €5-7; 1pm-midnight) This convivial *ouzerie* (a taverna serving food that complements ouzo) sits on a quiet crossroads in Ano Poli. In operation since the 19th century, it boasts a tile-floored, stove-heated dining room, a flower-scented deck for warm weather, and a great way with grilled sardines, roast aubergine, meatballs and other *ouzerie* staples. Tea, wine and other nonouzo drinks are easily obtained.

Mourgá   Greek €€
(2310 268 826; Christopoulou 12; mains €9-14; 1pm-midnight;) Elegant and relaxed,

yet serious about everything that issues from its open kitchen, Mourgá is everything that's delightful about Greek food, Thessaloniki style. The grilled catch of the day is always excellent, while the raw anchovies with Cretan rusk and pickles is a stunning combination. While local producers are a focus, you can try cheeses and wines from across the country.

Extravaganza   Mediterranean €€
(2310 529 791; Episkopou Amvrosiou 8; mains €8-14; 1.30-11.30pm Wed-Mon;) The humming open kitchen here keeps punters happy with food that's innovative yet rooted in the Greek fundamentals. Expect treats such as *garganelli* (short pasta) with pecorino, yogurt, smoked pancetta, egg yolk and truffle, and trust the excellent waiters to find a glass of something local to match your meal. Cocktails are another highlight here.

Ergon Agora   Greek €€
(2310 284 224; www.ergonfoods.com; Pavlou Mela 42; mains €9-13; 10am-midnight;) Agora restaurant is part of the Ergon chain, dedicated to the best Greek produce, from Pindos mountain truffles to Alonissos tuna. The food at this deli-bistro-grocer is generally excellent. Try the zucchini balls, the selection of cheeses and cured meats from around Greece and the juicy lamb chops. Take home, oils, jams and other regional goodies from the adjoining shop.

Radikal   Greek €€
(2310 202 007; http://radikal.gr; Stergiou 61; mains €8-12; 6pm-midnight Tue-Thu, 1pm-midnight Fri & Sat, 1-6pm Sun;) Up in the heights of Ano Poli, beneath one of the best-preserved stretches of the city's Byzantine walls, Radikal is a handsomely styled restaurant where the kitchen more than plays its part. From huge, spanking-fresh salads to slow dishes such as rooster stewed in wine with small pasta and sheep's cheese, the food's all seasonal and expertly handled. Great wines, too.

Cafes on Alexandras Papadopoulou

🍷 DRINKING & NIGHTLIFE

Café Palermo
Cafe

(☏2310 279 958; 1st fl, Plateia Aristotelous 8; coffee €2.50; ☺10am-midnight; 🛜) A lovely oasis of potted plants, geometric tiles, slanting coloured light, bentwood chairs and vintage ephemera awaits those who find Palermo, up an unpromising flight of stairs within Plateia Aristotelous 8. The coffee, tea and cake are all excellent, and the calm contrasts deliciously with the throng of the square below.

Coo
Bar

(☏2311 274 752; Vassiliou Irakliou 4; ☺7pm-late; 🛜) What started as a venue to promote the musical creations of a few friends morphed into Coo, the fantastic alternative bar of today. Coo often hosts live events, dancing and exhibitions. The top floor is open for drinks and coffee, and the basement hosts experimental theatre, photo exhibits and summer concerts.

Chatzi Bahtse
Bar

(☏2310 541 786; www.chatzi-bahtse.gr; Georgiou Tsontou 9; ☺9pm-2am Thu-Sat, 8pm-midnight

Sun) A little out of the way, this is the place to go for *rembetika* (urban 'blues') and other unamplified strains of traditional Greek song. Three brothers started it in the 1958 house of their father, and they ensure everything – the home-cooked food, the carafes of juicy wine, the tables draped with wine-splattered cloths, and the music – stays perfect.

Gorílas
Cocktail Bar

(☏6977590306; Verias 3; ☺9am-3am Sun, Tue & Wed, to 4am Thu, to 5am Fri & Sat; 🛜) This ultrapopular cocktail bar is all industrial interiors and serious attitudes – when it comes to cocktails. Thankfully the welcome comes without attitude, the music is eclectic and tasteful, and DJs select on weekend nights. Check out Gorílas' special cocktail mixes, which change seasonally.

Hoppy Pub
Craft Beer

(☏2310 269 203; Nikiforou Foka 6; ☺5.30pm-1.30am Tue-Sun; 🛜) With 18 beers on tap, and many more behind glass, Hoppy is Thessaloniki's most dedicated purveyor of craft and obscure froth. Beers change every week, quality rock plays on the stereo, and the smoke-free policy makes your cheese, charcuterie and other bar snacks taste all the better.

To Pikap   Cafe
(⏱2310 271 499; www.topikap.gr; Olimpou 57; ⏰noon-1am Tue-Sun, from 6.30pm Mon; 📶) This grab-bag of groovy businesses, anchored on a gregariously smoky cafe-bar, also accommodates a record shop, a few racks of designer T-shirts and even a radio station over two levels of clean lines and funky furniture.

TOMS Flagship   Cafe
(⏱2310 234 222; Tsimiski 22; ⏰10am-11pm Mon-Wed, 10am-1am Thu, Fri & Sun, noon-1am Sat; 📶) Set inside the courtyard of the Old Post Office building, this friendly, vintage-strewn space offers good coffee, drinks, brunches and books to browse. Freelancers making the most of the wi-fi, families resting from a day's shopping and friends catching up over a glass of wine disport themselves over many configurations of seating.

Vogatsikou 3   Cocktail Bar
(⏱2310 222 899; http://vogatsikou3.gr; Vogatsikou 3; cocktails €9-10; ⏰9am-3am; 📶) Locals consider this darkly stylish cocktail bar to be the best in town. If you like your drinks fancy and shaken, you'll enjoy poring over a long menu of classic and inventive cocktails. Whisky drinkers are very well catered to as well, and the nonsmoking policy comes as a great relief to many.

🎯 ENTERTAINMENT

Kismet   Live Music
(⏱2310 548 490; Katouni 11; ⏰10pm-4am) Set right among Ladadika's restaurants, Kismet is a fine, though crowded, spot for live bands, ranging from rock and pop to Greece's most popular *rembetika* acts.

Rover   Live Music
(⏱2310 544 304; Salaminos 6; ⏰4.30pm-4am Tue, Thu & Sun, 2.30pm-4am Wed, 4.30pm-6am Fri & Sat) Live music and arts events form an eclectic calendar at Rover bar. But

while the soundtrack could be anything from Slovenian dubstep to rock 'n' roll, the cocktail quality is thirst-quenchingly consistent.

ℹ️ INFORMATION

MEDICAL SERVICES

Whenever closed, Thessaloniki pharmacies must list nearby working pharmacies.

If going to hospital, bring an ID card/passport and insurance information (if possible). If you are an EU citizen, bring your EU health card.

Farmakeio Gouva (⏱2310 205 544; Agias Sofias 110; ⏰8.30am-9pm Mon-Fri, 9am-3.30pm Sat) Pharmacy in Ano Poli with experienced staff.

Farmakeio Sofia Tympanidou (⏱2310 522 155; Egnatia 17; ⏰8am-8pm) Well-stocked pharmacy on west Egnatia.

Ippokrateio (⏱2310 892 000; Kostantinoupoleos 49; ⏰24hr) Some 2km east of the city centre, this is Thessaloniki's largest public hospital.

MONEY

Except in Ano Poli, banks and ATMs are widespread. Commission-hungry exchange offices line western Egnatia.

TOURIST INFORMATION

For local happenings and other info, visit the frequently updated www.enjoythessaloniki.com website, run by local enthusiasts.

Mt Athos Pilgrims' Bureau (⏱2310 263 308; www.agioritikiestia.gr; Egnatia 109, Thessaloniki; ⏰9am-4pm Mon-Fri) Issues permits for Mt Athos monasteries to male pilgrims.

Tourism Office (⏱2310 229 070; www.thessaloniki.travel; Plateia Aristotelous 10; ⏰10am-6pm) The tourist office on Plateia Aristotelous can assist with hotel bookings, local information, and arranging tours and excursions beyond Thessaloniki.

ℹ️ GETTING THERE & AWAY

AIR

Besides Greece's **Aegean Airlines** (https://en.aegeanair.com), many foreign carriers use

Thessaloniki's Makedonia International Airport (p305).

Bus X1 (during the day) and N1 (at night) runs half-hourly from the airport (17km southeast of town), heading west through the city to the main bus station (KTEL Makedonia) via the train station. Tickets cost €2 from the airport to the bus station; €1 for short journeys.

Taxis to the airport cost €20 to €30, depending on the distance – it is a set rate, even if the meter reads a lower fee (this allows for airport charges and the differences in central locations). Call in advance if you need them to pick you up from town; the operator speaks English.

BOAT

Ferries from Thessaloniki port are limited and change annually. Consult www.ferries.gr or **Karacharisis Travel** (☑2310 513 005; www.thesferry.gr; Salaminos 10; ☺10am-6pm Mon-Fri, to 2pm Sat) for details and booking options.

BUS

Thessaloniki's main bus station, **Macedonia Intercity Bus Station** (☑2310 595 400; www.ktelmacedonia.gr; Giannitson 244), is 3km west of the city centre. Each destination has its own specific ticket counter, signposted in Greek and English.

For Athens *only,* avoid the trip out west by going instead to **Monastiriou bus station** (☑2310 500 111; http://ktelthes.gr; Monastiriou 67) – next to the train station – where Athens-bound buses start before calling in at KTEL Makedonia.

Buses leave for Halkidiki from the eastern Thessaloniki **Halkidiki bus terminal** (☑2310 316 555; www.ktel-chalkidikis.gr; Km 9 Thessaloniki-Halkidiki Rd). The terminal is out towards the airport, reached via city buses 45A or 45B. From the main bus station, buses stop en route at the train station and Plateia Aristotelous. With waiting time and traffic, this 'express' service to the bus terminal can take more than an hour.

TRAIN

Thessaloniki's **train station** (www.trainose.gr; Monastiriou) has ATMs, card phones and small

modern eateries, plus an Orthodox chapel. Self-serve luggage storage lockers start from €3.

ⓘ GETTING AROUND

BUS

Dependable city buses have electronic rolling signs listing the next destination, accompanied by an audio announcement in Greek and English. Screens above most bus stops note how many minutes until the next buses.

Bus X1 connects the main bus station (KTEL Makedonia) and the train station, while buses 45A and 45B stop at both (plus Plateia Aristotelous and Kamara) en route to the Halkidiki Bus Terminal. From the train station, major points on Egnatia are constantly served by buses such as Nos 10 and 14.

Buy tickets at *periptera* (street kiosks), or from on-board blue ticket machines (€1). Validate the former in the orange machines. Machines neither give change nor accept bills; when boarding, be sure you have the right change and buy your ticket immediately. Thessaloniki's ticket police pounce at any sign of confusion. If they nab you, you'll pay €60.

CAR

If driving, take note that Ano Poli's streets are steep and can be rather narrow, so avoid driving there if you're not used to such conditions. If you can't find free parking (a common problem in hectic Thessaloniki, where double parking is de rigueur), try the municipal parking at the port (per hour €2). For rental cars try the following:

Avance Rent a Car (☑2310 279 888; www.avance.gr; Agelaki 7)

Budget Rent a Car (☑2310 888 100; www.budget.gr; Papandreou 5; ☺8am-9pm Mon-Sat)

TAXI

Thessaloniki's blue-and-white taxis carry multiple passengers, and only take you if you're going the same way. The minimum fare is €3.40. A more expensive 'night rate' takes effect from midnight until 5am. To book a cab for an airport transfer, try **Taxi Way** (☑18 300, 2310 866 866; www.taxiway.gr).

DELPHI

Delphi at a Glance...

For the ancient Greeks, Delphi (from delphis, meaning womb) was a sacred space where human beings could communicate directly with the gods. The home of the all-seeing oracle retains a magical aura, standing in beautifully preserved splendour on a pristine mountainside 750m east of (and out of sight of) the modern village.

Delphi is a major tourist destination. Despite heavy commercialisation, the nearby village makes a pleasant place to stay, with hotels and restaurants to suit all budgets, and great views down to the Gulf of Corinth.

One Day in Delphi

To avoid the summer heat (and year-round crowds), aim to visit the **ancient site** (p108) early morning or late afternoon, allowing at least an hour to explore the site in full. Whenever you visit, be sure to check opening times ahead, as hours can vary.

Two Days in Delphi

On your second day undertake one of three popular day hikes that start and end at Delphi. Choose between walking all the way up to the mysterious **Korykeon Cave** (p113); just going as far as the dramatic **Kroki Viewpoint** (p113); or heading downhill to the sea and the ancient port of **Kirra** (p113).

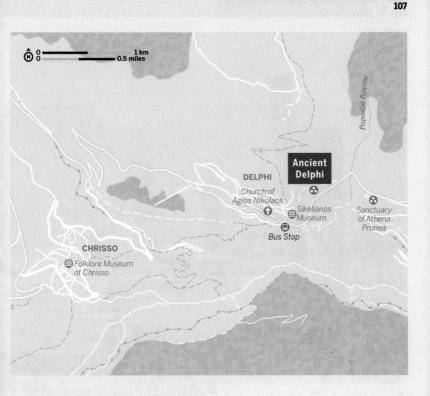

Arriving in Delphi

Buses (p114) depart from the eastern end of Vasileon Pavlou and Friderikis, outside the In Delphi restaurant, which sells tickets daily between 9am and 8pm (the time of the last bus). Buy tickets for early buses the day before, especially in high season. It's best to travel to Kalambaka/Meteora via Lamia and Trikala, rather than Larissa.

Where to Stay

Delphi offers sleeping options to suit every price level, from tent camping and camp site bungalows to simple village inns and boutique hotels.

Temple of Apollo

Ancient Delphi

Of all Greece's archaeological sites, Ancient Delphi has the most potent spirit of place. To this day, the haunting ruins – a short walk east of the modern town – look out over an unbroken expanse of olive trees, sloping down to the Gulf of Corinth.

Great For...

☑ Don't Miss

Views from the top row of the site's 4th-century-BC theatre are breathtaking.

Sanctuary of Athena Pronea

For ancient pilgrims, Delphi's first stop was the **Sanctuary of Athena Pronea** (☉24hr) **FREE**, now set just below the road 800m east of the Sanctuary of Apollo. This lovely spot is best known as home to the superbly photogenic Tholos, a graceful circular structure of unknown purpose that dates from the 4th century BC. Three of the 20 columns that stood on its three-stepped podium were re-erected in the 1940s; the white portions are original marble, the darker are new.

Sanctuary of Apollo

The hillside **Sanctuary of Apollo** (☎22650 82313; http://odysseus.culture.gr; combined ticket for site & Delphi Archaeological Museum adult/student/child €12/6/free; ☉8am-8pm

Charioteer statue, Delphi Archaeological Museum

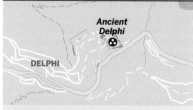

❶ Need to Know

http://ancient-greece.org/history/delphi.html

✕ Take a Break

Taverna Vakhos (p114) is an exceptional place that uses fresh local ingredients and mountain herbs in its dishes.

★ Top Tip

Really understand the site by taking a tour with an expert licensed guide such as Penny Kolomvotsou (p113).

May-Sep, 8.30am-7pm Apr & Oct, 8.30am-3pm Nov-Mar), 750m east of the village, was the heart of the Delphic oracle. The **Sacred Way**, the path that climbs to its centrepiece Temple of Apollo, was lined in ancient times by treasuries and statues, erected by city-states including Athens and Sparta to thank Apollo and assert their own wealth and might. Some stand complete, most lie in ruins, but together they form a magnificent spectacle.

As the home of Apollo himself, the **Temple of Apollo** dominated the entire sanctuary. Its surviving incarnation, from the 4th century BC, contained a statue of the god, guarded by an eternal flame, and was where the Pythia, the god's mouthpiece, delivered her pronouncements. Its vestibule bore the so-called Delphic Maxims, including 'Know Thyself' and 'Nothing in Excess', which Socrates mentioned in Plato's *Protagoras*. Congregations gathered not inside the temple, but out in the open air.

Delphi Archaeological Museum

Delphi's magnificent modern **museum** (☏22650 82312; http://odysseus.culture. gr; combined ticket for museum & site adult/ student/child €12/6/free; ⏰8am-8pm May-Sep, 8.30am-4pm Apr & Oct, 8.30am-3pm Nov-Mar), 500m east of town, perfectly complements the ancient site alongside. Which you visit first doesn't matter, but the treasures collected here will bring your image of ancient Delphi to life. Rich and powerful petitioners flocked to Delphi from the 8th century BC onwards, bringing fabulous gifts and erecting opulent monuments. Unearthed by archaeologists, these now fill a succession of mind-blowing galleries.

Ancient Delphi

A PILGRIM'S WALKING TOUR

Delphi's **Sanctuary of Apollo** remained in use for over 1200 years (8th century BC to 4th century AD), and reached its height between the 6th and 4th centuries BC. While the site today consists of ruins and reconstructions scattered across the beautiful slopes of Mt Parnassus, our illustration shows it at its peak. With a bit of imagination, modern visitors can walk in the footsteps of past pilgrims, and re-create their experience of this ancient place.

Worshippers would start by purifying themselves in the Castalian Spring (now closed to the public), then pay a pelanos (tribute). Those who hadn't brought a votive offering would buy one from ❶ **The Roman Market**, before setting off up the the ❷ **Sacred Way** towards the Temple of Apollo.

The sanctuary was adorned throughout with statues, sculptures and monuments dedicated to Apollo. In particular, victorious city-states would erect temple-like structures such as the ❸ **Athenian Treasury**, and fill them with the spoils of war. The nearby ❹ **omphalos** (navel stone), symbolising Delphi's status as the centre of the earth, was left by archaeologists where it was found.

Next, visitors pass the ❺ **Rock of the Sibyl** before arriving at the Stoa of the Athenians, behind which rises the amazing ❻ **polygonal wall**. Finally, they arrived at the ❼ **Temple of Apollo** at the sanctuary's core. It was here that consultations with the oracle took place, and the chants of the Pythia (priestess) were interpreted by the priests of Apollo. The ❽ **theatre** above the temple staged drama, music and poetry competitions.

TOP TIPS

➡ Visit in the morning or late afternoon to beat the heat and crowds.

➡ Wear comfortable shoes and a hat, and bring drinking water.

➡ Opening hours are subject to change, so check ahead.

➡ Don't miss the Delphi Museum, which helps to contextualise the site.

➡ Your ticket allows you to visit the sanctuary and museum on successive days.

Athenian Treasury
The impressive Athenian Treasury is among the sanctuary's most important buildings. Built to commemorate the Athenians' victory against the Persians at the battle of Marathon in 490 BC, it was reconstructed in the early 1900s.

Omphalos
Delphi was considered the omphalos (navel) of the world. There was another omphalos in the adyton (temple chamber) where the Pythia pronounced her oracles.

Siphnian Treasury

The Bouleuterion

The Sacred Way
The Sacred Way (so-named by modern archaeologists) leads to the Temple of Apollo. It was lined with monuments, statues and treasuries that commemorated victories (usually in war, sometimes the Pythian Games).

To Delphi Museum

Temple of Apollo
The most sacred building in the sanctuary, this was the third version of the temple to be constructed, in the 4th century BC. A large ramp leads to its interior, where the Pythia delivered her pronouncements.

Theatre
The Pythian Games, held in Delphi every four years, were not just about athletics – they also included music and drama contests (Apollo is the god of music). The original theatre was built in the 4th century BC; the current one dates fom the 1st century BC and could seat 5000 spectators.

To Stadium ⑧

Acanthus Column of Dancers

⑦

Sphinx of the Naxians

⑥

⑤

②

King of Argos Monument

Votive Offering of Lacedaemon

Stoa of the Athenians

Bull of Kerkyra

①

Polygonal Wall
This extraordinary retaining wall comprises interlocking polygonal stones. It features around 800 inscriptions that relate to the emancipation of slaves.

To Castalian Spring and Sanctuary of Athena Pronea

The Roman Market (Agora)
Pilgrims could buy small votives and offerings here. Wealthier and more powerful visitors, however, brought statues and valuable items from afar. The remains of many of these are in the Delphi Museum.

Rock of the Sibyl
Legend has it that this marks the spot where the first sibyl (an elderly prophetess, not to be confused with the later Pythia), stood to declare Delphi's earliest oracle.

⊙ SIGHTS

The main road through Delphi divides into two one-way sections. The lower route, running west–east and named Vasileon Pavlou & Friderikis, holds most of the village's commercial activity; more hotels and restaurants line the east–west Apollonos, parallel and slightly higher. Steep stairways connect these two roads, and also the much quieter Filellinon just below.

The ancient site (p108) and museum (p109) are an enjoyable 500m walk east of the village, around a curve in the road.

Sikelianos Museum   Museum

(Delphic Festivals Museum; ☑22650 82175; www. eccd.gr; cnr Sikelianos & Diakou; €1; ⊙8am-3pm; 🅿) Fans of Greek drama should head to this intimate 1920s mansion-turned-museum, which overlooks Delphi both ancient and modern. It's dedicated to Greek poet Angelos Sikelianos and his American-born wife Eva Palmer, who jointly reinvented Delphi as a modern Greek centre for drama and the arts. The museum displays intriguing photos of their attempts to re-create ancient festivals.

Folklore Museum
of Chrisso   Museum

(☑22650 83203; Chrisso; ⊙Tue-Sun 9am-3pm) **FREE** An imposing mansion and former school in the traditional village of Chrisso, 6km southwest of Delphi by road, now holds an enjoyable museum of local life. Fronted by colourful citrus trees, it shows off 19th-century costumes including a man's skirt with 400 pleats to symbolise 400 years of Ottoman rule, along with jewellery, pistols, paintings and photographs.

Church of Agios Nikolaos   Church

(Syngrou & Apollonos; 🅿) Even if it's just for the views, it's well worth the short climb up the steps from opposite Hotel Tholos to reach the Byzantine-style stone church of Agios Nikolaos. Come between 8am and 8.30am any morning to see its candles being lit.

Delphi to Ancient Kirra walk

ACTIVITIES

Recommended local guides offering walking and hiking tours include **Penny Kolomvotsou** (☑6944644427; kpagona@hotmail.com), **George Malissos** (☑6948181084; www.delphilocaltours.gr), **Christina Stoli** (☑6944987411; xristolh@gmail.com), **Georgia Hasioti** (☑6944943511; www.delphi-guide.gr) and Giorgos Korodimos at **Trekking Hellas** (☑22670 31901; www.trekking.gr) in Arahova.

Delphi to Ancient Kirra Walk   Hiking

The 14km downhill hike to the ancient port of Kirra, just east of modern Itea, starts from the E4 long-distance trailhead 100m east of the Hotel Acropole. Skirting the village of Crissa, it meanders to the gulf through Greece's largest olive grove. After your three-to-four-hour hike, and lunch or a swim, you can return to Delphi by bus (around €2).

Korykeon Cave Walk   Hiking

The Korykeon Cave, 800m above Delphi on the Parnassian slopes, is probably where the ancient prophetic cult first originated. The exhilarating E4 trail climbs all the way up, but it's a gruelling all-day hike – four hours up, perhaps less to come down – so many visitors take a taxi to a point 2km from the cave (around €30), then hike back.

While the entrance to the cavern is surprisingly small, it opens into a vast natural amphitheatre, filled with stalactites and stalagmites, that was sacred to Pan and his nymphs. Look out for eerie formations and ancient inscriptions carved into the rock.

Delphi to Kroki Viewpoint Walk   Hiking

(Kroki Observatory Walk) A shorter hike up the same well-signposted E4 trail that leads all the way to the Korykeon Cave takes you as far as the Kroki Viewpoint for superb views over the archaeological site (p108). Allow roughly 90 minutes each way (4km up and 4km down). Set off – carrying water – up the *kako skala* (evil steps) opposite upper Delphi's Sikelianos Museum.

The Delphic Oracle

The Delphic oracle ranked high among the sacred sites of Ancient Greece. Devotees flocked from far and wide to ask for the guidance of Apollo in making decisions. Wars were fought, colonies created, marriages sealed, leaders chosen and journeys begun on the strength of the oracle's advice.

Surprisingly little is known about how the oracle actually functioned. Apollo's instrument of communication, the Pythia (priestess), was usually an older woman who sat on a tripod in his temple. Although there's no evidence for the suggestion that she inhaled vapours from cracks or chasms in the rocks below the sanctuary, she certainly made her prophesies in a trance-like state.

The Pythia's pronouncements were notorious for their ambiguity, which left recipients to choose how they should be interpreted. Thus Croesus of Lydia was told that he would 'destroy a great empire' if he invaded Persia, but the empire that was destroyed was his own. Similarly, the Athenians were advised to trust their 'wooden walls' to defend against the Persians, but it took Themistocles to decide that the 'walls' in question were actually their ships.

17th-century engraving of the Delphic oracle
GIBON ART ALAMY STOCK PHOTO ©

✖ EATING

Dionysos Souvlaki   Greek €

(Apollonos 28; mains €2.50-7; ⊙11am-11pm)
Great-value budget diner run by a family
that conscientiously and efficiently whips up
tasty dishes such as well-prepared souvlaki
and Greek salads, to eat in or take away.

Taverna Gargadouas   Taverna €

(☑22650 82488; Vasileon Pavlou & Friderikis;
mains €6-9.50; ⊙1-11pm) Welcoming, no-frills
traditional taverna at the west end of the
village; it makes a snug retreat from the
tourist crowds. Daily specials can include
provatina (slow-roasted lamb), but on the
whole it's the grilled meats that keep bringing the locals back. Good value, but slightly
disorganised.

Taverna Vakhos   Taverna €€

(☑22650 83186; Apollonos 31; mains €8-16;
⊙noon-10.30pm; ☎🌐) Delphi's best restaurant, this exceptional place uses fresh local
ingredients and mountain herbs. Along with
generous salads and hearty lamb and rooster dishes, the menu includes delicious veggie options ranging from *horta* (wild greens)
to *trachanopita* (a savoury 'frumenty pie' of
cracked wheat, zucchini and feta). Reserve
for dinner; lunch tends to be less busy.

Taverna To Patriko Mas   Greek €€

(☑22650 82150; Vasileon Pavlou & Friderikis 69;
mains €9-21; ⊙lunch & dinner; ❄🌐) Set in a
19th-century stone building, this smart restaurant opens into a large rear room with
panoramic views, and also has an outdoor
patio. Something of a place to linger in, it
offers unusual salads and generous mezedhes, plus dishes including savoury pie with
leek and pork, and rabbit with mustard and
tarragon. Fine all-Greek wine list.

🍷 DRINKING & NIGHTLIFE

Café Apollon   Coffee

(☑22650 82842; Vasileon Pavlou & Friderikis
9; ⊙7am-late; 🌐) A happy blend of old and
new, Apollon is a charming, traditional *kaf-*

eneio (coffeehouse) on the inside, coupled
with a broad tiled terrace with stunning
views. Linger over a great-value breakfast,
coffees and snacks.

Melopoleio Cafe   Cafe

(☑22650 83247; Vasileon Pavlou & Friderikis 14;
⊙7am-midnight; 🌐) A smart little cafe on
the inland side of the main through road,
with a cosy interior plus streetside watch-
the-world-go-by seating. Over the course
of the day, it morphs from serving espresso drinks, teas from local herbs and fresh
juices, via savoury pies, into an afternoon
sandwich and ice-cream stop, and then
an evening wine bar with signature
cocktails.

★ ENTERTAINMENT

**European Cultural
Centre of Delphi**   Arts Centre

(ECC; ☑22650 82731; www.eccd.gr; Syngrou;
⊙no fixed hours) FREE Set in gardens
above the western end of the village, this
handsome facility generally comes to life in
spring and summer, with a programme of
photography and art exhibitions, lectures
and open-air theatre events.

ℹ INFORMATION

There are several ATMs along Vasileon Pavlou &
Friderikis.

Delphi has no tourist office, but there's a
staffed exhibition space at the town hall.

ℹ GETTING THERE & AWAY

Buses (☑22650 82317; www.ktel-fokidas.gr)
depart from the eastern end of Vasileon Pavlou
and Friderikis, outside the In Delphi restaurant,
which sells tickets daily between 9am and 8pm
(the time of the last bus). Buy tickets for early
buses the day before, especially in high season.
It's best to travel to Kalambaka/Meteora via
Lamia and Trikala, rather than Larissa.

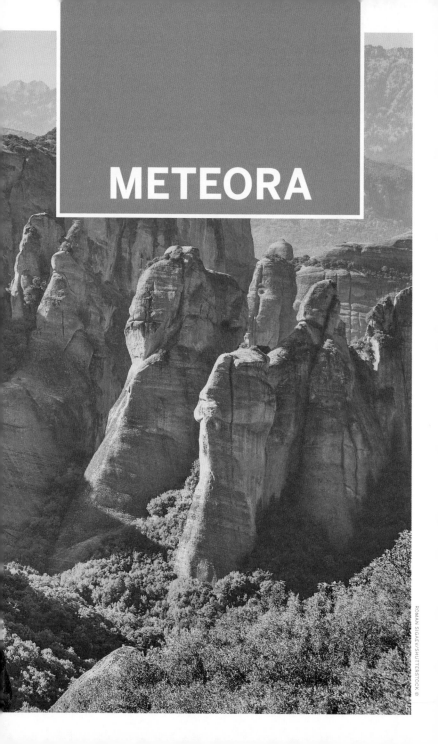

METEORA

Meteora at a Glance...

The extraordinary rock formations of the Meteora region would be an unmissable tourist attraction even if they weren't crowned by Byzantine monasteries. However, the sheer spectacle of those monasteries – somehow glued atop slender stone pinnacles by medieval masons and now collectively listed as a World Heritage Site – makes this one of the most visited attractions in all Greece. While there's abundant food and lodging nearby in the modern town of Kalambaka and the pretty village of Kastraki, there's almost no infrastructure among the actual monasteries themselves.

Two Days in Meteora

As it takes at least a day to see all the Meteora **monasteries** (p120), most visitors spend a night or two either in **Kalambaka** (p122) or the village of **Kastraki** (p127), which is 5km away. This strange and beautiful landscape also offers wonderful opportunities for walkers and climbers, which could easily fill another day.

Three Days in Meteora

Spend time in Kalambaka exploring its magnificent old Byzantine **church** (p122), plus a couple of enjoyable **museums** (p122) – one devoted to old schoolbooks and another to mushrooms. If you're in town on Friday, there's also a bustling fresh produce **market** (p123).

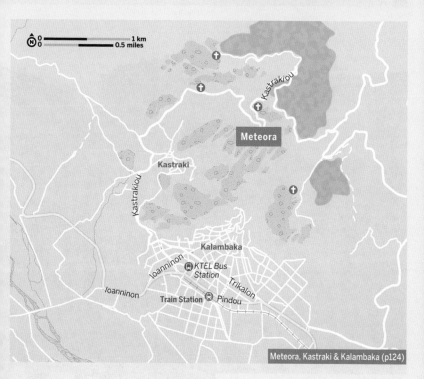

Meteora, Kastraki & Kalambaka (p124)

Arriving in Meteora

All public transport access to Meteora is via Kalambaka, which is served by both trains and buses. Once there, you can pick up local buses to Kastraki and the monasteries.

If you drive it yourself, it's just about possible to see all the monasteries that are open within a single day.

Where to Stay

Kalambaka and quieter Kastraki hold all the Meteora's lodging options, ranging from camping and budget hostels to boutique hotels.

Meteora

TRABANTOS/SHUTTERSTOCK ©

Monasteries of Meteora

The prime destinations in the Meteora are the monasteries, with their exqui-sitely decorated churches and stunning viewpoints, but there's plenty more to see. The scenery is consistently jaw-dropping, with traces left by former inhabitants everywhere you look.

Great For...

☑ **Don't Miss**

The superb frescoes in Moni Agias Var-varas Rousanou's beautiful chapel.

Moni Agiou Nikolaou

The 15th-century **Moni Agiou Nikolaou** (Monastery of St Nikolaou Anapafsa; ✆24320 22375; http://agiosnikolaosanapafsas.blogspot. gr; €3; ⊙9am-4pm Sat-Thu) is the first monastery you reach from Kastraki. Many visitors, keen to press on to the top of the massif, skip it altogether, but it's well worth making the steep climb up. Inside, it's very cosy and snug. Its small church, scooped into the rock, holds exceptional frescoes painted by the Cretan monk Theophanes Strelizas, including a gorgeous depiction of *The Naming of Animals* by Adam in Paradise.

Moni Megalou Meteorou

The Meteora's largest **monastery** (Grand Meteoron; ✆24320 22278; €3; ⊙9am-3pm Wed-

Fresco, Moni Megalou Meteorou

Meteora

Kastraki

Kalambaka

Train Station

ⓘ Need to Know

Strict dress codes apply: no bare shoulders are allowed, men must wear trousers and women must wear skirts below the knee.

✕ Take a Break

Seasonal trucks sell simple snacks at some monasteries; the nearest tavernas and cafes are in Kastraki and Kalambaka.

★ Top Tip

Monastery opening hours change frequently so check current schedules locally before you set off.

Mon Apr-Oct, to 2pm Fri-Mon Nov-Mar), founded by St Athanasios in the 14th century, looks down on Kastraki from the highest rock in the valley (613m). Visitors can view the large *katholikon* (church) topped by a magnificent 12-sided dome, and the unchanged 16th-century kitchen, plus a museum devoted to the struggle for Greek independence and WWII.

Moni Agias Varvaras Rousanou

Dramatically perched atop a steep pinnacle and accessed via a high narrow wooden bridge, **Rousanou convent** (☏24320 22649; €3; ☺9am-5pm Thu-Tue May-Oct, to 2pm Thu-Tue Nov-Apr) has an intimate atmosphere. Its small community of nuns engage with visitors by selling their

jam and honey, and leading group tours. There's little outdoor space, but it feels as though you could almost reach out across the abyss to touch the neighbouring monasteries.

Moni Agias Triados

Of all the Meteora monasteries, **Moni Agias Triados** (Holy Trinity; ☏24320 22220; €3; ☺9am-5pm Fri-Wed Apr-Oct, 10am-4pm Fri-Wed Nov-Mar), which featured in the 1981 James Bond film *For Your Eyes Only*, feels the most remote. A long down-then-up footpath reaches it from the road, with the final climb following a staircase beneath an overhang cut into the rock. Apart from some beautiful frescoes in the small church, the monastery buildings hold little to see, but the bare rocks beyond, topped by a white cross, offer stunning views over Kalambaka.

Meteora History

The name Meteora is derived from the Greek adjective *meteoros,* meaning 'suspended in the air' (the word 'meteor' comes from the same root).

Hermit monks (known as *meteorites*) began to make their homes in the scattered natural caverns of Meteora during the 11th century. By the 14th century, the power of the Byzantine Empire was waning, and with Turkish incursions into Greece on the rise, monks started to seek safe havens away from the bloodshed. The inaccessibility of the rocks of Meteora made them an ideal retreat.

At their peak, a total of 24 monasteries graced these remote pinnacles. As you explore the region, you'll spot the ruins of abandoned communities in sites that now seem utterly inaccessible. Only six now remain active, inhabited by monks or nuns and visited by the faithful and curious alike.

The earliest monasteries could only be reached by climbing removable ladders. Later on, windlasses were used to haul the monks up in nets. A famous story relates that when curious visitors asked how frequently the ropes were replaced, the monks' straight-faced reply was 'when the Lord lets them break'. These days, access is via steps that were hewn into the rocks in the 1920s, and a convenient road passes nearby.

Moni Agias Triados (p121)
MIKADUN/SHUTTERSTOCK ©

Kalambaka

Kalambaka, the town that guards the approach to the Meteora, was burned to the ground by the Nazis in WWII, and is now almost entirely of recent construction. While not especially attractive in itself, it does occupy a stunning location immediately in front of some gigantic rock formations.

◎ SIGHTS

Museum of Hellenic Culture
Museum

(☑24320 75219; www.bookmuseum.gr; cnr M Alexandros & Chatzipetrou; adult/student €5/4; ☺9am-5pm Mon-Fri, from 11am Sat & Sun) This enjoyable museum focuses on a beautifully displayed collection of antiquarian books, from versions of *Aesop's Fables* to a 1567 edition of Homer. The emphasis on children's literature and schoolbooks is brought to life in a reconstructed Greek classroom from a century ago. You can also try your hand at some fun science experiments, and see old films and photos of the Meteora monasteries.

Church of the Dormition of the Virgin Mary
Church

(€2; ☺8am-1pm & 3-8pm) The 14th-century frescoes in this Byzantine basilica, at Kalambaka's highest point where the footpath sets off to Moni Agias Triados (p121), are a match for anything you'll see in the Meteora monasteries. This is the world's only Orthodox church to centre on a free-standing pulpit, a relic of its 7th-century predecessor. Vespers are sung at 6.30pm.

Natural History & Mushroom Museum
Museum

(☑24320 24959; www.meteoramuseum.gr; Pindou 20; adult/child €5/4; ☺9am-5pm Mon-Fri, 10am-6pm Sat & Sun) Once you pass its forbidding modern exterior, this museum comes as a quirky surprise. Downstairs, dioramas display stuffed birds and animals ranging from beavers to flamingos, but the real joy comes upstairs, with a downright dotty collection of wax model mushrooms. Look out for the lurid *phallus impudicus*! You can also buy all sorts of dried and pickled mushrooms, with free tastings if you're lucky.

The museum staff can arrange truffle-hunting excursions in the nearby woods for groups.

ACTIVITIES

Visit Meteora Adventure Sports
(2 24320 23820; www.visitmeteora.travel; Patriarhou Dimitriou 2; ⊙8am-9pm) Besides running monastery van tours (€30), this sharp, friendly crew specialises in guided hiking and walking excursions (€25 to €35) of varying difficulties; the most popular, especially with photographers, is the Sunset Tour. They also offer fully equipped rock-climbing sessions; a three-hour beginners' course costs €60.

Their office doubles as a centre for general visitor advice, as does the branch they open in neighbouring Kastraki village between April and October.

Meteora Thrones Hiking
(2 24320 78455; www.meteora.com; Trikalon 28, Plateia Riga Fereou; ⊙8am-8pm) Very enthusiastic local operator offering four-hour hiking tours, either in the morning or to coincide with sunset, as well as a morning-only van tour of the monasteries. All cost €25. They also arrange Meteora tours by train from Athens (day trip €93, overnight €139) or Thessaloniki (€96/143).

SHOPPING

Friday Market Market
(To Pazari; Plateia Dimarhiou; ⊙8am-2pm Fri) Kalambaka's busy little fruit and vegetable market takes place on Friday mornings alongside the central roundabout.

EATING

Taverna Archontariki Taverna €
(2 6973767385; Trikalon 13, Plateia Riga Fereou; mains €6-10; ⊙lunch & dinner; ✿) Roomy traditional taverna at the corner of Plateia Riga Fereou, with some outdoor tables.

Church of the Dormition of the Virgin Mary

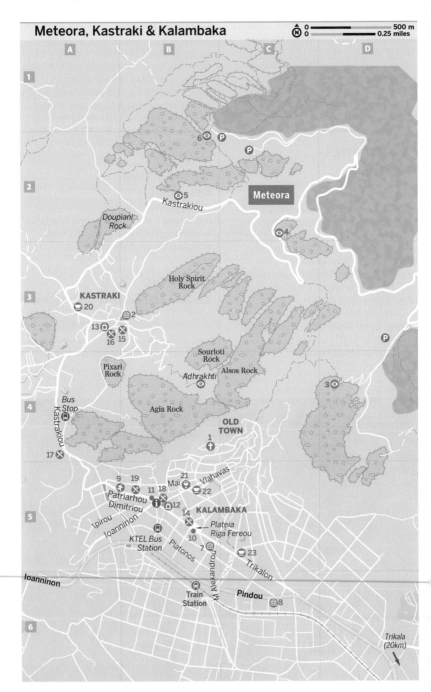

Meteora, Kastraki & Kalambaka

N 0 — 500 m
0 — 0.25 miles

Meteora

Kastrakiou

Doupiani Rock

Holy Spirit Rock

KASTRAKI

Sourloti Rock

Pixari Rock

Adhrakhti

Alsos Rock

Bus Stop

Kastrakiou

Agia Rock

OLD TOWN

Vlahavas

Mai

Patriarhou Dimitriou

KALAMBAKA

Ipirou

Ioanninon

Plateia Riga Fereou

KTEL Bus Station

Platonos

M Alexandrou

Trikalon

Ioanninon

Train Station

Pindou

Trikala (20km)

Meteora, Kastraki & Kalambaka

Mayirefta (ready-cooked dishes) such as *mousakas* are the mainstay, along with pasta, lamb chops, grilled feta and seasonal vegetables.

Taverna To Paramithi   Taverna €

(☑24320 24441; Patriarhou Dimitriou 14; mains €7.50-11; ⊗noon-11pm Mar-Dec; ❄🐾) This verdant taverna, slightly west of Plateia Dimarhiou, offers a tourist-friendly menu of Greek favourites, with nightly musical accompaniment from a guitar/bouzouki duo. Service can be perfunctory, as the place is usually packed, while the appetisers tend to taste better than the generally unremarkable mains.

Taverna Panellinion   Taverna €€

(☑24320 24735; Vlahavas 3, Plateia Dimarhiou; mains €8-13; ⊗lunch & dinner) The parasol-shaded tables of the popular Panellinion sprawl across Plateia Dimarhiou alongside the fountain, while the original taverna nearby is filled with antique bric-a-brac. As well as mezedhes including roasted feta and red peppers, they serve fine traditional dishes such as *pastitsio* (macaroni and meat bake), *briam* (mixed eggplant and veggies) and chicken fillet.

🍸 DRINKING & NIGHTLIFE

Fortounis   Bar

(☑24320 22555; Vlahavas 23; ⊗noon-midnight; 🛜) A favourite for snacks and drinks, with low-key music most evenings, this long-standing *ouzerie* (place serving ouzo and light snacks) attracts a young crowd that stays late.

Kafeneio Mikas   Cafe

(☑24320 22048; Vlahavas 32; ⊗8am-midnight; 🛜) The older generation of locals congregate at the simple pavement tables of this old-fashioned cafe, sipping coffee or ouzo and watching the modern world go about its business. Inside, the walls are clad with black-and-white photos of days gone by.

Rapsody   Cafe

(☑24320 22470; Trikalon 25, Plateia Dimola; ⊗7am-3am Mon-Fri, from 9am Sat & Sun; 🛜) Comfortable and inviting espresso and wine bar, with indoor/outdoor seating and decent prices for good coffee drinks, wine and sandwiches.

ℹ️ INFORMATION

Banks with ATMs surround the central Plateia Riga Fereou on Trikalon.

Info Tourist Centre (24323 50245; www.infotouristmeteora.gr; Plateia Dimarhiou; 8am-8pm Mon-Fri, to 2pm Sat) The town tourist office provides maps as well as recommendations for lodging and transport; much material can also be downloaded from their website.

Medical Centre of Kalambaka (24320 22222; Ioanninon 82) Located 1km west of the station, on the main road towards Thessaloniki.

Tourist Police (24320 76100; cnr Ipirou & Pindou)

Visit Meteora (p123) This local tour operator has up-to-date information on opening hours and public transport.

GETTING THERE & AWAY

Kalambaka's **KTEL bus station** (24320 22432; www.ktel-trikala.gr; Ikonomou 9), 150m down Roudou from the roundabout at Plateia Dimarhiou, is the arrival/departure point for regular Trikala bus connections. To reach Delphi, change first at Trikala, and then at Lamia. Two buses from Trikala each day connect at Lamia with direct onward services to Delphi, while another two connect with buses to Amfissa, where you'll have to change again for Delphi.

Meteora Car Rental (24320 75682; www.meteora-carrental.com; Patriarhou Dimitriou 12; 8am-8pm) is a useful car rental outlet.

Trains depart from Kalambaka's **train station** (24320 22451; www.trainose.gr; Pindou). To reach Athens and Thessaloniki, you may need to change at Paleofarsalos; for Volos, you must change at Larissa.

GETTING AROUND

Hobby Shop (6973743747, 24320 25262; www.meteora-bike-rentals.gr; Patriarhou Dimitriou 28; per 24hr bike €8-18, motorcycle & scooter €18-25; 8am-9pm Mon-Sat, to 2pm Sun) is a helpful service for bike and motorbike hire (helmets included); electric bikes available.

Every two hours, buses leave for Kastraki (€1) from beside the Plateia Dimarhiou fountain. Three daily Meteora-bound buses (one way/all day €1.80/5.50) depart from the KTEL station, with additional pick-ups at the fountain and Kastraki en route, between April and September.

Tavern, Kalambaka

Each of Kalambaka's squares has a taxi rank. Taxis can take you to Kastraki (€4) or the monasteries – Moni Megalou Meteorou (p120), for example, will cost around €10. Some drivers speak English, German or Italian, and offer tours for around €20 per hour.

Kastraki

Although the village of Kastraki stands less than 2km beyond bustling Kalambaka, you've now left the plain and found yourself amid the mighty rocks of the Meteora; it feels like another, very verdant world. Apart from the church in its sleepy central square, and the **geology museum** (🖉24323 22523; Plateia Pavlou; ⌚9am-5pm) **FREE** that faces it, almost every building here is a hotel, cafe or taverna. But it's all very laid-back, and the scenery is utterly breathtaking.

🄰 SHOPPING

Maro Theodorou   Ceramics
(🖉24320 22760, 6974483782; www.maro-theo dorou.gr; Kastrakiou; ⌚9am-8pm) Kalambaka-born ceramicist Maro Theodorou runs this delightful shop in the heart of Kastraki village, selling her own distinctive pottery as well as works by other local artists. Drop in to check out her tableware and one-off sculptures.

✖ EATING & DRINKING

Kastraki is filled with tavernas, and there's plenty of choice for where to eat, but few options are truly exceptional.

Taverna Harama   Taverna €
(Xarama; 🖉24320 23976; Kastrakiou; mains €7-12; ⌚lunch & dinner, closed Mon & Tue in low season; **P** ❄ 🕾) Good traditional taverna in a lovely rural setting a few steps down off the main Kalambaka–Kastraki road; it's a 10-minute walk from either village. All the usual standards, baked and grilled, are prepared with care, making this a fine spot to linger over a leisurely meal.

Taverna Bakaliarakia   Greek €€
(🖉24320 23170; mains €6-12; ⌚lunch & dinner; **P** 🕾 🍽) This long-time local favourite, below the church in the village centre, has reopened better than ever. Eat in the simple interior or on the garden terrace (heated in winter). As well as an excellent, chunky country sausage (one serving comfortably feeds two), they offer good veggie alternatives, and it's one of the few Kastraki places to serve fresh fish.

Taverna Batalogianni   Taverna €€
(🖉24320 23253; Kastrakiou; mains €7-13; ⌚8am-late; ❄ 🕾) Set on a terrace below the side road into the village centre, just before the church, this charming little spot serves up delicious 100% homemade *mayirefta* (ready-cooked meals), along with lemon-flavoured dolmadhes, grilled meats and fabulous views of the nearby rocks. All the fish is frozen, though.

ABG Cafe   Cafe
(🖉24320 78618; Kastrakiou; ⌚2pm-late; 🕾) With its colourful, well-shaded front garden, this lively cafe makes a good stop for wi-fi, coffee and cocktails. A cool jazz soundtrack makes for a mellow evening vibe.

It's next to the Revoil petrol station on the main road through Kastraki.

ℹ GETTING THERE & AWAY

The only buses that serve Kastraki are the shuttles that run to and from Kalambaka every two hours (€1), and the three daily services that stop here en route between Kalambaka and the Meteora monasteries (one way/all day €1.80/5.50). All long-distance buses start from Kalambaka.

PELOPONNESE

Peloponnese at a Glance...

Home to Ancient Olympia, the Peloponnese is literally the stuff of Greek legends. The region bears tangible traces of the many past civilisations, witnessed in its classical temples, Mycenaean palaces, Byzantine cities, and Ottoman, Frankish and Venetian fortresses. The very topography that kept invaders at bay for centuries – lofty, snowcapped mountains, vast gorges, plus sandy beaches and azure waters – now draws visitors of a different kind. The food is among Greece's best, and the region's vineyards are contributing to Greece's wine renaissance. Locals claim to have the best of everything to give. And that's no myth.

Two Days in Peloponnese

The **Archaeological Museum** (p139) and **Palamidi Fortress** (p139) are the main highlights of pretty and romantic Nafplio. There are also a couple of nearby beaches. On day two marvel at the ruins of **Ancient Olympia** (p132), the birthplace of the Olympic Games. Make time also for the **Olympia Archaeological Museum** (p134) and the **Kotsanas Museum** (p138).

Four Days in Peloponnese

Explore the southern reaches of the Peloponnese peninsula. Our driving route (p138) takes in the fortresslike stone towers that are a characteristic architectural feature of the region as well as the steep, forbidding mountains of the Lakonian Mani.

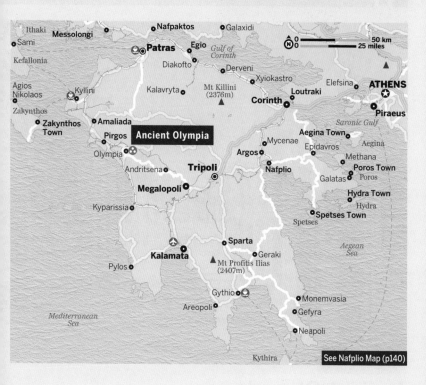

See Nafplio Map (p140)

Arriving in Peloponnese

The Peloponnese has one airport at Kalamata. Most visitors fly in to Athens, just over an hour away by car. Domestic and international ferries service the region, the main ones being from Patra (for Italy), Kyllini (for Kefallonia) and Gythio (for Crete). A good bus network services the region, but train (OSE) services are limited.

Where to Stay

Both Olympia and Nafplio are well-stocked with hotels covering all price points. In Olympia most are budget or midrange options; the best of them offer exceptional value. Nafplio has numerous boutique hotels and midrange guesthouses; its old town is chock-full of accommodation but can book out in summer.

Palaestra

GEORGE DAMIGOS/ALAMY STOCK PHOTO ©

Ancient Olympia

One of Greece's most evocative ancient sites, this is where the Olympic Games took place every four years for more than 1100 years. The Olympic flame is still lit here for the modern Games. Wandering amid the tree-shaded ruins, you can almost picture the athletes waiting inside the original stadium and the jostling crowds watching the proceedings from a nearby hill.

Great For...

☑ Don't Miss

The rectangular stadium with a track measuring 192.27m.

Entering the Site

Thanks to the destruction of the site ordered by Theodosius II in AD 420 and various subsequent earthquakes, little remains of the magnificent temples and athletic facilities, but enough exists to give you a hint of the sanctuary's former glory.

On your right as you descend, the first ruin encountered is the **gymnasium**, which dates from the 2nd century BC. South of here are the columns of the partly restored **palaestra** (wrestling school), where contestants practised and trained. Beyond is **Pheidias' workshop**, where the gargantuan ivory-and-gold Statue of Zeus, one of the Seven Wonders of the Ancient World, was sculpted by the Athenian master. Next is the **leonidaion**, an elaborate structure that accommodated dignitaries, built around 330 BC.

Inscription, Pheidias' workshop

❶ Need to Know

☎26240 22517; http://odysseus.culture.gr; adult/child €12/free; ⊘8am-8pm Apr-Oct, to 3pm Nov-Mar

✕ Take a Break

Zeus (☎26240 23913; Kondyli Praxiteli 59; ⊘8am-2am; 📶), in the middle of the town, is a good place to kick back with a coffee, cocktail or something from the decent wine list.

★ Top Tip

A visit to the archaeological museum (p134) before or after will provide context and help with visualising the ancient buildings.

Sacred Precinct of Zeus

The Altis, or **Sacred Precinct of Zeus**, lies on the left of the path you came down. Its most important building was the immense 5th-century-BC Doric **Temple of Zeus**, which enshrined Pheidias' statue, later removed to Constantinople by Theodosius II (where it was destroyed by fire in AD 475). One column of the temple has been restored and re-erected, and helps put into perspective the sheer size of the structure. To the east of the temple is the base for the **Nike (Victory statue)** that you can admire in the archaeological museum.

South of the Temple of Zeus is the **bouleuterion** (council house), which contains the **altar of oaths**, where competitors swore to abide by the rules decreed by the Olympic Senate and not to commit foul play. Here were kept the official records of the Games and its champions.

East of the temple is the **echo stoa**, with a Doric colonnade leading towards the stadium. Its remarkable acoustics meant that a sound uttered within was repeated seven times. Just east of the portico are the remains of a lavish **villa** used by Emperor Nero during his participation in the Games in AD 67; it replaced the original Sanctuary of Hestia.

The Stadium

The **stadium** lies to the east of the Altis and is entered through a stone archway. It could seat at least 45,000 spectators; slaves and women, however, had to be content to watch from outside on the Hill of Kronos. The stadium was used again in 2004, when it was the venue for the shotput at the Athens Olympics.

Temple of Hera

Further north is the late 7th-century-BC Doric **Temple of Hera**, the site's oldest temple. An altar in front of the temple would have maintained a continuous fire during the Games, symbolising the fire stolen from the gods by Prometheus; today, the Olympic flame is lit here.

Near the altar is the **nymphaeum** (AD 156–60), a once grandious building erected by the wealthy Roman banker Herodes Atticus. Despite its elaborate appearance, the nymphaeum had a practical purpose; it was a fountain house supplying Olympia with fresh spring water.

Beyond the nymphaeum and up a flight of stone steps, a row of 12 **treasuries** stretched to the stadium, each erected by a city-state for use as a storehouse for offerings to the gods; these were mainly used to advertise the city-state's prestige and wealth.

The foundations of the **philippeion**, west of the Temple of Hera, are the remains of a circular construction with Ionic columns built by Philip of Macedon to commemorate the Battle of Chaironeia (338 BC). North of the philippeion was the 5th-century-BC **prytaneum**, the magistrate's residence, where winning athletes feasted and were entertained.

Museums

Exhibits at the superb **Olympia Archaeological Museum** (☑26240 22742; http://odysseus.culture.gr; adult/child €12/free; ☺8am-8pm Apr-Oct, to 3pm Nov-Mar) span the sanctuary's past, from the prehistoric to the Roman periods. Artefacts include increasingly sophisti-

Temple pediments, Olympia Archaeological Museum

cated ceramics, votive offerings to Zeus and Hera, sacrificial cauldron adornments and statuary from the Temple of Hera. The main hall dramatically displays the biggest highlight: reassembled pediments and metopes from the Temple of Zeus.

The general entrance ticket also gives access to the excellent **Museum of the History of the Olympic Games in Antiquity** (26240 29119; http://odysseus.culture. gr; adult/child €12/free; ⊙8am-8pm Apr-Oct, to 3pm Nov-Mar). Learn about the Olympic Games' original core events (foot racing, wrestling, boxing and chariot racing), why it's associated with Hercules (or Pelops), and what fate befell women who tried to

It is worth visiting first thing in the morning or in the late afternoon; it's a magical experience to be there without the crowds.

watch the Games despite prohibitions. The sculptures, mosaics, pottery art and votive offerings all pay tribute to athletes and athleticism, while the bronze strigils were used by the athletes to scrape themselves down.

Tours

To really make the Ancient Olympia site come alive, it's worth considering a guide, especially if there are a few of you to split the cost. Tours start at around €120 for two or three people. Recommended bilingual guides include **Marieta Kolotourou** (6977526146) and **Niki Vlachou** (6972426085; www.olympictours.gr).

> To the north of the Temple of Zeus was the **pelopion**, a small, wooded hillock with an altar to Pelops, the first mythical hero of the Olympic Games.

SKLIFAS STEVEN/ALAMY STOCK PHOTO ©

The Lakonian Mani

Journeying south down Mani's west coast from Areopoli, you encounter a barren mountain landscape broken only by semideserted settlements with mighty towers.

Start Areopoli

Distance 112km

Duration Six to eight hours

1 From **Pyrgos Dirou**, packed with ceramics shops, you can detour to the Diros Caves.

Areopoli

START/FINISH

Omales

Diros Caves **1**

Pyrgos Dirou

2 *Drialos*

Vamvaka

2

2 The picturesque villages of **Drialos**, **Vamvaka**, **Briki** and **Mina** have fine examples of Maniot stonework.

2 *Briki*

2 *Mina*

Messinian Gulf

Tigani Peninsula

Mezapos

Stavri

Nomia **3** *Kita*

3 Kita has the lion's share of the west coast's war towers and fortified houses.

Gerolimenas

Alika

Take a Break...
Restaurant Akrotainaritis
(📞27330 54205; www.akrotainaritis. gr; mains €7-12; 🕐7am-midnight) in Gerolimenas serves home-cooked Greek standards, including local goat dishes.

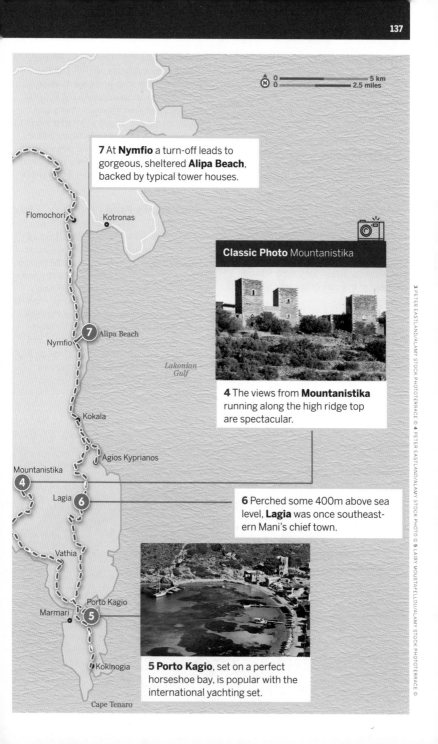

7 At **Nymfio** a turn-off leads to gorgeous, sheltered **Alipa Beach**, backed by typical tower houses.

Classic Photo Mountanistika

4 The views from **Mountanistika** running along the high ridge top are spectacular.

6 Perched some 400m above sea level, **Lagia** was once southeastern Mani's chief town.

5 **Porto Kagio**, set on a perfect horseshoe bay, is popular with the international yachting set.

Flomochori · Kotronas

Nymfio · Alipa Beach

Lakonian Gulf

Kokala

Agios Kyprianos

Mountanistika

Lagia

Vathia

Porto Kagio

Marmari

Kokinogia

Cape Tenaro

Olympia

◎ SIGHTS

Kotsanas Museum   Museum

(☑6931831530; www.kotsanas.com; Praxitelous Kondyli; by donation; ☺10am-8pm) This extraordinary private collection gets into the literal nuts and bolts behind the technological achievements of the Ancient Greeks. Marvel at the mechanics of the crane used to build the Parthenon, the Antikythera Mechanism (the 'first laptop'), and a statue servant that serves holy water, touted as the 'world's oldest vending machine'. Fascinating, educational and marvellous for kids, both young and old. Excellent English explanations. The pieces are on display courtesy of the collector, mechanical engineer Kostas Kotsanas.

⊕ ACTIVITIES & TOURS

Dig It!   Educational

(☑26240 26232; www.facebook.com/digit olympia; individual €9-15, family of 4 €30-50;

☺9am-3pm Mon-Fri, 10am-2pm Sat) Two young archaeologists run this fabulous programme for kids and parents designed to bridge the knowledge of what actually happens between a ruin discovery and museum display. To get your head around excavation and conservation, you participate in a 'dig' in one of three simulated archaeological sites. There are programs from 45 minutes to 1½ hours that must be prebooked.

Klio's Honey Farm   Food

(☑6977714530; www.klioshoneyfarm.com; ☺10am-6pm Jun-Aug, from 10.30am Mon-Sat May-Sep, 11am-4pm Mon-Sat Mar-Apr & Oct-Nov) Enterprising Klio, a professional beekeeper, has opened up the family home to provide a very local experience. She'll talk you through the beekeeping and honey-making process, before you sit at one of the lace-cloth-covered tables in the flower-filled garden, converse with Klio's mother and try honey drizzled over *diplas* (fried pastry curls). It's 500m from the centre, well signposted from the station.

Palamidi Fortress

NATALIYA NAZAROVA/SHUTTERSTOCK ©

Nemouta Waterfalls   Outdoors

(✆6978400540; siakkoulis@hotmail.com;
Namouta; 4-10 people from €60) For a nature-
based departure from Ancient Olympia,
guide Nick Siakkoulis will coordinate a trip
to three beautiful waterfalls, located near
the village of Nemouta, 26km northeast of
Olympia. The pick-up point is in Nemouta's weeny main plaza. From here you are
transported to the falls with guides from
the village (limited to no English spoken). A
relaxed, local experience, you would be hard
pushed to find these falls on your own.

✖ EATING

Symposio   Greek €

(✆26240 23620; mains €6-12; ⏱9am-midnight;
🖉) Warm-hearted taverna at the ruins at
the end of town with checked tablecloths
and a genuine welcome. Prices are fair for
large portions of dips, salads, Greek favourites and grilled meats.

Anesis   Grill €

(✆26240 22644; cnr Avgerinou & Spiliopoulou;
mains €6-9; ⏱7pm-midnight May-Sep) No-frills
grills. And excellent ones at that. Run by a
hard-working family, Anesis is a fabulous
budget option and will even deliver to your
hotel for no charge. Look for hearty homemade dishes including *pastitsio* (baked
pasta) and stuffed tomatoes. We love the
kontosouvli (spit-roasted pork).

Garden Taverna   Greek €€

(✆26240 22650; www.hoteleuropa.gr; Hotel
Europa; mains €10-17; ⏱noon-2pm & 7-10.30pm
May-Sep; 🛜) Nestled under olive trees in
a tranquil rose garden that overlooks the
valley, this restaurant is the most original
in Olympia. Alongside the excellent grilled
meats you'll find the likes of pasta in vodka
cream sauce with smoked salmon and dill.
A great spot to come for sunset drinks.

ⓘ GETTING THERE & AWAY

Buses depart from the train station, located in
the middle of town one block east of the main
street. There are three handy Athens connections (€30.10, four hours).

Nafplio

Though quite touristy, Nafplio is one of
Greece's prettiest and most romantic
towns. It occupies a knockout waterside
location beneath the towering Palamidi fortress, and is graced with attractive narrow
streets, elegant Venetian houses, neoclassical mansions and interesting museums. It's
also chock-full of tavernas, posh boutiques
and comfortable hotels and guesthouses.
Because it's a popular destination for locals
from Athens, it fills up on weekends and
gets overcrowded in high season.

Nafplio was the first capital of Greece
after Independence (between 1833 and
1834) and has been a major port since the
Bronze Age. So strategic was its position on
the Argolic Gulf that it had three fortresses:
the massive principal fortress of Palamidi,
the smaller Akronafplia, and the diminutive
Bourtzi on an islet west of the old town.

◎ SIGHTS

Archaeological Museum   Museum

(✆27520 27502; http://odysseus.culture.
gr; Plateia Syntagmatos; adult/child €6/free;
⏱8.30am-4pm Wed-Mon, to 3.30pm Nov-Feb)
Inside a splendid Venetian building, this
museum traces the social development
of Argolis, from the hunter-gatherers of
the Franchthi Cave to the sophisticated
Mycenaean-era civilisations, through beautifully presented archaeological finds from
the surrounding area. Exhibits include a
Palaeolithic hearth, Geometric-period pottery, a 6th-century-BC amphora that was a
prize from the Panathenaic Games, plus – a
real highlight – the only existing bronze armour from near Mycenae (3500 years old,
with a boar-tusk helmet). Excellent audio
guides available in several languages (leave
a government-issued ID).

Palamidi Fortress   Fortress

(✆27520 28036; http://odysseus.culture.gr;
adult/child €8/free; ⏱8am-8pm Apr-Aug, reduced
hours Sep-Mar) This vast, spectacular citadel,
reachable either by steep ascent on foot or a
short drive, stands on a 216m-high outcrop

Nafplio

Argolic Gulf

Bourtzi
(200m)

Mycenae
(24km)

Leoforos Argous

Thisseos

Stadium

Iraklepus

Vas Georgiou

Kilkis

Bouboulinas

Mineou

Vasileos Pavlou

Navarinou

Dervenakion

Sidiras Merarhias
Kolokotronis Park

Vasilissis Konstantinou

25 Martiou

Nikitara

Karathona Beach
(4.2km)

10 9

Former
Train
Station

Flessa

Syngrou

Plateia
Kapodistrias

Polizoidou

11

KTEL Argolis
Bus Station

Bouboulinas

Staikos Tours &
Rent-A-Car

12

Vasilissis Olgas

Sofroni

Amalias

Terzaki

Plateia Trion
Navarhon

Platonos

Town Hall

Moutzouridou

Papanikolau

Papoutta

5

Fotomara

Karathona Beach
(3.5km)

Polizoidou

Kotsonopoulou

Othonos

Blesi

Vasilissis Alexandrou

Ypsilandou

8

6

7

Siokou

Vasilissis Vasilissis Konstantinou

Kapodistriou

Plateia Agios
Spiridonos

Potamianou

Akronafplia

Argolic Gulf

Plateia
Fileitinon

Farmakopoulon

Miniati

Vyronos

Akti
Miaouli

Spiliadou

30 Noemvriou

13

Plateia
Syntagmatos

Staikopoulou

Konstantinoupoleos

Zygomala

Efthimiopoulou

Plateia
Politikou
Nosokomiou

Plateia Zygomala

1

3

N   200 m
    0.1 miles

Nafplio

of rock that gives all-encompassing views of Nafplio and the Argolic Gulf. It was built by the Venetians between 1711 and 1714, and is regarded as a masterpiece of military architecture despite being successfully stormed in one night by Greek troops in 1822, causing the Turkish garrison within to surrender without a fight.

Peloponnesian Folklore Foundation Museum
Museum

(☎27520 28379; www.pli.gr; Vasileos Alexandrou 1; adult/child €5/3; ⊙9am-2.30pm Mon-Sat, 9.30am-3pm Sun) Nafplio's award-winning museum is a beautifully arranged collection of folk costumes and household items from Nafplio's 19th- and early-20th-century history. Be wowed by the intricate embroidery of traditional costumes and the heavy silver adornments; admire the turn-of-the-20th-century couture; and look out for the cute horse-tricycle. The gift shop sells high-quality local crafts.

National Gallery – Nafplio Annex
Gallery

(☎27520 21915; www.nationalgallery.gr; Sidiras Merarhias 23; adult/concession €3/1.50; ⊙10am-3pm Mon, Thu & Sat, 10am-3pm & 5-8pm Wed & Fri, 10am-2pm Sun) This arm of the Athens National Gallery is housed in a stunningly restored neoclassical building (don't be deterred; the front door looks to be closed). It features numerous seascapes and different thematic takes on the 1821 Greek War of Independence, including paintings by Theodoros Vryzakis and Dionysios Tsokos, who are considered the most important Greek artists of the post-war years. Entry is free on Mondays.

Bourtzi
Fortress

(☎6977716998; www.odysseycruises.gr; return cruise €4.50) Odyssey Cruises runs boat excursions to this island fortress. Built in 1473, it lies about 600m west of the town's port and has served variously as a pirate deterrent, a home for executioners and a hotel. Note that the battlements are identical in design to Moscow's Kremlin; both were built by 15th-century Venetians. Boats leave from the northeastern end of Akti Miaouli. You can buy tickets from where the boats depart.

✪ ACTIVITIES

Nafplio Bio-Farms
Food

(☎6944184703; www.nafpliobiofarms.gr; tours per person €15-40) This fun, hands-on cultural experience is also tasty and informative. Guests visit a small organic farm, located just outside Nafplio, that produces oranges and olives and makes its own organic flour. Owners Petros and Panagiota run through the history of farming techniques that follow centuries-old practices; depending on the tour, you may sample and/or make local goodies.

✪ SHOPPING

Glykos Peirasmos
Food

(Plapouta 10; ⊙9am-9pm Mon-Thu, to 10pm Fri-Sun) *The* place for delicious chocolate, baklava, *loukoumi* (Turkish delight) and honey-sodden walnut cake.

Karonis
Wine

(☎27520 24446; www.karoniswineshop.gr; Amalias 5; ⊙8.30am-2pm & 6-9.30pm Mon-Sat)

 Beaches

Small and pebbly **Arvanitia Beach** is five minutes' walk south of town, tucked beside the Akronafplia Fortress, past the Land Gate. It's a nice place for a sunset bathe, with great views. For a scenic stroll, take the blustery, cactus-adorned path that skirts the headland from the bottom of the promenade.

A gorgeous pine-tree-lined 3km path runs from the car park next to Arvanitia Beach to the long, sandy **Karathona Beach** where there are places to eat and drink, as well as an operator offering water-skiing, flyboarding and more. It's a flat, easy walk, though the beach could be cleaner. Don't feel like walking? Head your car along 25 Martiou east of town. It's 5km from the centre.

Arvanitia Beach
BRIAN S/SHUTTERSTOCK ©

Wine enthusiasts can find a fine selection of wines from all over the country, including Nemean reds and spirits. Tastings are offered. Well-read owner Ioannis has a wide range of interests, from grapes to politics.

✕ EATING

Pidalio   Greek €
(📞27520 22603; www.pidalio.gr; 25 Martiou 5; mains €7-10; ⊙12.30pm-midnight Wed-Mon) One of several excellent spots in the new town frequented mainly by locals, Pidalio is a lovely taverna that serves excellent Greek fare at fair prices. It's warm and lively; you'll smell the cooking before you spot it.

I Gonia Tou Kavalari   Mezedhes €€
(Kavalaris Corner Mezedopoleio; 📞27525 00180; cnr Amalias & Koleti; mezedhes €4-9; ⊙8am-1am Tue-Sun; 🍴) Just off Plateia Syntagmatos and nestled into a cosy corner, this delightful spot whips, tosses and fries up some of the best mezedhes (tapas-style dishes) around. You can watch the chef at work in the open kitchen, though our guess is you'll be too busy munching on everything from *spetsofaï* (sausage) to *apaki* (fried pork). Excellent vegetarian options too. Traditional products but contemporary creations.

Menta   Greek €€
(📞27520 23603; 25 Martiou 7-19; dishes €8-15; ⊙noon-midnight Thu-Tue; 🛜🍴🐾) On an appealing eat street in the new town, this contemporary place re-creates a traditional *kafeneio* (coffee house) and blends it with millennial designer flair: mismatched chairs and tables, exposed light bulbs and an industrial interior. Service is very welcoming and the dishes – contemporary flair meets traditional ingredients – are delicious, though not all the food pairings are thought through.

Kakanarakis 1986   Greek €€
(📞27520 25371; Vasilissis Olgas 18; mains €8-15; ⊙1pm-1am Thu-Tue; 🛜🍴) This taverna bolsters its menu with stew-type specials like beef *stifado* and slow-cooked pork. There are numerous vegetarian options and the starters are a light meal in themselves. There's a certain elegance to the polished-floorboard, open-kitchen interior.

🍸 DRINKING & NIGHTLIFE

Mavros Gatos   Bar
(📞27520 26652; Sofroni 1; ⊙8am-3am) Chilled-out cafe by day, buzzy bar by night, the 'Black Cat' has live performers some nights and DJs always. There are comfy seats outside and an eclectic vintage vibe inside and upstairs.

Kontrabasso   Bar
(📞27520 27434; www.facebook.com/kontra bassocafe; Arvanitias 1; ⊙9am-midnight or later;

📶) Just by the steps up to the Palamidi fortress, this welcoming cafe-bar is an all-rounder that offers breakfasts and brunches, all-day sandwiches and salads, and pints of cold beer – just the thing after the hot staircase walk. We like it best in the evening, when a cocktail on the stepped wooden terrace is pleasantly removed from the centre's hubbub.

Sokaki   Bar

(📞27520 26032; www.sokakicafe.gr; Antistasis 8; ⏰9am-3am Mon-Sat, to midnight Sun; 📶) With an eclecticism of decor that runs from Buddhas to petrol pumps, this is a comfortably cluttered and cosy space both indoors and outdoors, with the shaded wraparound terrace a prime summer spot. It's a place to kick back with a cocktail or aperitif, but they also do decent coffee and crêpes, both savoury and sweet.

ℹ INFORMATION

Hospital (📞27523 61100; Kountouriotou 1) Nafplio's general hospital.

Staikos Tours (📞27520 27950; www.rentacar nafplio.gr; Bouboulinas 50; ⏰8.30am-2.30pm & 5.30-8.30pm Mon-Sat, 10am-noon & 6-8pm Sun) Run by the personable, English-speaking Christos. Has full travel services, including ferry tickets, plus Sixt rental cars.

Tourist Police (📞27520 98728; Eleftherias 2) At Nafplio's police station.

ℹ GETTING THERE & AWAY

The **KTEL Argolis bus station** (📞27520 27323; www.ktelargolida.gr; Syngrou) has buses to Athens (€14.40, 2½ hours, at least hourly), some via Corinth Isthmus (Peloponnese) KTEL bus station (€7.10, 1½ hours). Lockers available.

ℹ GETTING AROUND

Head to the taxi rank on Syngrou, which has a list of official prices for excursions in the area. Car-hire agencies include the following:

Hermes Car Rental (📞27520 25308; www. hermestravel.gr; Syngrou 20; ⏰9am-9pm)

Sixt Rent a Car Runs out of Staikos Tours.

Mavros Gatos

CORFU

Corfu at a Glance...

From the writings of Gerald and Lawrence Durrell to the place where the ship-wrecked Odysseus was soothed and sent on his way home, Corfu has been portrayed as an idyll for centuries. Today this reputation has led to parts of the island being defiled by mass tourism, but despite this, the Corfu of literature does still exist. All you need to do is sail around the corner, walk over the next headland or potter about the rugged interior and a place of bountiful produce, cypress-studded hills, vertiginous villages, and sandy coves lapped by cobalt-blue waters awaits.

Two Days in Corfu

Explore the Old Town making sure you don't to miss the excellent **Corfu Museum of Asian Art** (p150). Head inland to lose yourself for a happy hour or two amid the maze-like alleyways, seeking out sumptuous Orthodox churches or cosy cafes as the mood takes you. End the day taking in views from **Palaio Frourio** (p150). On day two stroll over to the **Mon Repos Estate** (p151) or hop on a boat to **Vidos Island** (p151) to relax on its beaches.

Four Days in Corfu

Escape the crowds by making a road trip to the southern tip of the island, pausing at sleepy fishing villages, like **Lefkimmi** (p157), as you go. On day four head to the west coast resort area of **Paleokastritsa** (p157). Hike or drive up the unspoilt villages of **Lakones** (p157) and **Krini** (p157). Consider dropping by the delightful old wine estate at **Ambelonas** (p155).

Cape Agia Ekaterinis

Cape Drastis
Sidhari
Perouladeso
Roda
Aharavi
Kassiopi

Agios
Stefanos
Cape Kefali
Arillaso

Mt Pantokrator
(906m)▲
Ksamil

ALBANIA

Kalami
Ano
Korakiana
Nisaki
Skripero
Barbati
Krini
Lakones
Ipsos
North
Kerkyra
Straits
Angelokastro
Liapades
Dasia
Paleokastritsa
Vidos
Island
Konispoli
Gouvia
Giannades
Agios
Ioannis
Corfu Town (Kerkyra)
Ermones
Mon Repos Estate
Ioannis Kapodistrias Airport
Glyfada
Kinopiastes
Perama
Sinarades
Achilleion Palace
GREECE
Agios
Gordios
Benitses
Strongyli
Agios
Matthaios
Moraïtika
Messonghi
South Kerkyra
Straits
Boukari
Petriti
Cape Lefkimmi
Lake Korission
Lefkimmi
Bay
Agios
Georgios
Lefkimmi

Ionian
Sea

Kavos
Cape Asprokavos

See Corfu Old Town Map (p152)

10 km
5 miles

Arriving in Corfu

Corfu's airport is on the southwestern fringes of Corfu Town, just over 2km southwest of the Old Town. Ferries depart from the Neo Limani (New Port), northwest of Corfu Town's Old Town. Green Buses (www.greenbuses.gr) goes to Athens and Thessaloniki, or you can take one of the many daily ferries to the mainland and catch the bus of your choice from there.

Where to Stay

Many visitors stay not in Corfu Town but in the various beach resorts scattered around the coast. The long strips of beach immediately north and south of Corfu Town, and along the north coast between Aharavi and Sidhari, are dominated by package holidaymakers. More appealing destinations for independent travellers include the harbour towns of Kassiopi, Kalami and Paleokastritsa (p157).

Corfu's Old Town

For this walk through Corfu's Old Town, be sure to pack your sun cream and swimming gear – you're going to need them along the way. Start at the southern end of the elegant, French-built Liston arcade.

Start Liston

Distance 2km

Duration Three to four hours

6 The church housing the **Antivouniotissa Museum** (p151) displays some sublime religious icons.

4 Settle down with a book in the library of the **Corfu Reading Society**.

7 Plateia Dimarchio, easily the Old Town's sweetest square, is lined with cafes and restaurants.

Arseniou

Donzelot

Plateia Kremasti

Apolodorou

Ag Theodoras

Mitropoleos

Vouthirotou

Kapodistriou

Nikiforou Theotoki

Filarmonikis

Ag Spyridonos
Kaloheretou
Pargas
Iperiou
Plateia
Agios Spyridon
Secastianou
Ag Panton

Velissariou

EVRAIKI

M Theotoki

Eleftherias

Old Cricket Ground

Voulgareos

Plateia Dimarchio

Voulgareos

Guilford

Kapodistriou

The Spianada

NEW TOWN

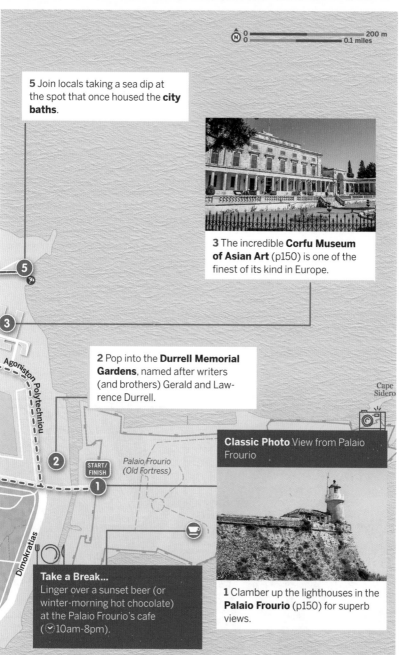

5 Join locals taking a sea dip at the spot that once housed the **city baths**.

3 The incredible **Corfu Museum of Asian Art** (p150) is one of the finest of its kind in Europe.

2 Pop into the **Durrell Memorial Gardens**, named after writers (and brothers) Gerald and Lawrence Durrell.

Agoniston Polytechniou

Cape Sidero

Classic Photo View from Palaio Frourio

Palaio Frourio (Old Fortress)

START/FINISH

Dimokratias

Take a Break...
Linger over a sunset beer (or winter-morning hot chocolate) at the Palaio Frourio's cafe (⏱10am-8pm).

1 Clamber up the lighthouses in the **Palaio Frourio** (p150) for superb views.

3 TATIANA DYUVBANOVA/SHUTTERSTOCK © 4 SKORDUS/SHUTTERSTOCK ©

Corfu Town

The Old Town's most eye-catching feature is the grand French-built **Liston** arcade, facing the Old Fort across the lawns of the **Spianada** and lined with packed cafes. The New Town, busy with everyday shops and services, revolves around Plateia G Theo-toki (also known as Plateia San Rocco). South, around the curving Bay of Garitsa, the ruin-strewn Mon Repos Estate marks the site of the ancient settlement of Palaeopolis.

◎ SIGHTS

Palaio Frourio   Fortress

(Old Fort; ☏26610 48310; adult/concession/child €6/3/free; ⊗8am-8pm Apr-Oct, 8.30am-3pm Nov-Mar) The rocky headland that juts east from Corfu Town is topped by the Venetian-built 14th-century Palaio Frourio. Before that, already enclosed within massive stone walls, it cradled the entire Byzantine city. A solitary bridge crosses its seawater moat.

Only parts of this huge site, which also holds later structures from the British era, are accessible to visitors; wander up to the **lighthouse** on the larger of the two hills for superb views.

Corfu Museum
of Asian Art   Museum

(☏26610 30443; www.matk.gr; Palace of St Michael & St George; adult/concession/child incl palace entry €6/3/free; ⊗8am-8pm Apr-Oct, 9am-4pm Tue-Sun Nov-Mar) Home to stunning artefacts ranging from prehistoric bronzes to works in onyx and ivory, this excellent museum occupies the central portions of the **Palace of St Michael and St George**. One gallery provides a chronological overview of Chinese ceramics, and showcases remarkable jade carvings and snuff bottles. The India section opens with Alexander the Great, 'When Greece Met India', and displays fascinating Graeco-Buddhist figures, including a blue-grey schist Buddha. A Japanese section incorporates magnificent samurai armour and Noh masks.

Achilleion Palace

Achilleion Palace Historic Building

(☎26610 56245; www.achilleion-corfu.gr;
Gastouri; adult/concession €8/6; ☺8am-8pm
Apr-Nov, to 4pm Dec-Mar) Set atop a steep
coastal hill 12km south of Corfu Town,
the Achilleion Palace was built during the
1890s as the summer palace of Austria's
Empress Elisabeth, the niece of King Otto
of Greece. The palace's two principal features are its intricately decorated central
staircase, rising in geometrical flights, and
its sweeping garden terraces, which com-
mand eye-popping views.

Antivouniotissa Museum Museum

(Byzantine Museum; ☎26610 38313; www.
antivouniotissamuseum.gr; adult/concession/
child €4/2/free; ☺8am-3pm Tue-Sun) Home
to an outstanding collection of Byzantine
and post-Byzantine icons and artefacts,
the exquisite, timber-roofed Church of Our
Lady of Antivouniotissa has a double role
as church and museum. It stands atop
a short, broad stairway that climbs from
shore-front Arseniou, and frames views out
towards wooded Vidos Island.

Archaeological Museum Museum

(☎26610 30680; www.amcorfu.gr; Vraïla 1;
adult/concession/child €6/3/free; ☺8am-8pm
Thu-Tue) Built in the 1960s, Corfu Town's Archaeological Museum has finally reopened
after nearly a decade of renovations. The
result of this work is a modern and well-lit
museum (although some of the English
labelling is a bit hit and miss) housing some
16,000 pieces found around Corfu. The
highlight of the fine collection is a massive
gorgon pediment (590–580 BC) from the
Temple of Artemis on the nearby Kanoni
Peninsula.

Mon Repos Estate Park

(Kanoni Peninsula; ☺8am-3pm Tue-Sun) `FREE`
This park-like wooded estate 2km around
the bay south of the Old Town was the site
of Corfu's most important ancient settlement, Palaeopolis. More recently, in 1921,
the secluded neoclassical villa that now

 **Joint Ticket**

A great-value joint ticket for the Corfu
Museum of Asian Art, Palaio Frourio,
Mon Repos Estate, Antivouniotissa
Museum and Archaeological Museum
costs €14 and is valid for 10 days.

Antivouniotissa Museum
IMAGEBROKER/ALAMY STOCK PHOTO ©

holds the **Museum of Palaeopolis**
(☎26610 32783; Mon Repos, Kanoni Peninsula;
adult/concession €4/2; ☺8am-3pm Tue-Sun)
was the birthplace of Prince Philip of
Greece, who went on to marry Britain's
Princess Elizabeth (now the current
queen). Footpaths lead through the woods
to ancient ruins, including those of a Doric
temple atop a small coastal cliff.

It takes half an hour to walk to Mon
Repos from town, or you can catch bus 2a
from the Spianada (€1.20, every 20 minutes). Bring a picnic and plenty of water;
there are no shops nearby.

Vidos Island Island

Hourly boats from the Old Port make the
10-minute crossing to tiny, thickly wooded
Vidos Island (€4 return), immediately off-
shore. The island is the final resting place
of thousands of Serbian soldiers killed
during WWII. There's a monument to them
here and also some abandoned buildings
once used by the scouts. There's a taverna
at the jetty, but the big attraction is to walk
the 600m across the island to reach a
couple of attractive beaches.

Corfu Old Town

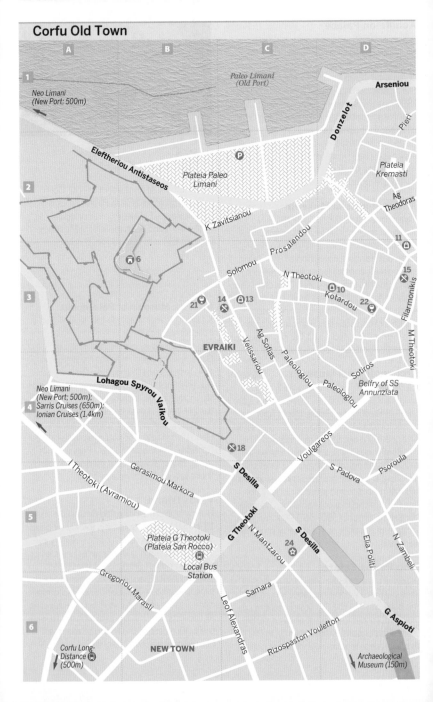

Neo Limani
(New Port; 500m)

Paleo Limani
(Old Port)

Arseniou

Eleftheriou Antistaseos

Donzelot

Pieri

Plateia
Kremasti

Plateia Paleo
Limani

Ag
Theodoras

K Zavitsianou

Prosalendou

11

Solomou

N Theotoki

15

6

10

Kotardou

Filarmonikis

21

14

13

22

M Theotoki

Ag Sofias

EVRAIKI

Velissariou

Paleologou

Paleologou

Sotiros

Belfry of SS
Annunziata

Lohagou Spyrou Vaïkou

Neo Limani
(New Port; 500m);
Sarris Cruises (650m);
Ionian Cruises (1.4km)

18

Voulgareos

S Padova

Psoroula

S Desilla

Gerasimou Markora

I Theotoki (Avramiou)

G Theotoki

N Mantzarou

S Desilla

Elia Politi

N Zambeli

Plateia G Theotoki
(Plateia San Rocco)

24

Local Bus
Station

Gregoriou Marasli

Samara

Leof Alexandras

G Asploti

Corfu Long-
Distance
(500m)

NEW TOWN

Rizospaston Vouleftion

Archaeological
Museum (150m)

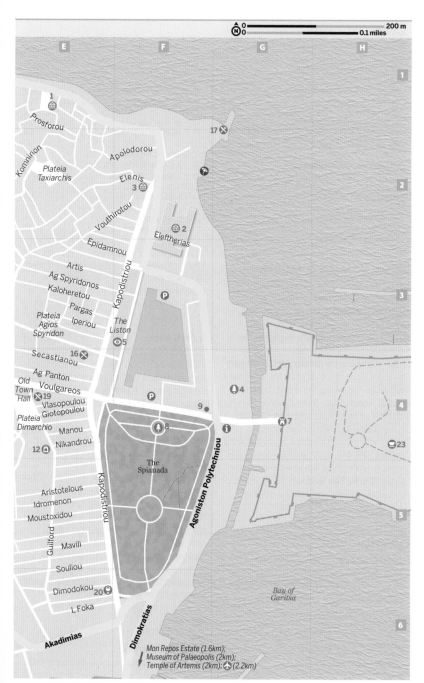

Corfu Old Town

⊕ ACTIVITIES & TOURS

All sorts of tours can help you explore in and around Corfu Town, whether on foot with **Corfu Walking Tours** (📞6932894466, 6945894450; www.corfuwalkingtours.com; €64-78), by bus with **Corfu Sightseeing** (📞26610 86000; www.corfusightseeing.gr; €19) or in the **horse-drawn carriage tours** (Dousmani, Spianada) that start from the Spianada. Cruises along the coast or to neighbouring islands start from the New Port, with operators including **Ionian Cruises** (📞26610 38690; www.ionian-cruises.com; Ethnikis Antistaseos 4; ⊙7am-8pm) and **Sarris Cruises** (📞26610 25317; www.sarriscruises.gr; Mouriki 1), while if you fancy learning to sail, contact **Corfu Sea School** (📞6945556821; www.corfuseaschool.com; Gouvia Marina) at Gouvia Marina not far northwest.

⊟ SHOPPING

Corfu Gallery   Art

(📞26610 25796; www.corfugallery.com; N Theotoki 72; ⊙10am-11pm) Fabulous sculptures, paintings and objets d'art are sold at this gallery. The pieces are uniformly expensive, but you're welcome to just browse.

Sweet'n'Spicy Bahar   Spices

(📞26610 33848; www.sweetnspicy.gr; Agias Sofias 12; ⊙9.45am-2pm) Gloriously aromatic spice and condiment shop, run by an ever-so-enthusiastic Greek-Canadian-Lebanese woman with a palpable love for devising her own enticing mixes of Greek and imported spices.

Icon Gallery   Arts & Crafts

(📞26614 00928; www.iconcraft.gr; Guilford 52; ⊙10am-10.30pm Mon-Sat; 🛜) True to its name, this hole-in-the-wall boutique sells stunning icons, handmade by an artists' co-op, as well as fine heraldic art and antiques. Some of the icons have a distinctly modern twist – Adam being titillated by a not-very-shy Eve, for example – that the Church surely wouldn't approve of!

Corfu Sandals   Shoes

(📞26610 47301; www.facebook.com/corfusandals; Philhellinon 9; ⊙9am-11pm) This standout shoe store, on the narrow lane that holds Corfu Town's heaviest (and tackiest) concentration of souvenir shops, sells well-priced handmade leather sandals in all styles and sizes, many with ergonomic bubble soles. To find it, look out for the sandals that only a giant could wear.

⊗ EATING

Pane & Souvlaki   Grill €

(📞26610 20100; www.panesouvlaki.com; Guilford 77; mains €6-13.50; ⊙noon-1am) Arguably the Old Town's best-value budget option (the locals rave), with outdoor tables on the town-hall square, this quick-fire restaurant does exactly what its name suggests, serving up three skewers of chicken or pork with chunky chips, dipping sauce and warm pitta in individual metal trays. The salads and burgers are good, too.

Chrisomalis
Taverna €

(☑26610 30342; N Theotoki 6; mains €7-13; ⊙noon-midnight) Going strong since 1904, this traditional little taverna was a haunt of the Durrell family and actor Anthony Quinn, and there are old pictures on the wall of Gerald and Lawrence Durrell with the owner. Follow your nose to the traditional grill for souvlaki, pork chops and swordfish. Warm service and pavement tables make it ideal for people-watching.

Abakas
Grill €€

(☑26613 04219; Velissariou; mains €8-15; ⊙6pm-midnight; ▓) Let your inner carnivore loose at this excellent grill house, which has a keen local following and is set a little way off the noisy tourist strip. Sit outside in the cobbled street to eat or head inside and savour the smell of sizzling meats.

Fishalida
Seafood €€

(☑26614 01213; Spirou Vlaikou 1; mains €12-20; ⊙11am-midnight; ▓) Right next to the market and a fishmongers, this is an easygoing, youthful place to eat inventive and highly superb seafood such as prawn tortellini with wild-mushroom sauce or the unexpectedly delightful octopus with hummus. There's a light-filled interior or you can eat outside at one of the couple of tables. Advance bookings almost essential.

Anthos
Seafood €€

(☑26610 32252; www.facebook.com/anthos restaurant; Maniarizi-Arlioti 15; mains €10-21; ⊙noon-midnight Mon-Sat, 6pm-midnight Sun; 🐾) Much-loved little back-alley restaurant with a handful of outdoor tables. Most diners are here for the seafood, savouring dishes such as squid carpaccio, octopus with fava-bean mousse, and grilled sea bass, but it also serves standard Greek meat favourites.

🍷🍽 Ambelonas

The delightful old estate at **Ambelonas** (☑6932158888; http://ambelonas-corfu. gr; ⊙7-11pm Wed-Fri Jun-Oct, 1-6pm Sun Dec-May), 6km west of Corfu Town towards Pelekas, produces enticing local products, from vinegars to olives to sweets. Tour the olive-oil mill and winery, and sample wines from local grapes (such as *kakotrygis*), along with Corfiot mezedhes (€9 to €15; prix fixe including wine €18 to €28).

Green olives
SZYMON MUCHA/ALAMY STOCK PHOTO ©

En Plo
Cafe €€

(☑26610 81813; www.enplocorfu.com; Gate of St Nicholas, Faliraki; mains €8-14; ⊙9.30am-11.30pm Mon-Sat, to 11pm Sun; 🐾) Cream-toned cafe in a magnificent setting, down at sea level away from everything at the northeastern tip of the Old Town. You can enjoy a simple meal of mixed appetisers or grilled meats, or settle back with a sunset drink. It's located in what used to be the city baths and today people still cool off in the sea here.

🍸 DRINKING & NIGHTLIFE

Firi Firi – The Beer House
Bar

(☑26610 33953; www.facebook.com/FiriFiriCor fu; Solomou 1; ⊙6pm-2am Tue-Sun; 🐾) Sample local and imported beers, either inside the custard-coloured villa at the foot of the steps leading up to the Neo Frourio or at the terraced tables beside the neighbouring church; if you find it hard to leave, it grills up some decent dishes, too.

Mikro Café   Bar
(📞26610 31009; N Theotoki 42; ⊙9am-midnight) You can smell the coffee beans roasting from 25m down the street, and whether your favoured beverage comes from these beans or is something a little more alcoholic, the Old Town holds no finer spot for drinking and people-watching than the delightful, multilevel, vine-shaded terrace of the convivial 'little cafe'.

Cavalieri Hotel Rooftop Bar   Bar
(📞26610 39041; www.cavalieri-hotel.com; Kapodistriou 4; ⊙6.30pm-late) Rather wonderful rooftop bar that makes an ideal venue for mellow predinner drinks, with stunning views across the Spianada to the Palaio Frourio. There's the hope that you'll stay for an Italian-flavoured meal, but you don't have to.

⊗ ENTERTAINMENT

Municipal Theatre   Performing Arts
(📞26610 40136; www.dipethek.gr; G Theotoki 68) This brutalist modern edifice at the edge of the Old Town serves as Corfu's cultural powerhouse, putting on performances of classical music, opera, dance and drama; some productions are also staged at the theatre next to Mon Repos (p151).

ⓘ INFORMATION

All Ways Travel (📞26610 33955; www.allways travel.com.gr; Plateia G Theotoki 34) Helpful English-speaking staff in the New Town's main square.

Aperghi Travel (📞26610 48713; www.aperghi travel.gr; I Polyla 1) Handles tours and accommodation, especially for walkers on the Corfu Trail (www.thecorfutrail.com).

Corfu General Hospital (📞26613 60400; www. gnkerkyras.gr; Kontokali) About 8km west of the town centre.

Municipal Tourist Kiosk (www.corfu.gr; Spianada; ⊙8am-4pm Mon-Fri Mar-Nov) Helps

with accommodation, transport and things to do around Corfu.

Pachis Travel (📞26610 28298; www.pachis travel.com; Guilford 7; ⊙9.30am-3pm & 6-8.30pm Mon-Fri, 9.30am-2pm Sat) Busy little agency that's useful for hotels, ferry and plane tickets, and excursions to Paxi.

ⓘ GETTING THERE & AWAY

Corfu Town is home to both the island's **airport** (CFU; 📞26610 89600; www.corfu-airport.com), 2km southwest of the centre, and its main ferry port. Ferries to Italy, the Greek mainland and Paxi depart from the Neo Limani (New Port), west of the Old Town.

Local bus 15 (€1.70, hourly Monday to Saturday, 10 daily Sunday) connects the airport with the Neo Limani, and also stops between the two at Plateia G Theotoki (Plateia San Rocco) in the New Town. Buy tickets at kiosks (or sometimes on board).

Corfu Town is at the centre of an efficient network of local buses, and you can get pretty much anywhere on the island from the **long-distance bus station** (📞26610 28900; https://greenbus es.gr; Lefkimmis 13) in the New Town.

ⓘ GETTING AROUND

Most Corfu Town rental companies, including **Budget** (📞26610 24404; www.budget.gr; Eleftheriou Antistaseos 6), **Sunrise** (📞26610 44325; www.corfusunrise.com; Ethnikis Antistaseos 16) and **Top Cars** (📞26610 35237; www.carrental corfu.com; Donzelot 25), are based along the northern waterfront.

Local blue buses depart from the **local bus station** (📞26610 31595; www.astikoktelkerkyras. gr; Plateia G Theotoki) in the Old Town. Journeys cost €1.20 or €1.70. Buy tickets at the booth on Plateia G Theotoki or on the bus itself. All trips are less than 30 minutes. Service is reduced at weekends.

Southern Corfu

The first resort that you reach as you head south on the coast road from Corfu Town is

Angelokastro

sleepy **Benitses**, 14km along. This pleasant old village backs a sand-and-gravel beach and is home to a ruined Roman villa, with footpaths ascending the wooded slopes.

Further south again, beyond the popular but uninspiring beach resorts of **Moraïtika** and **Messonghi**, the coastal road winds through sun-dappled woods, passing prettier and much less developed little coves. Tiny **Boukari** cradles a small harbour and has some narrow pebble beaches (alas, these wouldn't win a beauty award), while the fishing port of **Petriti**, where the road finally turns away from the shoreline, holds a row of welcoming seafood tavernas. Nearing the southern tip of Corfu, **Lefkimmi** is an elongated little town where everyday life simply carries on as usual, untroubled by visitors.

Western Corfu

The popular resort area of **Paleokastritsa**, 23km northwest of Corfu Town, stretches for nearly 3km through a series of small, picturesque bays. Craggy mountains swathed in cypress and olive trees tower above. The real treat comes at the resort's end, where an exquisite little beach is said to be where the weary Odysseus washed ashore. Boat trips from the jetty include **Paradise Sunset** (☎6972276442; Paleokastritsa; per person €10-20) cruises to nearby grottoes.

Set amid splendid gardens on the rocky promontory above, an easy 10-minute walk from the beach, **Moni Theotokou monastery** (Paleokastritsa; ⊙7am-1pm & 3-8pm) FREE dates to the 13th century. It's home to an interesting little **museum** (⊙Apr-Oct) FREE and a shop selling oils and herbs.

A circuitous hike or drive west from Paleokastritsa will take you along a high, winding road through the unspoilt villages of **Lakones** and **Krini**. A minor track that drops west of Krini dead-ends far above the waves at a mighty isolated crag, where a broad stone stairway climbs to the impregnable Byzantine fortress of **Angelokastro**. Though its ramparts remain largely intact, luxuriant wildflowers now fill its interior; the views back to Paleokastritsa are unforgettable.

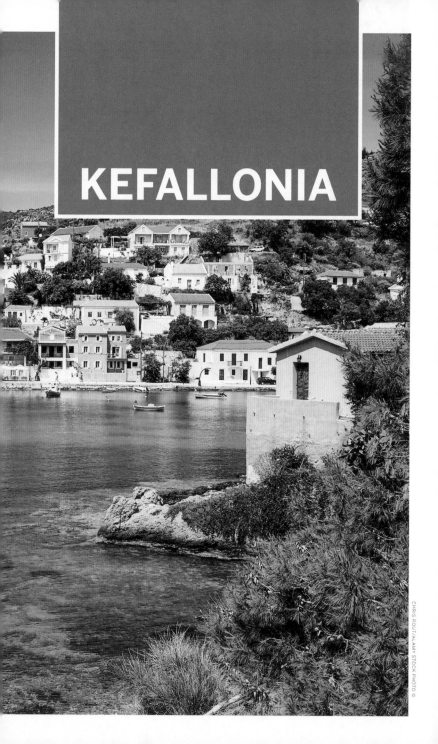

KEFALLONIA

Kefallonia at a Glance...

It's easy to lose yourself on magical Kefallonia, amid air thick with oleander and the sound of goat bells. The largest, and perhaps the most varied, of the Ionian islands, Kefallonia has a convoluted coastline that conceals captivating coves and beach-lined bays lapped by gin-clear waters teeming with colourful fish. Despite the devastating earthquake of 1953 that razed much of the island's historic Venetian architecture, ravishing harbour-front villages such as Fiskardo and Assos still show off Italianate good looks, while the lush and mountainous interior, dotted with wild meadows, Mediterranean oak forests and vineyards, invites endless exploration.

Two Days in Kefallonia

Spend a day in Argostoli, the island's main town, learning about Kefallonia's past at the **Korgialenio History & Folklore Museum** (p166), breathing in the scented air of **Cephalonia Botanica** (p166) and perhaps going on a winery tour. On day two, strike out for postcard-perfect **Assos** (p167), stopping by beautiful **Myrtos Beach** (p170) either on the way there or back.

Four Days in Kefallonia

Enjoy the old Venetian architecture of **Fiskardo** (p169) and dining at its excellent but pricey restaurants. There are beaches nearby or you could arrange to go diving with **Fiskardo Divers** (p165). On your final day take your pick between sea kayaking or hiking in the **Ainos National Park** – get up early and you could easily fit in both!

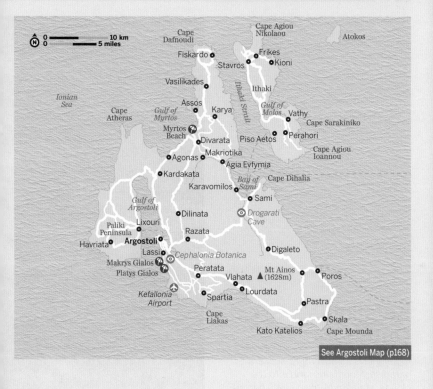

See Argostoli Map (p168)

Arriving in Kefallonia

The airport (p169) is 9km south of Argostoli. Three daily buses from the KTEL bus station in Argostoli use the ferry from Poros to make the journey to Athens (€33, seven hours, three daily). The main ferry ports are Sami and Poros. Between July and September there are ferry services connecting Sami and Bari and Brindsi in Italy.

Where to Stay

Accommodation options are scattered all over Kefallonia; hotels and guesthouses are limited but apartment and villa rentals abound. The main town is Argostoli, the nicest beach resorts are Karavomilos and Agia Evfymia on the Bay of Sami in the east, and Xi Beach at the southern tip of the Paliki Peninsula. Assos and Fiskardo are delightful upmarket enclaves in the north.

Loggerhead turtle

Kefallonia's Great Outdoors

*Kefallonia is an adventure-seekers'
paradise. Mountains swirl into the
clouds, stalagmite-filled caves burrow
deep into the earth, walking trails caress
coastal cliffs and slip through olive
groves, and then there's the sea and the
beaches. The opportunities for diving,
snorkelling, boating and kayaking –
from one hidden cove to the next – are
almost limitless.*

Great For...

❶ Need to Know

Book any organised activities as far
ahead as possible. Demand can be
heavy in high season.

★ **Top Tip**

Loggerhead turtles can occasionally be seen paddling patiently through Kefallonian waters. May to June is the best period.

Hiking

Kefallonia offers abundant and wonderful hiking, as detailed in many commercial maps and on noticeboards around the island. The area around **Fiskardo** offers some especially rewarding coastal hiking. An information panel in the car park just above town gives basic route suggestions and descriptions for three very well-marked short hikes.

For the best hiking on the island, though, you have to go much higher. Standing proud over the island is the lumbering hulk of **Mt Ainos** (1628m), most of which falls within Ainos National Park.

Horse & Donkey Trekking

A higher perspective of the island's walking trails can be achieved from atop a horse or donkey. Two companies, both based just outside Sami, can organise treks – ideal if you're travelling with children.

Ride sturdy Bavarian horses through the Kefallonian countryside with **Bavarian Horse Riding** (☑6977533203; www.kephalonia.com; Koulourata; 1-8hr €25-130). Day trips range from one to eight hours, with your choice of route. One longer trek leads across Mt Ainos and down to the sea, where you can take the horses for a swim. Multiday itineraries are also possible.

Slow-paced donkey treks aimed at children (the maximum weight allowed on a donkey is 50kg) explore ruined villages

Drogarati Cave

and evergreen valleys in the hilly country south of Sami. Contact **Donkey Trekking** (📞6980059630; www.donkeytrekkingkefalonia. com). The donkeys are well cared for.

Kayaking

It's on, around and under the water that Kefallonia truly excels. The island has some of the most jaw-droppingly beautiful beaches in the world, with white sand and pebbles caressed by the shimmering turquoise waters of the Mediterranean.

> ☑ **Don't Miss**
>
> **Drogarati Cave** (📞26740 23302; adult/child €5/3; ⏱10am-5pm Jun-Sep, shorter hours in low season) is a natural cavern hollowed into the hillside 4km south of Sami.

SIMURG/GETTY IMAGES ©

One of the nicest ways to enjoy this bounty is by lazily paddling from one perfect cove to another in a kayak. **Sea Kayaking Kefallonia** (📞6934010400; www.seakayak ingkefalonia-greece.com; day trips from €65) offers a full range of day-long kayak tours, with lunch and snorkelling gear included, plus some adventurous multiday excursions that will see you paddling to out-of-the-way coves and beaches, and even hopping between islands. It also does certified courses.

Diving & Snorkelling

The rugged coastline around the pretty port of Fiskardo has some of the best diving in this part of Greece. Eco-award-winning **Fiskardo Divers** (📞6970206172; www.fiskardo-divers.com; 3hr beginner courses €55, 4-day PADI open-water courses €430; ⏱9.30am-2pm & 5-7pm Mon-Sat, from 10.30am Sun) organises trips to caves, wrecks, reefs and a downed Bristol Beaufort WWII bomber. The ultra-clear waters in the area make this a perfect place to learn to dive, so the outfit also offers beginner courses.

If you're not up for scuba diving but still want to ogle the fish, take note that the snorkelling is good almost anywhere along Kefallonia's coastline, but with its small coves and generally more rocky coast, the eastern flank tends to be better than the western side (though the bay of Assos is pretty good as well).

> ✕ **Take a Break**
>
> **Paradise Beach** (📞26740 61392; www. paradisebeachtaverna.com; Agia Evfymia; mains €7-22; ⏱noon-11pm Apr-Oct; 🛜) will satisfy hunger pangs after a morning snorkelling or kayaking along the east coast near Sami.

Argostoli

Shielded from the open sea, its waterfront stretching along the landward side of a short peninsula, Argostoli was once renowned for its elegant Venetian-era architecture. Almost all of that was destroyed by earthquake in 1953, but Argostoli is now a lively, forward-looking town. The main focus of activity is just inland, centred on charming, freshly pedestrianised Plateia Valianou, where locals come to chat and eat at the many restaurants. In summer, musicians stroll the streets singing *kantades* (traditional songs accompanied by guitar and mandolin). Lithostroto, the pedestrian shopping street immediately south, is lined with stylish boutiques and cafes.

◉ SIGHTS

Korgialenio History & Folklore Museum
Museum

(☏26710 28835; Ilia Zervou 12; €3; ⊙9am-2pm Mon-Sat) Dedicated to preserving Kefallonian art and culture, this fine museum houses icons, assorted furniture, clothes and artwork from the homes of gentry and farm workers.

Cephalonia Botanica
Gardens

(☏26710 24866; www.focas-cosmetatos.gr; ⊙9am-2pm) **FREE** This lovely botanical garden, designed for the study, preservation and display of the island's plants and herbs, is located 2km south of central Argostoli. It also holds a small artificial lake. Last admission is 45 minutes before closing.

Platys Gialos
Beach

This little 'pocket' beach, just beyond Makrys Gialos, has plenty of shade and very clear water, as well as a few places to eat.

✪ ACTIVITIES

Robola Cooperative of Kefallonia
Wine

(☏26710 86301; www.robola.gr; Omala; ⊙9am-9pm daily Jul & Aug, to 6pm May, Jun, Sep & Oct, to 3pm Mon-Fri Nov-Apr) A cooperative winery comprising 300 members, at the heart of the verdant Omala Valley in the highlands southeast of Argostoli. A short guided tour

Katavothres (p169)

is offered, with a tasting afterwards and the chance to buy some bottles (from €6.20). *Robola* grapes, introduced by the Venetians, produce a dry white wine of subtle yet lively flavour.

Gentilini
Wine

(☑26710 41618; www.gentilini.gr; Minies; tastings & tour from €5; ⊙11am-8pm) This small but distinguished vineyard, 5km south of Argostoli on the airport road, has a charming setting and produces a range of superb wines, including the scintillating Classico. It offers informative short tours of the winery, complete with that all-important tasting.

✖ EATING

Ladokolla
Grill €

(☑26710 25522; Kalypsous Vergoti; dishes €2-8; ⊙12.30pm-2am) Lively and hugely popular grill house, where piping-hot and irresistibly flavourful chicken, pork or lamb kebabs and pittas are served up straight onto tabletop covers (no plates). It also delivers.

Tzivras
Greek €

(☑26710 24259; Vandorou 1; mains €7-9; ⊙1-5pm) Slightly grungy and brilliantly atmospheric, this veteran restaurant a block inland from the waterfront market is where locals lunch on hearty, great-value baked standards, such as veal with okra, goat with potatoes or cod pie. Choose your meal of choice from the display counter. Everything on the menu is less than €10.

Casa Grec
Mediterranean €€

(☑26710 24091; S Metaxa 12; mains €11-23; ⊙7.30pm-midnight May-Sep, Thu-Sat Oct-Apr) Centring on a verdant terracotta courtyard complete with fountain, this romantic restaurant is (despite the name) more Italian than Greek. It features chicken with rosemary or salmon with thyme, with either pasta or rice, succulent steaks, delicious desserts and a varied wine list.

Kiani Akti
Seafood €€

(☑26710 26680; Antoni Tritsi; mains €8-20; ⊙1pm-2am; 🐾) This restaurant has a huge wooden deck on stilts stretching out into

 Assos

It's almost hard to believe that a place as picture-perfect as Assos (population 88) can really exist. The pint-sized village is a confection of Italianate cream- and ochre-coloured houses, with a pretty crescent-shaped cove that's protected by a wooded peninsula. The fortress atop the headland makes a great hike (3.6km return), while the bay is eminently swimmable, and the water's so clear that you hardly need to put on a snorkel and mask in order to ogle the fish.

A mouth-watering array of tasty tavernas, such as **Molos** (☑26740 51220; Assos; mains €7-14; ⊙9.30am-late; 🐾) or **Platanos** (☑26740 51143; Assos; mains €7-15; ⊙9am-midnight Easter-Oct; 🐾🍴), plus a pace so slow you can palpably feel your pulse dropping, are compelling reasons to visit. **Apartment Linardos** (☑26740 51563; www.linardosapartments.gr; Assos; d/tr/q €80/90/120; ⊙May-Sep; ❄🐾) and **Vassilis Retreat** (☑26740 51174; www.vassilis-retreat.gr; Assos; apt €100; ❄🐾) are both great places to stay.

Want a local secret? There's a **hidden beach** around the other side of the headland from the jetty at the northern end of the village, but it can only be reached by boat or a 15-minute swim!

Assos
MARAP/SHUTTERSTOCK ©

the harbour, which allows you to peer guiltily down into the water at the brothers and sisters of the fish on your plate. The wide-ranging menu includes tasty Greek

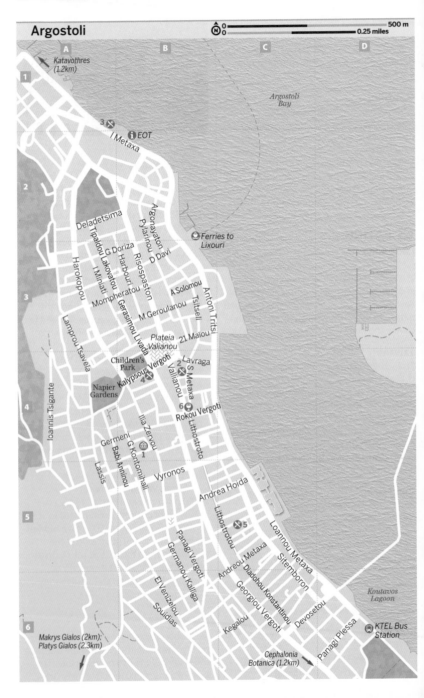

Argostoli

N 0   500 m
0   0.25 miles

A   **B**   **C**   **D**

Katavothres
(1.2km)

Argostoli
Bay

3

EOT
I Metaxa

Deladetsima

Argonaviton
Pylarinou

Risospaston

D Davi

Ferries to
Lixouri

Harokopou

Tripaldou Lakovatou
I Minlati

G Doriza
Harbouri

Mompheratou

Gerasimou Livada

M Geroulanou

A Solomou

Tsitseli

Antoni Tritsi

Lamprou Tsavela

Plateia
Valianou

21 Maïou

Children's
Park

Kalypsous Vergoti

2

Lavraga

Napier
Gardens

Valianou

S Metaxa

6

Rokou Vergoti

Lithostroto

Ioannis Tsigante

Germeni

G Kontomihali

Ilia Zervou

1

Babi Anninou

Vyronos

Lassis

Andrea Hoida

Lithostrotou

5

Loannou Metaxa

Panagi Vergoti

Andreou Metaxa

Sitemboron

Germanou Kalliga

Diadohou Konstantinou

Georgiou Vergoti

Devosetou

El Venizelou

Kegalou

Koutavos
Lagoon

Souidias

KTEL Bus
Station

Makrys Gialos (2km);
Platys Gialos (2.3km)

Cephalonia
Botanica (1.2km)

Panagi Plessa

Argostoli

appetisers, along with daily seafood specials and meaty classics. You can also just drop in for a drink.

To find it, follow the waterfront north to the cruise-ship dock.

🍷 DRINKING & NIGHTLIFE

Katavothres Club
(☎26710 22221; www.katavothres.gr; Mikeli Davi 10; ☺noon-midnight Mon-Thu & Sun, 24hr Fri & Sat; 🛜) A rather extraordinary hybrid, this popular club-restaurant at the tip of the Argostoli peninsula combines strange geological formations with iconic futuristic furnishings, and hosts big-name DJs for a varied crowd.

Bass Club Club
(☎26710 25020; www.bassclub.gr; cnr S Metaxa & Vergoti; ☺noon-7am; 🛜) Stylish, dimly lit and very central, the Bass Club pulses at night with Greek and Western music, often with guest DJs on the decks, and also operates a cool cafe by day that's the ideal spot to kick-start an evening.

ℹ️ INFORMATION

Banks with ATMs line the northern waterfront and Lithostroto.

EOT (Greek National Tourist Organisation; ☎26710 22248; ☺7am-2.30pm Mon-Fri)

ℹ️ GETTING THERE & AWAY

The **airport** (☎26710 29900; http://kefalonia airport.info) is 9km south of Argostoli. There's no airport bus; taxis to Argostoli cost around €20.

The **KTEL Bus Station** (☎26710 22281; www. ktelkefalonias.gr; A Tritsi 5) on Argostoli's south-

ern waterfront is the epicentre of the island's public-transport network. Buses run on Sunday in high season only.

The main ferry quay is at the northern end of the waterfront, close to the EOT information office. Car ferries connect Argostoli with Lixouri on the Paliki Peninsula (per person/car €2.80/4, 30 minutes, 7am to 10.30pm). Between May and September they run half-hourly from noon to 5.30pm and hourly at other times. From October to April they run a little less frequently.

First Class Travel (☎26710 20026; www. firstclasstravel.gr; D Davi) offers car hire from €25 a day.

Fiskardo

One of the prettiest towns in the Ionians, the little port of Fiskardo curves serenely beside coral-blue waters, gazing out towards Ithaki. Thanks to its colourful crop of Venetian villas, spared from earthquake damage because they rest on a sturdy bed of flat rock, Fiskardo is the island's most exclusive resort, home to upmarket restaurants and choice accommodation. There's no real dock or jetty here; ferries from Lefkada arrive unceremoniously at the northern end, while yachts jostle for space along the rest of the harbour. While it can get very crowded in summer, it has a cosmopolitan buzz unmatched elsewhere on the island.

🎿 ACTIVITIES

There are two small **pebble beaches** in Fiskardo. The best is just over the headland to the east. It's backed by Venetian-style houses and olive trees, and is as nice a town beach as you could

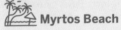 **Myrtos Beach**

From the road that zigzags down to it you'll understand why **Myrtos** is touted as one of the most breathtaking beaches in all of Greece. From afar it's certainly a stunning sight, with electric-blue waters offset by what appears to be searing-white 'sand' (in reality it's white pebbles). Unfortunately, a scrappy car park rather spoils the idyll. Even so, it's a beautiful spot and once you're in the sea it's heavenly. The closest village is Divarata, which has a couple of tavernas, including **Alexandros** (📱26740 61777; https://alexandros restaurant-myrtos.gr; Divarata; mains €7-9; ⏰noon-midnight).

Myrtos Beach
CHRIS ROUT/ALAMY STOCK PHOTO ©

hope for. The other is just next to where the ferries dock and almost within the town centre itself, but it's only a so-so beach. Much better beaches can be found further north, where the gorgeous sand at **Emblissi** is shaded by olive trees, and to the south, where **Foki Bay** is home to an attractive taverna.

✖ EATING & DRINKING

Café Tselenti — Mediterranean €€
(📱26740 41344; mains €8-26; ⏰8am-midnight May-Oct) Owned by the Tselenti family since 1893, this popular restaurant serves Italian-influenced dishes such as a terrific linguine with prawns, mussels and crayfish, as well as local specialities such as lamb shank, beef *stifadho* (stew) and grilled swordfish. It has a romantic terrace on the village square as well as quayside tables.

If you just want a quick snack, it also does pitta *gyros* (meat slivers cooked on a vertical rotisserie; €3).

Tassia — Taverna €€
(📱26740 41205; www.tassia.gr; mains €9-19; ⏰noon-2am May-Oct) Step straight off your yacht and into a waterside seat at this taverna run by well-known Kefallonian chef Tassia, who delights diners with her homemade pies, mezedhes and courgette croquettes. Try the 'fisherman's pasta', incorporating finely chopped squid, octopus, mussels and prawns in a magical combination with a dash of cognac.

Irida — International €€€
(📱26740 41343; mains €9-35; ⏰9am-late; ❄🛜) Whether you dine in the shadowy boho interior with its lamp made from a deep-sea diver's mask or out on the waterfront, there's something for everyone at this 200-year-old salt store. Dishes include meatballs, stuffed aubergine, and the much pricier lobster risotto or spaghetti, and it's all scrupulously prepared and presented.

Vasso's — Seafood €€€
(📱26740 41276; mains €9-48; ⏰lunch & dinner May-Oct; 🛜) Vasso's is renowned for its high-quality seafood, with highlights including honeyed octopus with mashed fava, mussels, *saganaki* (fried cheese) and *sofigado* (veal in tomato sauce).

Le Passage — Cafe
(📱26740 41505; ⏰9am-midnight; 🛜) Cool, very mellow quayside cafe festooned with little white lamps, and with a soothing soft-grey palette and cosy cushioned banquettes beside the water. Come early for simple breakfasts, at any hour for espresso with a smile, or in the evening for classy cocktails.

GETTING THERE & AWAY

Two or three surprisingly large **West Ferry** (www.westferry.gr) boats arrive from and return daily to the big package-tourism resort of Nydri on the east coast of Lefkada. Buy tickets from **Nautilus Travel** (26740 41440; 9am-1.30pm & 5-9pm).

KTEL (www.ktelkefalonias.gr) buses connect Fiskardo with Argostoli (€6.40, 1¾ hours, two daily), and with Sami via Agia Evfymia (€4.70, one hour, one or two daily).

Ainos National Park

Standing proud over the island is the lumbering hulk of **Mt Ainos** (1628m), most of which falls within Ainos National Park. The mountain's upper reaches are dominated by ancient, gnarled Greek fir and black pine, through which afternoon mist and cloud frequently swirl. In winter the mountain can be blanketed by snow, and at any time of year the views from close to the top (the actual summit has a crown of radio masts) are astounding.

Visitor facilities within the park are fairly undeveloped, but five **walking trails** have been established. The trails themselves are well signposted and very clear, though the trailheads are a little less obvious (a road runs right through the middle of the park and up to the summit; to find the trailheads, keep an eye out for information panels). The two most popular trails go up to the summit from opposite sides of the mountain and then loop back around to their respective starting points. Each is around 6.5km and easy, with a fairly gentle ascent. Unfortunately, in both cases the return route is back along the road, so it's best to ignore this and just retrace your steps along the footpath in the forest. Allow 1½ hours, excluding stops.

Another, much more challenging, route heads to the summit from the village of Digaleto, on the road between Sami and Poros. It's a 13km return walk with an altitude gain of 1096m.

If walking isn't your thing, you can drive pretty much all the way to the summit.

Mt Ainos

ZOONAR GMBH/ALAMY STOCK PHOTO ©

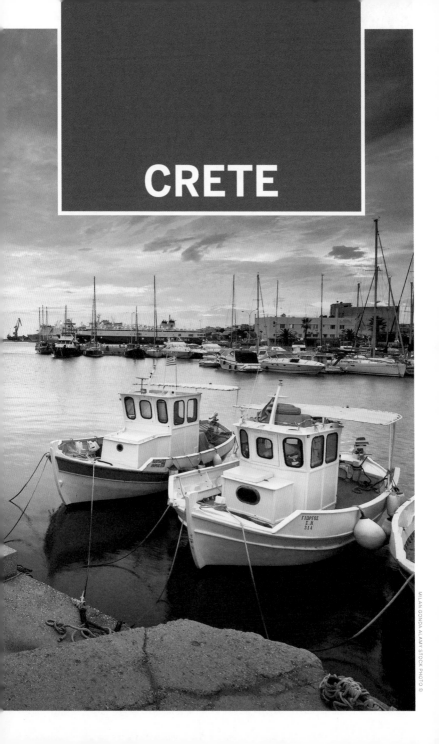

CRETE

Crete at a Glance...

Crete's landscape is beautiful – from the sun-drenched beaches in the north to the rugged canyons spilling out at the cliff-lined southern coast. In between, valleys cradle moody villages, and round-shouldered hills are the overture to often snow-dabbed mountains. Use charismatic Hania with its remnants of Venetian and Turkish architecture and or the capital, Iraklio, as a base for exploring the island. Go on a driving tour, plant your footprints on a sandy beach, trek through Europe's longest gorge and survey the Palace of Knossos, one of many vestiges of the mysterious ancient Minoan civilisation.

Two Days in Crete

Start in **Iraklio** (p188), checking out the superb museums such as **Heraklion Archaeological Museum** (p188) and **Historical Museum of Crete** (p188) before heading to the **Palace of Knossos** (p176) and enjoying the fruits of the **Iraklio Wine Country** (p182).

Four Days in Crete

Zip west to **Hania** (p195), your next base. Explore around the beautiful **Venetian Harbour** (p198) and pay visits to the **Hania Archaeological Museum** (p195) and the **Maritime Museum of Crete** (p198). When you've had your fill of Hania's historic beauty, take the early bus to **Samaria Gorge** (p186) and trek to Agia Roumeli.

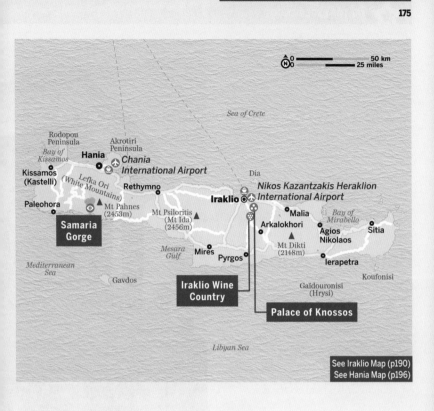

Arriving in Crete

Crete is easy to reach by air or sea – particularly in summer when it opens its arms (and schedules) wide. Iraklio's Nikos Kazantzakis Heraklion International Airport (p305) is Crete's busiest airport, although Hania (p201) is convenient for travellers heading to western Crete. There's at least one daily ferry from Piraeus (near Athens) to Iraklio and Hania year-round.

Where to Stay

The Iraklio region and the northern coast has Crete's most developed resorts and sandy beaches. Hania is a ravishing town and has beach resorts to the west; it is ideal if you're looking for a wide range of outdoor pursuits. For a quiet rural retreat, head for the hills or the remote villages and beaches along the southern and eastern coasts.

Palace of Knossos

Palace of Knossos

Crete's most famous historical attraction is the Palace of Knossos, the grand capital of Minoan Crete, located 5km south of Iraklio. The setting is evocative and the ruins and re-creations impressive, incorporating an immense palace, courtyards, private apartments, baths, lively frescoes and more. Reckon on a couple of hours to do the place justice.

Great For...

❶ Need to Know

http://odysseus.culture.gr; Knossos; adult/concession €15/8, incl Heraklion Archaeological Museum €16/8; ⊗8am-8pm Apr-Sep, to 7pm Oct, to 3pm Nov-Mar; Ⓟ; ⨭2

★ **Top Tip**

Get to Knossos either at 8am to stay a few steps ahead of the tour buses, or later in the afternoon, when it's cooler and the light is good for photographs.

Knossos History

Knossos' first palace (1900 BC) was destroyed by an earthquake around 1700 BC and rebuilt to a grander and more sophisticated design. It was partially destroyed again between 1500 and 1450 BC, and inhabited for another 50 years before finally burning down.

The complex comprised domestic quarters, public reception rooms, shrines, workshops, treasuries and storerooms, all flanking a paved central courtyard.

Excavation of the site started in 1878 with Cretan archaeologist Minos Kalokerinos, and continued from 1900 to 1930 with British archaeologist Sir Arthur Evans, who controversially restored parts of the site. Evans' reconstructions bring to life the palace's most significant parts, including the columns, which are painted deep brown-red with gold-trimmed black capitals and taper gracefully at the bottom. Vibrant frescoes add dramatic flourishes. The advanced drainage system and a clever floor plan that kept rooms cool in summer and warm in winter are further evidence of Minoan high standards.

Site Highlights

Enter the site from the **West Court**, taking note of a trio of circular pits on your left. Called **kouloures**, they were used for grain storage. Continue counterclockwise, walking along the **Processional Walkway** that leads to the **South Propylaion**, where you can admire the **Cup Bearer Fresco**. From here, a staircase leads past giant storage jars to an upper floor that Evans called the

Queen's Megaron

Piano Nobile because it reminded him of Italian Renaissance palazzi and where he supposed the reception and staterooms were located. On your left, are **west magazines** (storage rooms), where giant *pithoi* (clay jars) once held oil, wine and other staples.

At the northern end of the Piano Nobile is the **Fresco Gallery**, with replicas of Knossos' most famous frescoes. From the balcony, a great view unfolds of the **Central Court**, which was hemmed in by high walls during Minoan times. Follow the stairs down to the courtyard and then turn left

☑ **Don't Miss**

The Queen's Megaron, with its painted pillars and playful Dolphin Fresco on the far wall.

EWABEACHGIRL/SHUTTERSTOCK ©

to peek inside the beautifully proportioned **Throne Room**.

In the east wing the **Grand Staircase** drops down to the royal apartments. Get there via the ramp off the southeastern corner, but not without first popping by the south entrance to admire a replica of the **Prince of the Lilies fresco**. Down below you can peek inside the **Queen's Megaron** (bedroom). Continue to the king's quarters in the **Hall of the Double Axes**; the latter takes its name from the double axe marks (*labrys*) on its light well, a sacred symbol to the Minoans and the origin of the word 'labyrinth'.

Beyond, admire the Minoans' surprisingly sophisticated **water and drainage system**, pop by a stonemason's workshop and check out more giant storage jars before jogging around to the palace's north side for a good view of the partly reconstructed north entrance, easily recognised by the **Charging Bull Fresco**.

Tickets & Transport

Unlike at other ruins around Iraklio, visitors make their way through the site on platform walkways, which can get very crowded. This makes it all the more important to time your visit for outside the tour-bus onslaught. Avoid ticket lines by buying in advance through the **Archaeological Resources Fund e-Ticketing System** (www.etickets.tap.gr).

City bus 2 (€1.70, every 10 to 30 minutes) leaves from its own stop on the site of Iraklio's old long-distance bus station, 200m or so northwest of the new KTEL bus station. The bus also stops at Plateia Eleftherias outside the Capsis Astoria hotel.

✕ **Take a Break**

Foodie destination Elia & Diosmos (p184) in Iraklio Wine Country is a good spot for dining close by Knossos.

Palace of Knossos

THE HIGHLIGHTS IN TWO HOURS

The Palace of Knossos is Crete's busiest tourist attraction, and for good reason. A spin around the partially and imaginatively reconstructed complex (shown here as it was thought to be at its peak) delivers an eye-opening glimpse into the remarkably sophisticated society of the Minoans, who dominated southern Europe some 4000 years ago.

From the ticket booth, follow the marked trail to the ❶ **North Entrance** where the Charging Bull fresco gives you a first taste of Minoan artistry. Continue to the Central Court and join the queue waiting to glimpse the mystical ❷ **Throne Room**, which probably hosted religious rituals. Turn right as you exit and follow the stairs up to the so-called Piano Nobile, where replicas of the palace's most famous artworks conveniently cluster in the ❸ **Fresco Room**. Walk the length of the Piano Nobile, pausing to look at the clay storage vessels in the West Magazine. Circle back and descend to the ❹ **South Portico**, beautifully decorated with the Cup Bearer fresco. Make your way back to the Central Court and head to the palace's eastern wing to admire the architecture of the ❺ **Grand Staircase** that led to what Sir Arthur Evans imagined to be the royal family's private quarters. For a closer look at some rooms, walk to the south end of the courtyard, stopping for a peek at the ❻ **Prince of the Lilies Fresco**, and head down to the lower floor. A highlight here is the ❼ **Queen's Megaron** (Evans imagined this was the Queen's chambers), playfully adorned with a fresco of frolicking dolphins. Stay on the lower level and make your way to the ❽ **Giant Pithoi**, huge clay jars used for storage.

PLANNING

To beat the crowds and avoid the heat, arrive bang on opening or two hours before closing. Budget one or two hours to explore the site thoroughly.

Fresco Room
Take in sweeping views of the palace grounds from the west wing's upper floor, the Piano Nobile, before studying copies of the palace's most famous artworks in its Fresco Room.

South Portico
Fine frescoes, most famously the Cup Bearer, embellish this palace entrance anchored by a massive open staircase leading to the Piano Nobile. The Horns of Consecration recreated nearby once topped the entire south facade.

West Court

West Magazines

❹ Horns of Consecration

Prince of the Lilies Fresco
One of Knossos' most beloved frescoes was controversially cobbled together from various fragments and shows a young man adorned in lilies and peacock feathers.

Throne Room

Sir Arthur Evans, who began excavating the
Palace of Knossos in 1900, imagined the mythical
King Minos himself holding court seated on the
alabaster throne of this beautifully proportioned
room. However, the lustral basin and griffin
frescoes suggest a religious purpose, possibly
under a priestess.

North Entrance

Bulls held a special status in Minoan society,
as evidenced by the famous relief fresco of
a charging beast gracing the columned west
bastion of the north palace, which harboured
workshops and storage rooms.

Grand Staircase

The royal apartments
in the eastern wing
were accessed via this
monumental staircase
sporting four flights
of gypsum steps
supported by columns.
The lower two flights are
original. It's closed to
the public.

**Piano
Nobile**

**Central
Court**

**Royal
Apartments**

Queen's Megaron

The queen's room is
among the prettiest in
the residential eastern
wing thanks to the
playful Dolphin Fresco.
The adjacent bathroom
(with clay tub) and
toilet are evidence of a
sophisticated drainage
system.

Giant Pithoi

These massive clay jars are rare remnants from
the Old Palace period and were used to store
wine, oil and grain. The jars were transported by
slinging ropes through a series of handles.

Grapes on the vine, Arhanes

GEORGIOS PAGOMENOS/ALAMY STOCK PHOTO ©

Iraklio Wine Country

Almost two-dozen wineries are embedded in this harmonious landscape of rounded hills, sunbaked slopes and lush valleys. Winemakers produce Cretan grape varietals, while many estates offer tours, wine museums and wine tastings.

Winemakers in this region cultivate many indigenous, nearly extinct Cretan grape varietals – be sure to introduce your nose and taste buds to Kotsifali, Mandilari, Malvasia and Liatiko, among others.

Iraklio to Arhanes

Driving from Iraklio, follow the Knossos road south. Reserve ahead for a tour and tasting at **Koronekes** (28107 31722; http://koronekes.gr; Kapnistou Metochi, Spilia; tour & tasting €5; ☺9am-3pm) 🍃, a wonderful olive estate corralling more than 2000 trees clocking in at 200 to 300 years old. It's a great spot for stocking up on olive oil pressed in the traditional way and other Cretan products.

Great For...

☑ **Don't Miss**

Bakaliko offers some 45 island wines by the glass.

Ancient wine press, Vathypetro

❶ Need to Know

Made in Crete (☑6975626830; www.
tours.madeincrete.com; €100) leads the
most highly recommended wine-tasting
tours around Iraklio Wine Country.

✕ Take a Break

Clued-in gourmets make the trip to
Roussos Taverna (☑6936156835;
Houdetsi; mains €4.50-9.50; ⊗7am-4pm &
5pm-2am Apr-Oct, Fri-Sun only Nov-Mar; 🕏)
to dine on home-style Cretan cooking,
including fantastic lamb chops and local
horta (wild greens).

★ Top Tip

Check Wines of Crete (www.winesof
crete.gr) for tourist info. Look for the
burgundy-red road signs directing you
to local wineries.

Arhanes itself is a wine-country hub with
Minoan roots. After visiting the village's
small museum, soak up the atmosphere on
the leafy plaza over a glass of wine or more
at **Bakaliko** (www.bakalikocrete.com; Plateia
Eleftheriou Venizelou, Arhanes; mains €7.50-9.50;
⊗10am-11pm Apr-Oct, 5-10pm Fri, 10am-10pm
Sat & Sun Nov-Mar; 🕏) ✦. Afterwards,
detour up **Mt Yiouhtas** for spellbinding
wine-country views and a look at a Minoan
peak sanctuary.

Houdetsi to Skalani

Back in Arhanes, head south towards
Houdetsi, stopping at **Vathypetro**
(⊗8.30am-4pm Wed-Mon) **FREE** to see what
a Minoan stomping vat looked like (the

one discovered here is the oldest known
wine press in existence). From here it's a
quick drive north to **Peza**, the centre of
wine production in Crete, with several
wineries nearby offering tastings and
tours.

About 6km south of Peza, visitor-friendly
Lyrarakis (☑6981050681; www.lyrarakis.gr;
Alagni; tastings €10-60; ⊗11am-7pm Mon-Sat
Apr-Oct, by appointment rest of year) should be
your go-to if you must pick only one winery.
It rakes in awards and is known for reviving
three nearly extinct white varietals (Dafni,
Plyto and Melissaki). Also don't miss the
modern **Digenakis Winery** (☑28103 22846;
www.digenakis.gr; Katakouzinon 7, Kaloni; tastings €7; ⊗by appointment 10am-5pm), 1.7km

south of the village, with an art-driven tasting room.

From here, follow signs to Myrtia to pay your respects to Nikos Kazantzakis, the Cretan-born author of *Zorba the Greek*, at the excellent **museum** (☎2810 741689; www.kazantzaki.gr; Myrtia; adult/concessions €5/3; ☺9am-5pm daily Apr-Oct, 10am-3pm Mon-Fri & Sun Nov-Mar) right on the town square. Conclude the day by indulging in a gourmet Cretan dinner paired with excellent local wines at the delightful **Elia & Diosmos** (☎2810 731283; www.olivemint.gr; Dimokratias 263, Skalani; mains €8-15; ☺11am-midnight Tue-Sun; ☜) ✎ in Skalani, before you drive back to Iraklio.

Other Wineries

Founded in 1879, **Boutari** (☎22860 81011; www.boutari.gr; Megalohori; €15; ☺10am-7pm) is one of Greece's biggest wine producers. Visits to its Crete winery, which is near Skalani about 8km from Iraklio, start with a short tour to learn about local grapes and winemaking, followed by an optional 15-minute video on the island and/or the company and the chance to sample the product in the vast, airy tasting room overlooking the vineyard.

Based in Vorias, about 20km south of Peza, **Domaine Gavalas** (☎28940 51060, 6974642006; www.gavalascretewines.gr; Vorias; tastings €7-10; ☺10am-5pm Mon-Fri) ✎ is a

Wine tasting, Boutari

family operation dating back to 1906. Today it is one of Crete's largest organic wineries, producing award-winning wines such as the Fragospito Syrah/Cabernet Sauvignon, the Vilana (100% Vilana) and the Monahikos Cabernet Sauvignon.

Rustic, down-to-earth, boutique **Stilianou** (☎69364 30368; www.stilianou wines.gr; Kounavi; tastings €5, with tour €7; ◷11am-7pm Apr-Oct, 10am-5pm Mon-Sat Nov-Mar) ✎ sits above Kounavi (your GPS will never get you there, but it will get you to the signs, which are then easy to follow). It specialises in Minoan-strength organic wines with local varietals only, such as the

Cellars, Boutari

It's a good idea to phone ahead, as some wineries are not staffed to the point that they can handle multiple walk-ins at the same time.

Theon Dora blend (Vidiano, Vilana, Thrap-sathiri; 13%!), and small-batch olive oils. Be sure to try the unique Kotsifali dessert wine, too.

Striking architecture and steeply terraced vineyards characterise state-of-the-art **Domaine Zacharioudakis** (www. zacharioudakis.com; Plouti; tastings & tour €15-30; ◷10am-4pm Mon-Sat Apr-Sep) in Plouti, about 7km south of Zaros. The tasting room with views out to sea is a nice spot for sampling its fine wines.

Phylloxera in the 1970s nearly wiped out all the region's vines. But the area rebounded and today about 70% of Cretan wine comes from this region.

Bridge along the gorge floor

DANA DAVID/SHUTTERSTOCK ©

Samaria Gorge

Hiking the 16km-long Samaria Gorge, one of Europe's longest canyons, is high on the list of must-dos for many visitors to Crete. There's an undeniable raw beauty to the canyon, with its soaring cliffs and needlenose passageways. The hike begins at an elevation of 1230m just south of Omalos at Xyloskalo and ends in the coastal village of Agia Roumeli.

Great For...

☑ **Don't Miss**

The Sideroportes (Iron Gates).

Hiking the Gorge

From the trailhead at Xyloskalo, a steep, serpentine stone path descends some 600m into the canyon to arrive at the simple, cypress-framed **Chapel of Agios Nikolaos**. Beyond here the gorge is wide and open and not particularly scenic for the next 6km until you reach the abandoned settlement of Samaria. This is the main rest stop, with toilets, water and benches.

Just south of the village is a 14th-century **chapel** dedicated to St Maria of Egypt, after whom the gorge is named. Further on, the gorge narrows and becomes more dramatic until, at 11km, the walls are only 3.5m apart and you'll find the famous **Sideroportes** (Iron Gates), where a rickety wooden pathway leads hikers the 20m or so across the water.

Mountain goat

ⓘ Need to Know

☑ 28210 45570; www.samaria.gr; Omalos; adult/child €5/free; ⏱7.30am-4pm May–mid-Oct

✕ Take a Break

There are tavernas in Agia Roumeli and Omalos, including one located right by the gorge entrance. There's also a snack stall at the national-park exit selling beer, coffee and other refreshments.

★ Top Tip

The best time for the Samaria trek is in April and May, when wildflowers brighten the trail.

The gorge ends at the 13km mark just north of the almost abandoned village of **Palea** (Old) **Agia Roumeli**. From here it's a further 3km to the seaside village of **Agia Roumeli**, whose fine pebble beach and sparkling water are a most welcome sight. Few people miss taking a refreshing dip or at least bathing their aching feet before they fill up at one of the seaside tavernas.

The entire trek takes about four hours (for sprinters) to six hours (for strollers). This is a rocky trail and suitable footwear is essential.

It's also possible to do it the 'lazy way': hiking a shorter distance by starting at Agia Roumeli. The only way out of Agia Roumeli is by taking the boat to Sougia or Hora Sfakion, which are served by bus and taxi back to Hania.

Getting There & Away

Most people hike Samaria one way, going north–south on a day trip that can be arranged from every sizeable town and resort in Crete. Confirm whether tour prices include gorge admission (€5) and the boat ride from Agia Roumeli to Sougia or Hora Sfakion.

With some planning, it's possible to do the trek on your own. There are early-morning public buses to Omalos from Hania (€7.50, one hour) once or twice daily in high season. Check www.e-ktel.com for the schedule, which changes seasonally. Taxis are another option.

Iraklio

Crete's capital, Iraklio (also called Heraklion), is Greece's fifth-largest city and the island's economic and administrative hub. Though not pretty in a conventional way, Iraklio definitely grows on you if you take the time to explore its layers and wander its backstreets. You'll discover a low-key urban sophistication with a thriving cafe and restaurant scene, good shopping and bustling nightlife. A revitalised waterfront invites strolling, and the pedestrianised historic centre is punctuated by bustling squares flanked by buildings from the time when Christopher Columbus first set sail.

◉ SIGHTS

Heraklion
Archaeological Museum   Museum
(www.heraklionmuseum.gr; Xanthoudidou 2; adult/concession/child €10/5/free, combined ticket with Palace of Knossos adult/concession €16/8; ⊙8am-8pm Mon & Wed-Sun, 10am-8pm Tue mid-Apr–Oct, 8am-4pm Nov–mid-Apr) This state-of-the-art museum is one of the largest and most important in Greece. The two-storey revamped 1930s Bauhaus building makes a gleaming showcase for artefacts spanning 5500 years from Neolithic to Roman times, including a Minoan collection of unparalleled richness. The rooms are colour coded and displays are arranged both chronologically and thematically, and presented with descriptions in English. A visit here will greatly enhance your understanding of Crete's rich history. Don't skip it.

Koules Fortress   Fortress
(Rocca al Mare; http://koules.efah.gr; Venetian Harbour; adult/concession €2/1; ⊙8am-8pm May-Sep, to 4pm Oct-Apr) After six years of restoration, Iraklio's symbol, the 16th-century fortress called Rocca al Mare by the Venetians, reopened in August 2016 with a brand-new exhibition. It tells the story of the building, zeroes in on milestones in the city's history, and displays ancient amphorae, Venetian cannons and other finds recovered from shipwrecks around Dia Island by Jacques Cousteau in 1976.

Historical Museum of Crete   Museum
(www.historical-museum.gr; Sofokli Venizelou 27; adult/concession €5/3; ⊙9am-5pm Mon-Sat, 10.30am-3pm Sun Apr-Oct, to 3.30pm daily Nov-Mar) If you're wondering what Crete's been up to for the past, say, 1700 years, a spin around this engagingly curated museum is in order. Exhibits hopscotch from the Byzantine to the Venetian and Turkish periods, culminating with WWII. Quality English labelling, interactive stations throughout and audio-guides (€3) in five languages greatly enhance the experience.

Monastery of
St Peter & St Paul   Ruins
(Sofokli Venizelou 19; admission by donation; ⊙10am-2.30pm May-Sep) One of Iraklio's most striking ruins, this 13th-century Dominican monastery has been rebuilt and repackaged (mosque, movie theatre) numerous times throughout the centuries. Unusually located right on the sea wall, the monastery contains some beautiful 15th-century frescoes, as well as a modern mosaic exhibition by Loukas Peiniris that is well worth checking out.

Museum of Christian Art   Museum
(St Catherine of Sinai; St Catherine's Sq; adult/concession €4/2; ⊙9.30am-7.30pm Apr-Oct, to 5pm Nov-Mar; 🚻) Housed in a 13th-century monastery that was later a mosque, this tiny but fascinating museum features well-displayed historic religious artworks from monasteries around Crete. Paintings, woodcraft, manuscripts and stone carvings are presented in a clear manner with English descriptions. Star exhibits include works by 15th-century icon hagiographer Angelos Akotantos and post-Byzantine painter Michael Damaskinos.

⊕ ACTIVITIES
Ammoudara, about 4km west of Iraklio, and Amnisos, 2km to the east, are the closest beaches; the latter is just past the airport and gets quite a bit of noise. The strands

Monastery of St Peter & St Paul

in Agia Pelagia, some 20km west of town, are nicer.

Cretan Adventures   Outdoors
(☎6944790771; www.cretanadventures.gr) ♠
This well-regarded local company, run by
friendly and knowledgeable English-
speaking Fondas, organises hiking tours,
mountain biking and extreme outdoor
excursions.

Mountaineering
Club of Iraklio   Outdoors
(☎2810 227609; www.eos-her.gr; Dikeosynis 53;
⊙8.30-10.30pm Mon-Fri) The club arranges
hiking trips across Crete most weekends
(trip programs are published on the website). Anyone is welcome to join in.

🔒 SHOPPING
Zalo   Gifts & Souvenirs
(www.zalo.gr; Papa Aleksandrou 2; ⊙9am-9pm
Mon-Sat, to 4pm Sun) This recommended
shop specialises in the kinds of souvenirs
that won't embarrass you a year down
the track: designer art prints, jewellery,
notebooks, frameable postcards, funky
handbags and the like, all 100% made in
Greece from a network of cutting-edge,
contemporary artists and designers.

Ora Gentleman   Clothing
(☎2810 331164; www.oragentleman.com; Korone-
ou 18; ⊙10am-2pm & 5.30-9.30pm Mon-Sat)
Cretan pursuer of finer things Nikos
Makridakas designs his own top-shelf clothing for men (including made-to-measure
options), combining the best of British- and
Italian-inspired design with his own epicure-
an Greek ethos. His popular pocket squares
(from €25) are fashioned from Soufli silk,
but the linen shirts, colourful polos and
restrained T-shirts (all perfect upscale island
wear) are enticing, too.

Aerakis Music   Music
(☎2810 225758; www.aerakis.net; Korai 14;
⊙9am-9pm Mon-Fri, to 5pm Sat) An Iraklio
landmark since 1974, this little shop stocks
an expertly curated selection of Cretan and
Greek music, from old and rare recordings
to the latest releases, many on its own
record labels, Cretan Musical Workshop
and Seistron.

Iraklio

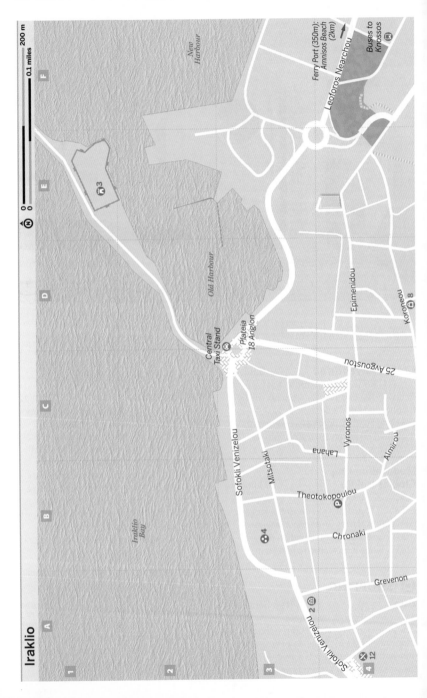

New Harbour

Old Harbour

Iraklio Bay

Central Taxi Stand

Plateia 18 Anglon

Sofokli Venizelou

Mitsotaki

Lahana

Vyronos

Theotokopoulou

Chronaki

Grevenon

Almirou

25 Avgoustou

Epimenidou

Koronaiou

Leoforos Nearchou

Ferry Port (350m);
Amnisos Beach
(2km)

Buses to
Knossos

Sofokli Venizelou

200 m
0.1 miles

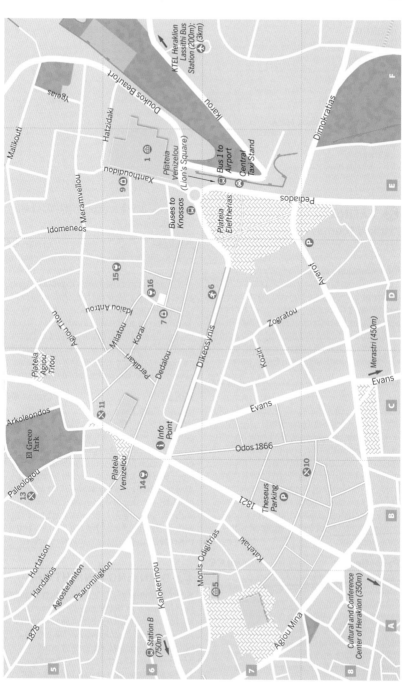

KTEL Heraklion
Lassithi Bus
Station (200m);
Airport (3km)

Ikarou

Ygeias

Doukos Beaufort

Malliouti

Hatzidaki

Meramvellou

1

Plateia
Venizelou
(Lion's Square)

Xanthoudidou

Bus 1 to
Airport

Central
Taxi Stand

9

Idomeneos

Buses to
Knossos

Plateia
Eleftherias

Pediados

Dimokratias

Agiou Titou

Plateia
Agiou
Titou

Milatou

Idaion Antron

15

16

Averof

Arkoleondos

El Greco
Park

Perdikari

Korai

Dedalou

7

Dikeosynis

6

Zogratou

Kozizi

Merastri (450m)

Paleologou

13

11

Plateia
Venizelou

14

Info
Point

Evans

Evans

Odos 1866

10

Theseus
Parking

Hortatson

Handakos

Agiostefaniton

Psaromiligkon

Kalokerinou

1821

Katehaki

Station B
(750m)

Monis Odigitras

5

Agiou Mina

Cultural and Conference
Center of Heraklion (350m)

1878

Iraklio

ⓧ EATING

Kritikos Fournos   Cafe €
(www.kritikosfournosgeuseis.gr; Plateia Kallergon 3; snacks €1-5; ⓞ6am-midnight; ⓞⓟ) This fun cafe-bakery is a Cretan chain, and it's a dependable stop for good espresso (it opens at 6am!), baked goods, pastries and sandwiches (including tasty vegan focaccia options) and even a craft beer or two. Perch yourself in a choice people-watching spot overlooking Lion Sq and banter with the hip, friendly staff. Signed in Greek only.

Merastri   Cretan €€
(ⓟ2810 221910; www.facebook.com/merastri; Chrisostomou 17; mains €5-13; ⓞ6pm-midnight Tue-Sun Jun-Aug, 6pm-midnight Tue-Sat, noon-midnight Sun Sep-May; ⓟ) Enjoying one of the most authentic Cretan meals in town, served in this stunning home (a former music building), is a highlight of dining in Iraklio. The family of owners is passionate about its products (including oil and wine), and will conjure up everything from slow-cooked lamb to porterhouse steak with wine and sage.

Parasties   Greek €€
(ⓟ2810 225009; www.parastiescrete.gr; Handakos 81; mains €9-43; ⓞnoon-1am; ⓟ) Parasties' owner, Haris, is genuine about serving great-quality local produce and top Cretan wines. And his passion shows in his gourmet menu of inventively updated traditional fare, including a daily special. Grab a seat under an annexe with a bar, in the roomy dining area or on the side patio with sea views.

Peskesi   Cretan €€
(ⓟ2810 288887; www.peskesicrete.gr; Kapetan Haralampi 6-8; mains €9-14; ⓞ1pm-2am; ⓟⓟ) ⓟ It's almost impossible to overstate how good Peskesi's resurrected, slow-cooked Cretan dishes are, nor the beauty of the revamped Venetian villa in which you'll partake of them: this is Crete's finest culinary moment. Nearly everything is forged from heirloom produce and organic meats and olive oils from the restaurant's own farm.

Athali   Cretan €€
(ⓟ2815 200012; www.athali.gr; Karterou 20; mains €8.50-15.50; ⓞnoon-midnight; ⓟ) This colourful, crowd-pleasing restaurant is a true family affair: Dad oversees a massive central open fire, roasting spits of succulent lamb and pork for hours, while Mum handles traditional hearty stews such as rustic chicken, rooster and youvetsi (baked lamb with tomatoes and kritharaki pasta served with anthotiro cheese) in the kitchen and their three personable daughters serve.

ⓞ DRINKING & NIGHTLIFE

Solo Brewery   Microbrewery
(www.solobeer.gr; Kointoirioti 35; ⓞnoon-5pm; ⓟ) Norwegian brewer Kjetil Jikiun started Norway's first craft brewery (Nøgne Ø) before he founded Crete's first craft brewery (he's clearly a man of firsts). There's no taproom per se, but drinking

here is a worthwhile excursion for beer connoisseurs. A wealth of IPAs, stouts and porters, and hoppy saisons across five taps and numerous bottles await for makeshift front-patio consumption.

Xalavro
Cocktail Bar

(www.facebook.com/xalavro; Milatou 10; ☺10am-3am; 🖥) This rather idyllic open-air bar gets a whole lot right, with charming servers slinging creative cocktails to a diverse crowd of holidaymakers and locals in the ruins of an archaeologically protected roofless stone house. It exudes *Ef Zin* – the Greek art of living well.

Bitters Bar
Cocktail Bar

(www.thebittersbar.com; Plateia Venizelou; ☺8pm-3am Mon-Thu, to 5am Fri-Sun; 🖥) The indisputable frontrunner of Iraklio's mixology scene is this den of Prohibition-inspired decadence centred on a retail alcove just off Lion Sq. Throwback cocktails dominate the classics on the list, but let the bartenders shine with creations such as Bitters House (gin, ginger syrup, pink-grapefruit and lemon juice, cardamom bitters) and

Attaboy (vodka, mango puree, lemon juice, aromatic bitters).

Crop
Craft Beer

(www.crop.coffee; Aretousas 4; ☺7am-1am; 🖥) Crop divides its focus equally between two vices: caffeine and craft beer. At the time of writing it was Iraklio's only craft-focused bar, with five independent taps (including Crete's own Solo Brewing and Brewdog, and 25 or so bottled; beers cost €4 to €6). It's also a highly recommended roastery specialising in Third Wave coffee preparations such as V60 and Chemex.

⊛ ENTERTAINMENT

Cultural and Conference Center of Heraklion
Arts Centre

(🖉2810 229618; Plastira 10) This new and modern five-building complex, opened in 2019, is Crete's most important cultural and events venue. It includes the gorgeous 800-seat Andreas and Maria Kalokairinou Hall, designed for theatre, opera and classical-music performances.

Peskesi

ℹ️ INFORMATION

Banks with ATMs are plentiful, especially along 25 Avgoustou.

Tourist Info Point (📞28134 09777; www.heraklion.gr; Plateia Venizelou; ⏰8.30am-2.30pm Mon-Fri)

University Hospital of Heraklion (📞28103 92111; www.pagni.gr; Stavrakia; ⏰24hr)

Venizelio General Hospital (📞28134 08000; www.venizeleio.gr; Knossos Rd; ⏰24hr emergency)

ℹ️ GETTING THERE & AWAY

The airport (p305) is just off the E75, about 5km east of the city centre. Buses run to points in the city, including the port, the regional (and local) bus stations and Plateia Eleftherias, from 6am to midnight (€1.20, every 10 to 15 minutes) from a stop about 50m in front of the departures door. Buy tickets at the bus-stop machine or with the attendant (on board the fare is €2).

Taxis wait outside the arrivals terminal. The fare into town is a fixed rate €15 (outlying destinations are by meter).

The **ferry port** (📞28103 38000; www.port heraklion.gr) is 500m east of Koules Fortress and the old harbour. Iraklio is a major port for access to many of the Greek islands, though services are spotty outside high season. Tickets can be purchased online or through travel agencies, including central **Paleologos** (📞28103 46185; www.paleologos.gr; 25 Avgoustou 5; ⏰9am-8pm Mon-Fri, to 3pm Sat).

Iraklio's long-distance **bus station** (📞28102 46530; www.ktelherlas.gr; Leoforos Ikarou 9; 📶) serves major destinations in eastern and western Crete, including Hania.

For destinations around Crete, you can order a cab from **Crete Taxi Services** (📞6970021970; www.crete-taxi.gr; ⏰24hr) or **Crete Cab** (📞6955171473; www.crete.cab). There are also long-distance cabs waiting at the airport, at Plateia Eleftherias (outside the Capsis Astoria hotel) and at KTEL Heraklion Lassithi Bus Station.

ℹ️ GETTING AROUND

BUS

KTEL (www.ktelherlas.gr) runs Iraklio's blue-and-white city buses. Fares are €1.20 (€2 if

Passenger ferry, Iraklio

purchased on board). Two lines are free. The blue line runs hourly from 9.30am to 4.30pm, starting at Hotel Apollonia and stopping at the Heraklion Archaeological Museum, the Historical Museum of Crete, Koules Fortress and Knossos, while the red line runs hourly from 9.15am to 4.15pm from the port, making more or less the same stops. (These buses are not to be confused with the pay hop-on, hop-off blue-and-red buses.) A daily bus pass is €5. For the airport, catch **bus 1** (Plateia Eleftherias).

CAR & MOTORCYCLE

Iraklio's streets are narrow and chaotic, so it's best to drop your vehicle in a car park – between €5 and €12 per day; though not the cheapest option, it doesn't get much more central than **Theseus Parking** (www.facebook.com/theseus parking; Thiseos 18; 1st hour €4.80, per additional hour €.80, overnight €12) – and explore on foot. All the international car-hire companies have branches at the airport, local outlets line the northern end of 25 Avgoustou.

TAXI

There are small taxi stands all over town, but the main ones are at the Regional Bus Station, on Plateia Eleftherias and at the northern end of 25 Avgoustou. You can also phone for one on 28140 03084.

Useful taxi apps include Aegean Taxi (www. aegeantaxi.com).

Hania

Hania (also spelled Chania) is Crete's most evocative city, with its pretty Venetian quarter criss-crossed by narrow lanes and culminating at a magnificent harbour. Remnants of Venetian and Turkish architecture abound, with old townhouses now transformed into atmospheric restaurants and boutique hotels.

Although all this beauty means the old town is deluged with tourists in summer, it's still a great place to unwind. The Venetian Harbour is ideal for a stroll and a coffee or cocktail. Thanks to an active modern centre, the city retains its charm in winter. Indie boutiques and an entire lane (Skryd-

Hania for Families

If your youngster has lost interest in Venetian architecture, head to the Park of Peace and Friendship between Tzanakaki and A Papandreou, where there's a playground and a shady cafe. Eight kilometres south of town, the giant water park **Limnoupolis** (28210 33246; www.limnoupolis.gr; Varypetro; day pass adult/4-12yr €25/18, afternoon pass €17/14; ⊙10am-6pm mid-May–mid-Jun & Sep, to 7pm mid-Jun–Aug) has enough slides and pools to keep kids amused, and cafes and pool bars for adults. Buses leave regularly from the KTEL bus station.

Limnoupolis
IAN WOOLCOCK/ALAMY STOCK PHOTO ©

lof) dedicated to leather products provide good shopping, and a multitude of creative restaurants means you'll eat very well here.

⊙ SIGHTS

Hania Archaeological Museum
Museum

(28210 90334; http://chaniamuseum.culture. gr; Halidon 28; adult/concession/child €4/2/ free; ⊙8.30am-8pm Wed-Mon Apr-Oct, to 4pm Wed-Mon Nov-Mar) The setting alone in the beautifully restored 16th-century Venetian Church of San Francisco is reason to visit this fine collection of artefacts from Neolithic to Roman times. Late-Minoan clay baths used as coffins catch the eye, along with a large glass case with an entire herd of clay bulls (used to worship Poseidon). Other standouts include Roman floor mosaics, Hellenistic gold jewellery, clay tablets

Hania

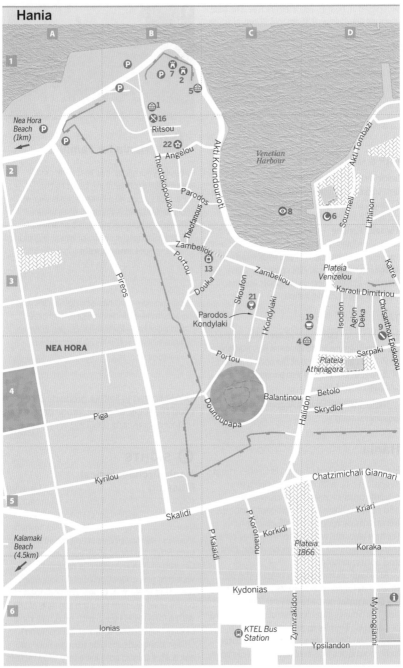

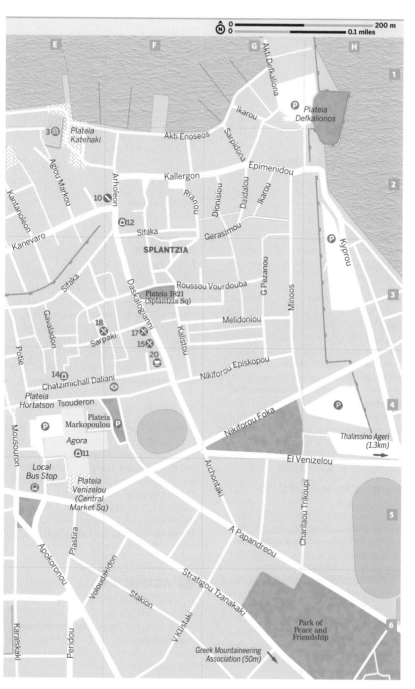

Hania

with Linear A and Linear B script, and a marble sculpture of the head of Roman emperor Hadrian.

Venetian Harbour   Historic Site
FREE There are few places where Hania's historic charm and grandeur are more palpable than in the old Venetian Harbour. It's lined by pastel-coloured buildings that punctuate a maze of narrow lanes lined with shops and tavernas. The eastern side is dominated by the domed **Mosque of Kioutsouk Hasan** (Mosque of the Janissaries), now an exhibition hall, while a few steps further east the impressively restored **Grand Arsenal** (☑28210 34200; Plateia Katehaki; ⊗varies by exhibit) **FREE** houses the Centre of Mediterranean Architecture.

Maritime Museum of Crete   Museum
(☑28210 91875; www.mar-mus-crete.gr; Akti Koundourioti; adult/concession €3/2; ⊗9am-5pm May-Oct, to 3.30pm Nov-Apr) Part of the hulking Venetian-built **Firkas Fortress** (⊗8am-2pm Mon-Fri) at the western port entrance, this museum celebrates Crete's nautical tradition with model ships, naval instruments, paintings, photographs, maps and memorabilia. One room is dedicated to historical sea battles, while upstairs there's thorough documentation of the WWII-era Battle of Crete. You might be lucky enough to see artists working on new model ships in the ship workroom.

Byzantine & Post-Byzantine Collection   Museum
(☑28210 96046; Theotokopoulou 78; adult/concession/child €2/1/free; ⊗8am-4pm Wed-Mon) In the impressively restored Venetian Church of San Salvatore, this small but fascinating collection of artefacts, icons, jewellery and coins spans the period from AD 62 to 1913. Highlights include a segment of a mosaic floor from an early Christian basilica, an icon of St George slaying the dragon, and a panel recently attributed to El Greco.

Venetian Fortifications   Fortress
Part of a defensive system begun in 1538 by Michele Sanmichele, who also designed Iraklio's defences, Hania's massive fortifications remain impressive. Best preserved is the western wall, running from the Firkas Fortress to the **Siavo Bastion**. Entrance to the fortress is via the gates next to the Maritime Museum. The bastion offers good views of the old town.

⊕ ACTIVITIES
Hania is a popular gateway for guided excursions to Samaria Gorge and other hiking trips; the **Greek Mountaineering Association** (EOS; ☑28210 44647; www.eoshanion.gr; Tzanakaki 90; ⊗9-11pm Mon-Fri) has information.

Diving outfits, including **Blue Adventures** (☎28210 40608; www.blueadventures.gr; Chrysanthou Episkopou 39; 2 dives incl gear €90, snorkelling tour €50; ⏰9am-9pm Mon-Sat May-Oct) and **Chania Diving** (☎28210 58939; www.chaniadiving.gr; Arholeon 1; 2 dives €90, snorkelling tour €55), offer boat dives and snorkelling trips around the area.

For something more sybaritic, you can opt for a **private cruise** (☎69471 81990; www.notos-sailing.com; full-day trip for 3/8 people €550/880) to islands nearby for a spot of swimming and light snorkelling.

🔒 SHOPPING

Sifis Stavroulakis   Jewellery
(☎28210 50335; www.sifisjewellery.gr; Chatzimichali Daliani 54; ⏰10am-2pm Mon-Sat, plus 5.30-8.30pm Tue, Thu & Fri) Beautiful naturalistic jewellery made with semi-precious stones and metals takes on floral and human forms in this small shopfront and jeweller's workshop.

Roka Carpets   Arts & Crafts
(☎28210 74736; Zambeliou 61; ⏰11am-9pm Mon-Sat) One of the few places in Crete where you can buy genuine, hand-woven goods (note, though, that they're not antiques). Amiable Mihalis Manousakis and his wife, Annie, weave wondrous rugs on a 400-year-old loom, using methods that have remained essentially unchanged since Minoan times.

Miden Agan   Food & Drinks
(☎28210 27068; www.midenaganshop.gr; Daskalogianni 70; ⏰10am-5pm Mon-Wed & Sat, to 9pm Thu & Fri) Food and wine lovers are spoilt for choice at this excellent shop, which stocks more than 800 Greek wines as well as its own wines and liquors, along with local gourmet deli foods, including its own line of spoon sweets (try the white pumpkin). Wine tastings are also available (by appointment; 15 minutes to one hour from €15 per person).

Agora   Market
(Covered Market; Chatzimichali Giannari; ⏰8am-5pm Mon, Wed & Sat, 8am-9pm Tue, Thu & Fri) Hania's cross-shaped market hall

🏖️ Beaches

The town beach 2km west of the Venetian Harbour at **Nea Hora** (Akti Papanikoli) is crowded but convenient if you just want to cool off and get some rays. Koum Kapi is less used (and less clean). For better swimming, keep heading west to the beaches (in order) of **Hrysi Akti** (Nea Kydonia), **Agioi Apostoli** and **Kalamaki**, which are all served by local buses heading towards Platanias.

Kalamaki

opened in 1913 and bustles mostly with souvenir-hunting tourists, though a few stands selling traditional Cretan produce and products (herbs, honey, baked goods, raki, cheese) – along with cafes – are still part of the mix.

🍴 EATING

Kouzina EPE   Cretan €
(☎28210 42391; www.facebook.com/kouzinaepe; Daskalogianni 25; dishes €5-10; ⏰noon-7.30pm Mon-Sat; 🛜🌱) This cheery lunch spot gets contemporary designer flair from the cement floor and hip lighting. It wins the area's 'local favourite' hands down, by serving a mix of modern à la carte options and great-value, delicious blackboard-listed *mayirefta* (ready-cooked meals); you can inspect what you're about to eat in the open kitchen. Good veg options, too.

Pulse   Vegan €
(Theotokopoulou 70; mains €9.50; ⏰noon-midnight daily May-Oct, noon-9pm Mon-Sat Nov-Mar; 🌱) Settle in at an outdoor table with sea

Thalassino Ageri

views for fantastic vegan dishes at meat-free Pulse, located at the western end of Firkas Fortress. The mezes boards are great for snacking on, as are the potato cakes with chilli jam; mains include a tasty cheeseburger and a beef-free red-wine casserole. The *mousakas* is an absolute highlight.

To Maridaki   Seafood €€
(☑28210 08880; www.tomaridaki.gr; Daskalogianni 33; dishes €6-13; ⊗noon-midnight Mon-Sat) This modern seafood *mezedhopoleio* (restaurant specialising in mezedhes) is often packed to the gills with chatty locals and tourists. Dishes straddle the line between tradition and innovation with to-die-for mussels *saganaki,* charcoal-grilled fresh fish, and delicious house white wine. The complimentary panna cotta is a worthy finish.

Well of the Turk   Middle Eastern €€
(☑28210 54547; www.welloftheturk.gr; Sarpaki 1-3; mains €10-15; ⊗6pm-midnight Wed-Mon; ✳🛜) In an age-old stone building that used to house a *hammam*, and flanking a quiet square, this romantic taverna serves richly

textured dishes with a strong French and Moroccan identity, prepared with the finest Cretan ingredients. Specialities include the shish kebab, and slow-cooked lamb with preserved lemons and couscous. The cheesecake with orange blossom is an imaginative culinary coda.

Thalassino Ageri   Seafood €€€
(☑28210 51136; www.thalasino-ageri.gr; Vivilaki 35; fish per kg €55-65; ⊗6.30pm-midnight Mon-Sat, 12.30pm-midnight Sun Apr & May, from 7pm daily Jun-Oct) This solitary fish taverna among the vestiges of Hania's old tanneries in Halepa, 2km east of the centre, is one of Crete's top restaurants. Take in the sunset from the superb waterside setting and peruse the changing menu, dictated by the day's catch, which is cooked over charcoal. The fried calamari melts in your mouth.

🍷 DRINKING & NIGHTLIFE

Monogram   Coffee
(☑28215 07046; www.facebook.com/monogram chania; Daskalogianni 5; ⊗8am-9pm) Soak up the sun at a street-side table with music

wafting from this hip coffee spot. Beans are sourced from around the globe, including Guatemala and Ethiopia, then roasted locally in Iraklio. It also has a large range of teas you'd be hard-pressed to find elsewhere in Greece, and a few tempting cakes.

Sinagogi   Bar
(☑28210 95242; Parodos Kondylaki 15; ⊗noon-5am May-Oct; 🛜) Housed in a roofless Venetian building on a small lane next to the synagogue, this popular summer-only lounge bar with eclectic decor is a laid-back place to relax and take it all in. After dark it's bathed in a romantic glow while DJs play soft electro and bartenders whip up mojitos and daiquiris.

Bohème   Cafe
(☑28210 95955; www.boheme-chania.gr; Halidon 26-28; ⊗8am-3am; 🛜) Bohème's pretty, tree-shaded terrace and vine-covered pastel-pink stone building provide the perfect retreat. Sip coffee, craft beer or cocktails while relaxing on bright, cushioned wrought-iron chairs; it's especially atmospheric under fairy lights at night. Inside, the multispace cafe-bar evokes modern Med vibes and does a menu of everything from brunch pancakes to bao (steamed buns) and burgers.

⭐ ENTERTAINMENT
Fagotto Jazz Bar   Live Music
(☑28210 71877; Angelou 16; ⊗8.30am-2pm & 9pm-late) Established in 1978, this Hania institution in a Venetian building offers smooth jazz and blues, and occasionally live bands or DJs, in an intimate setting in a narrow lane close to the Maritime Museum. The action picks up after 10pm. It opens in the mornings as a cafe and does great breakfasts, too.

ℹ INFORMATION
Banks cluster around Plateia Markopoulou in the new city, but there are also ATMs in the old town on Halidon.

Alpha Bank (cnr Halidon & Skalidi; ⊗8am-6pm Mon-Fri, 10am-5pm Sat, ATM 24hr)

Municipal Tourist Office (☑28213 36155; Kydonias 29; ⊗9am-3pm Mon-Fri) Modest selection of brochures, maps and transport timetables.

National Bank of Greece (cnr Tzanakaki & Giannari; ⊗8am-2pm)

ℹ GETTING THERE & AWAY
Hania's **airport** (☑28210 83800; www.chania-airport.com) is 14km east of town on the Akrotiri Peninsula, and is served year-round from Athens and Thessaloniki and seasonally from throughout Europe. A taxi from the airport to anywhere in Hania costs €25. Public buses into town stop right outside the terminal (€2.50, 30 minutes) and run between 5.30am and 11pm daily.

Hania's port is at Souda, 7km southeast of town. The port is linked to town by bus (€2, or €2.50 if bought aboard) and taxi (€10). Hania buses meet each boat.

Anek Lines (www.anek.gr) runs an overnight ferry between Piraeus (near Athens) and Hania (from €38 per person, nine hours). Buy tickets online or at the port; reserve ahead for cars.

Hania's **KTEL bus station** (☑info 28210 93052, tickets 28210 93306; www.e-ktel.com; Kelaidi 73-77; 🛜) has an information kiosk with helpful staff and timetables, a cafeteria, a minimarket and a left-luggage service. Check the excellent website for the current schedule.

ℹ GETTING AROUND
Hania town is best navigated on foot, since most of it is pedestrianised.

Local buses are operated by **Chania Urban Buses** (☑28210 98115; http://chaniabus.gr). Zone A/B tickets cost €1.20/1.70 if bought from a kiosk or vending machine and €2/2.50 from the driver.

Major car-hire outlets are at the airport and you'll find outlets on Halidon in the old town, including recommendable **Kriti Plus** (☑6947404801; www.kritiplus.gr; Halidon 99; ⊗8.30am-9pm).

For a taxi contact **Taxi** (☑28210 98700; www.chaniataxi.gr).

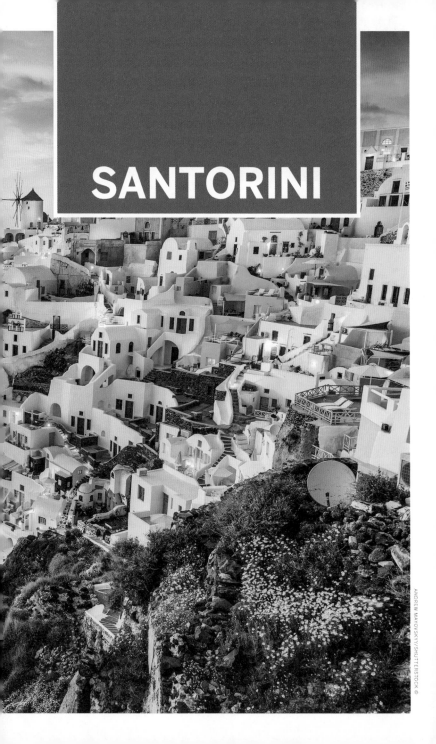

SANTORINI

Santorini at a Glance...

If you approach Santorini (Thira) from the water, it's hard not to be awed by the sheer cliffs that soar above a turquoise sea, by the fact that you're sailing in an immense crater of a drowned volcano and that before you lies an island shaped by an ancient eruption cataclysmic beyond imagining. High above, the main villages of Fira and Oia are a snow-drift of white Cycladic houses that line the cliff tops and spill like icy cornices down the terraced rock. And then there are the sunsets, with crowds breaking into applause as the sun disappears below the horizon.

Two Days in Santorini

Before heading to **Ancient Akrotiri** (p213) and **Ancient Thira** (p213) check out the **Museum of Prehistoric Thera** (p212) and **Archaeological Museum** (p220) both in **Fira** (p212). Walk up to the caldera-edge pathway (or ride the **Santorini Cable Car** (p213)) and continue on to **Oia** (p218)making sure you time your arrival well in advance of the showstopper sunsets.

Four Days in Santorini

Join a **wine tasting tour** (p218) or create your own sipping itinerary around the island's dozen or so wineries that are open to the public; **Art Space** (p218) is a good one that also show-cases contemporary art. Spend a day beach hopping or simply opt for red sand at **Kokkini** (p211), white at **Aspri** (p211) or black at **Perissa** (p210).

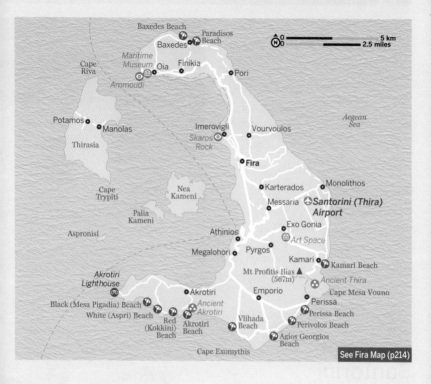

Baxedes Beach
Paradisos Beach
Baxedes
Maritime Museum
Oia
Finikia
Cape Riva
Ammoudi
Pori

5 km
2.5 miles

Potamos
Manolas
Thirasia

Imerovigli
Vourvoulos
Skaros Rock

Aegean Sea

Fira

Nea Kameni

Karterados
Monolithos
Messaria
Santorini (Thira) Airport

Cape Trypiti

Palia Kameni

Exo Gonia
Art Space

Aspronisi

Athinios

Megalohori
Pyrgos

Kamari
Kamari Beach

Mt Profitis Ilias ▲ (567m)
Ancient Thira
Cape Mesa Vouno

Akrotiri Lighthouse

Akrotiri

Emporio

Perissa

Black (Mesa Pigadia) Beach
White (Aspri) Beach
Ancient Akrotiri
Red (Kokkini) Beach
Akrotiri Beach
Vlihada Beach

Perissa Beach
Perivolos Beach

Agios Georgios Beach

Cape Exomythis

See Fira Map (p214)

Arriving in Santorini

Santorini Airport has flights year-round to/from Athens; seasonal connections are plentiful with various European cities. There are plenty of ferries each day to and from Piraeus, Athens' main port, and many Cyclades islands.

Where to Stay

Most accommodation (mostly midrange and top end) is concentrated in Fira and Oia, along with a few 'budget' pensions. For a caldera view, expect to pay a premium. Away from these main villages, the biggest concentration of midrange and budget rooms can be found in and around Kamari, Perissa and Messaria.

Fried shrimp

Gourmet Santorini

Beyond caldera views, infinity pools and black-sand beaches, Santorini has become a magnet both for foodies and oenophiles, drawn to the island by one of the best dining scenes in Greece and its reputation for excellent wine. Edible offerings include dishes cooked according to traditional recipes using only local ingredients in family-run tavernas, and stellar fusion by internationally renowned chefs.

Great For...

☑ Don't Miss

Lauda (p219) in Oia is one of Greece's top fine dining restaurants.

❶ Need to Know

Some wineries require advance bookings for wine tastings, particularly in peak season.

✕ Take a Break

In between wine tastings, squeeze in a traditional meal at **Tzanakis** (☎22860 81929; http://tavernatzanakis.com; Megalohori; mains €8-14; ☺noon-midnight).

★ Top Tip

In love with Santorini's traditional dishes? You can learn to cook them as well at the cooking school run by **Selene** (☎22860 22249; www.selene.gr; Pyrgos; cooking class €85-100).

MURAT AN/ALAMY STOCK PHOTO ©

Local Ingredients

Santorini's traditional food draws heavily on its unique volcanic soil that endows its vegetables with qualities not found elsewhere in Greece. The island is best known in Greece for its white aubergines (eggplants), capers, cherry tomatoes and fava (yellow split peas, not unlike lentils).

The island's tiny tomatoes with a high sugar content are turned into tomato paste with capers, olive oil, salt, basil and oregano and served with bread, or else turned into *pseudokeftethes* (tomato fritters). Santorini was 'tomato island' before the volcanic eruption of 1950 and throughout the tourism boom during the island's recovery period, though only one of 13 former tomato processing factories is still in operation. The small white Santorini aubergine turns up in stews and salads, or is smoked and pureed. Capers and pickled caper leaves make a regular appearance in salads. Cooked and puréed, the popular fava bean dish is traditionally eaten warm (sometimes with caramelised onions), as an appetiser (or dip), or accompanying a main course of meat or fish. Less well-known is *katsuni*, the Santorini cucumber that acquires a sweet, melon-like flavour if not picked in time, and is used in salads. In spring, wild greens are picked in Santorini's fields and served as an accompaniment to fish.

Greek salad

Typical Dishes

Typical Santorini dishes include *skordo-makarona* (homemade pasta with Santorini tomatoes, garlic, olive oil and salt) and *apochti* (spiced pork carpaccio), which has Byzantian roots and takes days to prepare with salt, vinegar and sun-dried cinnamon, pepper and parsley.

Made with barley, raisins and sesame seeds, *kopania* is a traditional Santorini sweet. *Melitinia* (a festive sweet made with salted sheep's cheese and yoghurt) is also found in traditional bakeries on the island, as is baklava made with local pistachios.

Not found elsewhere in Greece, *chlorotyri* is a soft, creamy goat's cheese that gives a local twist to the traditional Greek salad.

Octopus, squid and grilled fish are not unique to Santorini but they have been a staple of the local diet for millennia.

Old Vines & Varietals

Not only is Santorini blessed with a dry volcanic microclimate that results in some of the best wine in Greece, but its vines are also Europe's oldest, impervious to the phylloxera bug that wiped out most of Europe's vines in the late 19th century.

Grapes are grown close to the ground, in a *kouloura* (nest) of vines to make the most of the moisture and protect the grapes from fierce winds.

Santorini's most lauded wine is a crisp dry white *asyrtiko*, as well as the amber-coloured, unfortified dessert wine known as Vinsanto. Both wines are made from the heritage-protected, indigenous grape variety, *asyrtiko*, as is Nykteri (*asyrtiko* made at night). *Asyrtiko* grapes are grown across the Cyclades, but the Santorini variety stands out in terms of unique flavour. You'll also come across *mavrotragano* (full-bodied red), and the medium-bodied *mandelaria* red.

Most local vineyards host tastings (usually for a small charge), with snacks or full meals on the side, with scenery and local produce combining to great effect.

Santorini's contemporary dining scene is among the most exciting in Greece, with some local chefs taking traditional ingredients and using them in unusual and interesting combinations.

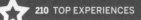

Red (Kokkini) Beach

OLGA GAVRILOVA/SHUTTERSTOCK ©

Santorini's Beaches

Volcanic Santorini has beaches to suit everyone. There's lively beaches a stone's throw from a plethora of tavernas, secluded coves, stretches of sand to bare all on and places where you can combine sunbathing with appreciation of remarkable natural beauty.

Great For...

☑ **Don't Miss**

Red (Kokkini) Beach is particularly worth visiting in the afternoon when it's at its photogenic best.

East & South Coasts

Santorini's best beaches are on the east and south coasts. Some of the beaches have no facilities at all, whereas others come fully equipped with sunbeds, beach bars and the odd water-sports operator.

The long stretches of black sand, pebbles and pumice stones at **Perissa**, **Perivolos** and **Agios Georgios** are backed by bars, tavernas, hotels and shops and remain fairly relaxed.

Among the recommended places to eat at Perissa are **Apollon Taverna** (☎22860 85340; Perissa; mains €9-14; ☺10am-midnight) and **Fratzeskos Fish Tavern** (☎22860 83488; www.facebook.com/fishtavernfrageskos1; Perissa; mains from €8; ☺noon-11.30pm).

Lighthouse, Akrotiri

RICHARD CUMMINS/ALAMY STOCK PHOTO ©

❶ Need to Know

Take a mat or rent a sun lounger at black-sand beaches as the sand gets extremely hot.

✖ Take a Break

Hungry after a stint on Kamari Beach? Skip the mediocre seafront offerings and visit **Aroma Avlis** (☏22860 33794; www.artemiskaramolegos-winery.com; Messaria–Kamari Rd; mains €13-48; ⓘ1-11pm) ✔ for lunch instead.

★ Top Tip

Detour to **Akrotiri Lighthouse** for sunset to enjoy the light show without Oia's crowds.

There's also a 24-hour bar that plays DJ sets on summer nights.

Red (Kokkini) Beach, near Ancient Akrotiri in the south, has particularly impressive red cliffs. Caïques from **Akrotiri Beach** can take you there and on to the sheltered cove of **White (Aspri) Beach** and the sunbed-studded sand at the **Black (Mesa Pigadia) Beach** for about €5 return. Mesa Pigadia has a beachside tavern, and there are several restaurants up from Kokkini Beach.

Vlihada, also on the south coast, has a **beach** backed by weirdly eroded cliffs as well as tavernas; it also has a photogenic fishing harbour with an excellent restaurant above it. The further along the beach you go, the less clothes you see; it's a favourite with naturists.

Kamari

Kamari is Santorini's best-developed resort, with a long beach of black sand. The beachfront road is dense with restaurants and bars, and things get extremely busy in high season. Boats connect Kamari with Perissa in summer.

North Coast

On the north coast, a short drive from Oia, there is the long, narrow stretch of sand that is the **Baxedes Beach** that flows seamlessly into **Paradisos Beach**. There are no facilities there, and the water isn't as sheltered for swimming as it is on the south coast, but there are relatively few people as well.

Fira

⊙ SIGHTS

Museum of Prehistoric Thera
Museum

(☎22860 22217; www.santorini.com/museums; Mitropoleos; adult/under 18 €6/3; ⊗8.30am-3pm Wed-Mon) Opposite the bus station, this well-presented museum houses extraordinary finds excavated from Akrotiri, which has been settled since neolithic times. Check out the wealth of wall paintings, ceramics with a heavy Minoan influence and the glowing gold ibex figurine, dating from the 17th century BC and in mint condition. Also look for fossilised olive tree leaves from within the caldera, which date back to 60,000 BC.

Gyzi Megaron
Museum

(☎22860 23077; www.megarogyzi.gr; Erythrou Stavrou; adult/child €3/free; ⊗10am-9pm Mon-Sat, 10.30am-4.30pm Sun May-Oct) At the north end of Fira, this museum displays fascinating before-and-after photographs of the 1956 earthquake, along with centuries-old maps of the Cyclades, paintings, striking photography by Christos Simatos and 15th-century manuscripts.

Old Port
Port

Sitting 220m below Fira – three minutes by cable car, or 587 steps by foot – the Old Port, also known as Fira Skala, is now mainly used by cruise ship passengers visiting Fira for the day. They generally arrive in the morning, then head back in the afternoon. The little port has restaurants, tavernas and small shops, and presents a stunning view from the foot of the caldera cliffs.

Skaros Rock
Landmark

From Imerovigli, a sign points west for the track to Skaros, the conical peninsula jutting out into the caldera. Not only geologically interesting, it is also historically important, as it was the first of five *kasteli* (fortresses) built on Santorini in the 15th century to protect the islanders from pirate attacks. Earthquakes put an end to that, however, and the inhabitants moved to Fira. Walk out for great views and a perfectly situated church, but expect plenty of steps.

Skaros Rock

NATALIYA NAZAROVA/ALAMY STOCK PHOTO ©

⚙ ACTIVITIES

Santorini Cable Car   Cable Car

(https://scc.gr/cablecar.htm; one way €6; ⏱7am-9.20pm May-Sep, reduced hours Oct-Apr) Fira's efficient cable car links the caldera-top town with the Old Port, 220m below, in three minutes. It can be totally swamped with cruise ship passengers coming up in the morning and heading back down in the afternoon. One option: walk the 587 steps down, then come back up by cable car.

🛍 SHOPPING

Ceramic Art Studio   Ceramics

(☑22860 24750; next to the conference centre; ⏱9am-9pm) Ceramics artist Andreas Ale-fragkis has been perfecting his craft over the course of three decades and the results are striking. Behold the hanging amphorae in an aquamarine or artfully cracked cream glaze and the one-of-a-kind vases, as well as utility drinking vessels and platters.

Eduart Gjopalaj Gallery   Art

(☑69424 39225; www.facebook.com/gjopalaj eduart; Agiou Ioannou; ⏱10am-9pm) This gallery is filled with the sinuous, surreal woodwork of Albanian-born sculptor Edu-art Gjopalaj: delicate, lattice-like platters, serene faces seemingly floating out of undulating waves of wood. If you're lucky, you'll catch the artist at work.

Ergon Deli   Food & Drinks

(☑22860 28360; www.ergonfoods.com; Erythrou Stavrou; ⏱9.30am-9pm) Not only do these guys produce some of Santorini's hottest craft beer (Volkan, served at their caldera-edge cafe; p215), but this deli is also a terrific place to shop for island edibles (superb olive oil, preserves, pickled caper leaves) and drinkables, including Vinsanto dessert wine.

Mati Art Gallery   Art

(☑22860 23814; www.matiartgallery.com; Cathedral Plateau; ⏱10am-9.30pm) The shark-head installation piece outside is sure to catch your attention. This is the main exhibition

📷 Ancient Santorini Sights

First settled by the Dorians in the 9th century BC, **Ancient Thira** (☑22860 25405; http://odysseus.culture.gr; adult/child €4/free; ⏱8am-3pm Tue-Sun) consists of Hellenistic, Roman and Byzantine ruins and is an atmospheric and rewarding site to visit. The ruins include temples, houses with mosaics, an agora (market), a theatre and a gymnasium. Views are splendid. If you're driving, take the narrow, switchbacked road from Kamari for 3km. From Perissa, a hike up a dusty path takes a bit over an hour to reach the site.

In 1967, excavations at **Akrotiri** (☑22860 81366; http://odysseus.culture.gr; adult/concession €12/6; ⏱8am-8pm May-Sep, to 3pm Oct-Apr) in the island's south-west uncovered an ancient Minoan city buried deep beneath volcanic ash from the catastrophic eruption of 1613 BC. Housed within a cool, protective structure, wooden walkways allow you to pass through the city. Peek inside three-storey buildings that survived, and see roads, drainage systems and stashes of pottery. It's best to visit with a guide and to stop by the Museum of Prehistoric Thera before coming here.

Ancient Thira
STAVROS PAPAVASILIOU/SHUTTERSTOCK ©

space of Yorgos Kypris, an internationally celebrated artist who takes much of his inspiration from Santorini and the sea. From the larger pieces featuring bright silver darts of sardine shoals to glass-and-metal

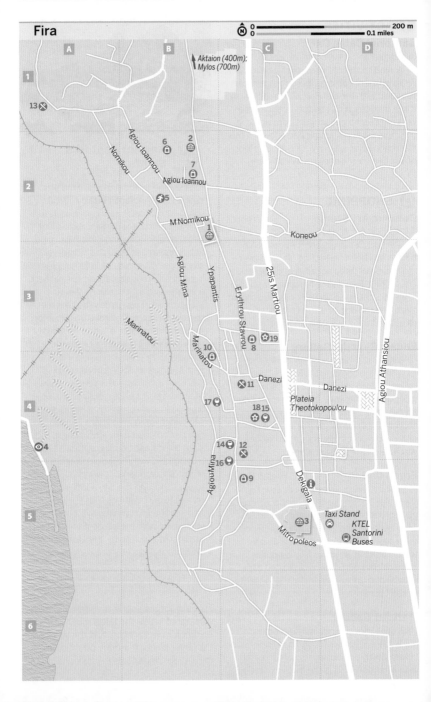

Fira

0   200 m
0   0.1 miles

Aktaion (400m);
Mylos (700m)

Fira

denizens of the deep, his work is striking and unique.

Tzamia-Krystalla Art Gallery Santorini
Art

(☏22860 21226; www.tzamia-krystallagallery. gr; Marinatou; ⊙10am-10pm) Near the top of the steps leading down to the Old Port, this gallery specialises in Greek contemporary art, both from established artists and up-and-coming young talent. All the ceramic sculptures – including ones inspired by Santorini's volcanic origins and created especially for this gallery – are made by Manousos Chalkiadakis, one of the most distinguished ceramic artists in Greece.

⊗ EATING

Volkan on the Rocks
Cafe €€

(☏22860 28360; https://ergonfoods.com; mains €10-13; ⊙9am-midnight May-Oct; 🖥) With a breezy clifftop terrace overlooking the caldera, this cafe is the home of Volkan craft beer, which is nicely paired with Santorini's fire in the sky. Come for breakfast, swing by for the selection of imaginative hot and cold mezedhes made from local produce, or visit in the evenings for the open-air movie screenings.

Aktaion
Taverna €€

(☏22860 22336; www.aktaionsantorini.com; Firostefani; mains €13-23; ⊙1pm-midnight; 🖉)

Just off the tiny Firostefani square, this taverna has been around since 1922 and continues to specialise in traditional island recipes, such as octopus with fava and capers, *skordomakarona*, steamed seasonal greens and *mousakas*. Sit in the atmospheric cavern or on the outside terrace.

Idol Restaurant Bar
Fusion €€€

(☏22860 23292; https://idolsantorini.gr; Ypapantis; mains €22-35; ⊙11am-11pm) This caldera-edge, three-level restaurant and bar serves up stupendous views and intelligent dishes full of depth, fire and vivacity. The chef dares combine squid with kimchi, raisins and chickpeas, alongside the more classic slow-cooked pork belly with sweet potato puree. And what could be more Greek than *mastika* (mastic liqueur) ice cream?

Excellent wine list, too; perfect for a romantic sunset dinner.

Koukoumavlos
Greek €€€

(☏22860 23807; www.koukoumavlos.com; mains €28-36; ⊙7pm-late Apr–Oct) Award-winning fresh, modern Aegean cuisine (including a worthwhile degustation at €82), with obligatory caldera views from the terrace. Daring pairings of ingredients include sea bass with passionfruit and Jerusalem artichoke, and tiramisu with white Santorini aubergine. Excellent selection of local wines (including by the glass). It's located 30m north of the cathedral.

Mylos   Greek €€€

(☎22860 25640; www.mylossantorini.com; Firostefani; mains €24-29; ⊗5.30pm-midnight) Located in a converted windmill on the caldera edge in Firostefani, this uber-glam venue has upscale food that's ambitious in its techniques and beautifully presented. Try crispy fish 'covered with sea snow', or lamb with Greek coffee and shellfish powder. Book ahead.

Ovac   Fusion €€€

(☎22860 27900; http://ovac.gr; Imerovigli; mains €35-52; ⊗1pm-midnight) Helmed by one of Greece's hottest chefs, this Greek-Asian fusion place is all rough slate-grey rock and caldera views. The flavour combinations are bold and the presentation is impeccable; try the beetroot salmon tartare with roasted fennel or the bao buns with chilli jam. The original cocktails are terrific but the wine list is only for those with deep pockets.

🍸 DRINKING & NIGHTLIFE

Kira Thira   Bar

(☎22860 22770; Erythrou Stavrou; ⊗8pm-3am daily) The oldest bar in Fira and one of the best. Dark wood and vaulted ceilings give it an intimate, cave-like atmosphere. There's smooth cocktails and smoother jazz, and a huge viola hanging from the ceiling. This tiny bar is so popular it often gets swamped, especially when there is live music on offer.

MoMix Bar Santorini   Bar

(☎6974350179; www.momixbar.com; Agiou Mina; ⊗8pm-3am) It might take a minute to get your head around this, but MoMix is short for Molecular Mixology. This popular party spot offers innovative cocktails (to help your mind travel) and cool interior colours in its cave-like bar. Head outside for stunning caldera views.

Crystal Cocktail Bar   Cocktail Bar

(☎22860 22480; www.crystal-santorini.gr; Marinatou, Loucas Hotel; ⊗10am-1am) Relax at Crystal, and its views to die for, with coffee in the

Mylos

morning and cocktails as your day evolves. This is one of those spots that you won't want to leave. Part of Loucas Hotel, Crystal is a top spot, with stupendous sunsets.

Tango   Cocktail Bar
(☑6947453999; www.tangosantorini.gr; Marinatou; ⊙8pm-5am) This is edge-of-the-caldera stuff, with stupendous views, delicious cocktails – its champagne cocktails are a speciality – a fashionable crowd and brilliant tunes that get louder and funkier as the sun goes down. Come for sunset and stay for hours and hours – or until your wallet is empty.

⊛ ENTERTAINMENT

White Door Theatro   Theatre
(☑22860 21770; www.whitedoorsantorini.com; €55; ⊙9pm May, Sep & Oct, 9.30pm Jun-Aug) Fira's popular *Greek Wedding Show* is a hit with visitors, featuring lots of traditional music, dance, fun and audience participation. Small plates (mezedhes) and local wine are included in the ticket, which can be booked online – advisable in the high season. The show is in an atmospheric open-air courtyard surrounded by whitewashed buildings.

Casablanca Soul Bar   Live Music
(☑6977575191; www.facebook.com/casablanca soul; Ypapantis; ⊙10pm-3.30am) This cocktail and absinthe bar is a Fira hotspot with live bands, visiting DJs and soul well into the wee hours. Expect tasty cocktails and a relaxed vibe.

ⓘ INFORMATION

There are numerous ATMs scattered around town. There are public toilets near the taxi station. You may need to brace yourself (they're of squat vintage).

Alpha Bank (Plateia Theotokopoulou) Has an ATM.

National Bank of Greece (Dekigala) South of Plateia Theotokopoulou, on the caldera side of the road. Has an ATM.

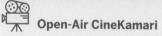

Open-Air CineKamari

After the caldera sunset **CineKamari** (☑22860 33452; www.cinekamari.gr; Kamari; €10; ⊙9.30pm) is one of the finest ways to spend a Santorini evening. On the road into Kamari, this tree-surrounded, open-air cinema screens movies in their original language throughout the summer. Pull up a deckchair, request a blanket if you're feeling chilly, and relax. Drinks and snacks available.

CineKamari
FOTOHELIN/ALAMY STOCK PHOTO ©

Central Clinic of Santorini (☑22860 21728; www.santorinicentralclinic.gr; Agiou Athanasiou; ⊙24hr) Health clinic just east of the town centre. Open 24 hours for emergencies.

Dakoutros Travel (☑22860 22958; www. dakoutrostravel.gr; Fira; ⊙8.30am-midnight Jul & Aug, 9am-9pm Sep-Jun) Helpful travel agency and de facto tourist office on the main street, just before Plateia Theotokopoulou. It sells ferry and air tickets, and provides assistance with excursions, accommodation and transfers.

Information Kiosk (Dekigala; ⊙9am-8pm Mon-Fri May-Sep) Seasonal information.

Police Station (☑22860 22649; 25 Martiou) In the centre of Fira.

ⓘ GETTING THERE & AWAY

There are frequent bus connections between Fira's bus station and the airport, located 6km east of Fira. The first leaves Fira around 5.30am and the last leaves around 10.15pm (€1.80, 20 minutes).

Wine Tasting

Santorini Wine Adventure (☎22860 34123; www.winetoursantorini.com; half-day tours from €120) and **Santorini Wine Tour** (☎22860 28358; www.santoriniwinetour.com; ⏱half-day tour from €145) are operators with knowledgeable guides and tours that blend food, wine, scenery and history, but it's most fun to explore under your own steam. A dozen or so of the island's 20 wineries are open to the public. Those not to miss include the following:

Estate Argyros (☎22860 31489; https:// estateargyros.com; Messaria–Kamari Rd; 4/7 tastings €15/40; ⏱10am-8pm) Terrific, internationally renowned wines. A short tour and snacks are included.

Gavalas Winery (☎22860 82552; www. gavalaswines.gr; Megalohori; tastings €9-24; ⏱10am-8pm) Small, family-run winery with award-winning Vinsanto and opportunities to join in traditional grape-crushing in August.

Canava Roussos (☎22860 31278; www. canavaroussos.gr; Mesa Gonia; ⏱10am-6pm May-Oct) Santorini's oldest winery's aged dessert wines are a speciality.

Art Space (☎22860 32774; www.art space-santorini.com; Exo Gonia; ⏱11am-sunset Apr-Oct) FREE Santorini's smallest winery combined with an atmospheric art gallery.

Hatzidakis Winery (☎22860 32466, 6970013556; www.hatzidakiswines.gr; Pyrgos; ⏱by appointment) The island's only organic winery.

Wine and snacks
SWEETRIVER/SHUTTERSTOCK ©

In summer buses leave Fira twice hourly for Oia (€1.80), Akrotiri/Red Beach (€2) and Kamari (€1.80), plus Perissa and Perivolos Beach (€2.40) and Kamari via Messaria (€1.80).

Buses leave Fira for the port of Athinios (€2.30, 30 minutes) seven times per day, but it's wise to check times in advance.

Fira's taxi stand is on Dekigala, just around the corner from the bus station. A taxi from the port of Athinios to Fira costs €25 and a trip from Fira to Oia €25 to €30. Expect to add a few euro if the taxi is booked ahead or if you have luggage. A taxi to Kamari is about €18, to Perissa €25.

Oia

Perched on the northern tip of the island, this once centre of trade in antiquity now reflects the renaissance of Santorini after the devastating earthquake of 1956. Restoration work has restored the beauty overwhelmingly enjoyed by visitors, though signs imploring visitors to be quiet and respectful remind you that for some, Oia is home year-round and a functioning village. You will struggle to find a more stunning spot in the Cyclades. Built on a steep slope of the caldera, many of its dwellings nestle in niches hewn into the volcanic rock.

Not surprisingly, Oia draws enormous numbers of tourists, and overcrowding is the price it pays for its good looks. Try to visit in the morning or spend the night here; afternoons and evenings often bring busloads from the cruise ships moored in the bay. At sunset the town feels like a magnet for every traveller on the island.

◎ SIGHTS

Ammoudi   Port
This tiny port of colourful fishing boats lies 300 steps below Oia. It's a steep haul down and up again but well worth it for the views of the blood-red cliffs, the harbour and back up at Oia. Once you're down there, have lunch at one of the excellent, if pricey, fish tavernas right on the water's edge.

In summer, boats and tours go from Ammoudi to Thirasia daily; check with travel agencies in Fira for departure times.

Maritime Museum   Museum
(☏22860 71156; €3; ☉10am-2pm & 5-8pm Wed-Mon) This museum is located along a narrow lane that leads off north from Nikolaou Nomikou. It's housed in a renovated and converted 19th-century mansion and has endearing displays on Santorini's maritime history. Oia's prosperity was based on its merchant fleet, which serviced the eastern Mediterranean, especially between Alexandria and Russia.

🜁 ACTIVITIES

Atlantis Oia   Diving
(☏22860 71158; https://atlantisoia.com; 1 dive €70, PADI course from €230; ☉8am-10pm) Helmed by stellar diving instructor Apostolos, this five-star diving outfit has been going strong for years and is the first of its kind – a member of Cousteau Divers – in all of Greece. Its deep commitment to marine conservation and enthusiastic, professional divemasters make Atlantis Oia a top pick for all manner of dives. Snorkelling outings also (€45). Find it off the main road.

Apostolos works closely with Pierre Cousteau, the son of legendary marine biologist Jacques Cousteau, in a bid to try to convince the Greek government to create a protected marine reserve around Santorini.

🔒 SHOPPING

Atlantis Books   Books
(☏22860 72346; www.atlantisbooks.org; Nikolaou Nomikou; ☉11am-8pm) Follow quotes and words that wind their way down the steep stairs into a little cavern with floor-to-ceiling shelves of books: fiction, philosophy, history, art and more. Staff are friendly and knowledgeable, and musicians and other events are hosted on the rooftop.

B.Loose   Clothing
(☏22860 27309; https://b-loose.gr; Pliarchon; ☉10am-9pm) Going strong for almost a decade, this is the Oia outlet of the Athens casual fashion label that specialises in comfortable, loose-fitting streetwear handmade from high-quality cotton and linen.

🍴 EATING

PitoGyros   Kebab €
(☏22860 71119; https://pitogyros.com; mains €3-11; ☉11am-11pm) You'll rarely find 'cheap' and 'Oia' in the same sentence, yet both apply to this souvlaki joint, a model of its kind. Go for a pitta filled with smoky, crisped meat with notes of tangy tzatziki and the crunch of onion, or fill your belly with a mixed grill platter, washed down with a Donkey craft beer.

Armeni   Seafood €€
(☏22860 71053; http://armenisantorinirestaurant.gr; mains €13-27; ☉10am-11pm) With the seashore literally at your table, this gem of a tavern is worth the steep ascent on foot to Armeni Bay (though you can also catch a boat from Amoudi Bay). This is an altar to seafood with a short and brilliantly executed menu of grilled sardines, calamari stuffed with local cheese, and fresh catch seared on the grill.

Karma   Greek €€
(☏22860 71404; www.karma.bz; mains €13-18; ☉dinner) With fountains, flickering candles, golden-coloured walls and wine-coloured cushions, this courtyard restaurant feels rather royal and august. The food is traditional and hearty (eg fava beans with caramelised onions and grilled sea bream with capers), and what you lack in caldera views you make up for with reasonable prices.

Lauda   Modern Greek €€€
(☏22860 72182; www.laudarestaurant.com; mains €48-135; ☉1-4.30pm & 6.30-10pm) One of the top fine dining experiences in Santorini – natch, in Greece! – Lauda

Special Ticket Package

A 'special ticket package' is available for the historic and cultural sites of Santorini. The four-day ticket (adult/child €14/7) covers entry to Ancient Thira (p213), Akrotiri (p213), the **Archaeological Museum** (Museum of Akrotiri; ☑22860 22217; M Nomikou; adult/concession €6/3; ⊙8.30am-4pm Wed-Mon), the Museum of Prehistoric Thera (p212) and the **Collection of Icons and Ecclesiastical Artefacts** at Pyrgos. Ask at any of these places.

Museum of Prehistoric Thera
HACKENBERG-PHOTO-COLOGNE/ALAMY STOCK PHOTO ©

morphed from Oia's humble first restaurant into a destination in its own right. Chef Emmanuel Renaut combines local produce with international cooking techniques, with stellar results. Splurge on a tasting menu or go for fish marinated with caper leaves, or slow-cooked lamb with gnocchi.

To Krinaki
Taverna €€€

(☑22860 71993; Finikia; mains €17-27; ⊙noon-late) All-fresh, all-local ingredients, such as wild greens, white aubergine, hand-crushed fava, caper leaves and wild asparagus go into top-notch taverna dishes at this homey spot in tiny Finikia, just east of Oia. Local beer and wine made from grape varieties grown in Santorini since antiquity, plus a sea (but not caldera) view looking north to Ios.

Catch
Fusion €€€

(☑22860 72063; https://catchrestaurant.gr; mains €26-39; ⊙6.30pm-2am) This new kid on the block stands out among Oia's other fusion offerings because it gets everything right. Service is efficient, ingredient-driven dishes – from sea bass tartare and grilled asparagus with Myconian cheese to wild mushroom risotto – are spot on, with beautiful presentation. There are terrific original cocktails, divided into four elements, plus sunset views from the terrace. Near the bus station.

1800
Greek €€€

(☑22860 71485; www.oia-1800.com; Nikolaou Nomikou; mains €15-38; ⊙noon-midnight) Housed in a restored sea captain's mansion, the artistically prepared, modern Greek cuisine has won this restaurant accolades for years. Sea bass with an aromatic spell of quinoa, artichoke and fennel puree or grilled lamb with sweet-and-sour green apple sauce give you a glimpse at the creative menu. Dine inside or on the caldera-view rooftop. Book ahead.

ℹ️ INFORMATION

ATMs can be found on Nikolaou Nomikou and also by the bus terminus.

Travel agencies such as **NS Travel** (☑22860 71199; www.nst-santorinitravel.com; ⊙9am-9pm) are found by the bus area; purchase ferry tickets here.

ℹ️ GETTING THERE & AWAY

In summer, buses leave Fira twice-hourly for Oia, with more services pre-sunset (€1.80). From the bus terminal, head left and uphill to reach the rather stark central square and the beautiful marble-lined main street, Nikolaou Nomikou, which skirts the caldera.

It's about a 15-minute drive or ride from Fira to Oia. There's public parking (follow the signs).

It takes around three hours to walk from Fira to Oia on a spectacular, well-trodden path along the top of the caldera.

A trip from Fira to Oia costs about €25 to €30. The taxi stop is at the bus station.

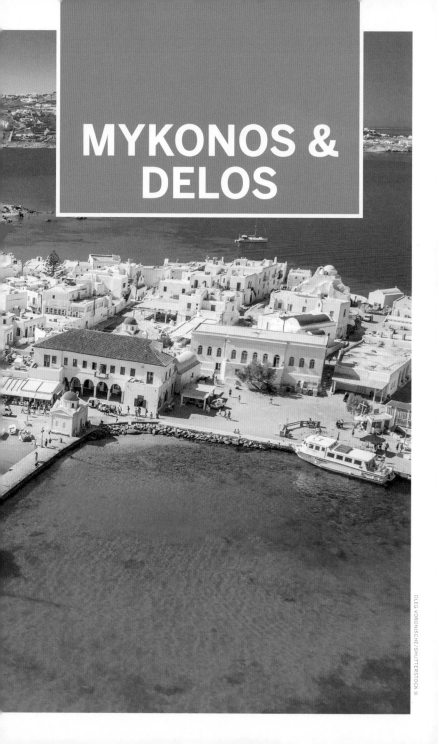

MYKONOS & DELOS

Mykonos & Delos at a Glance...

Mykonos is the great glamour island of Greece and flaunts its sizzling St-Tropez-meets-Ibiza style and party-hard reputation. Mykonos Town (aka Hora), the island's well-preserved port and capital, is a traditional whitewashed Cycladic maze, delighting in its cubist charms and its chichi cafe-bar-boutique scene. In the heart of the waterfront Little Venice quarter, tiny flower-bedecked churches jostle with glossy boutiques, and there's a cascade of bougainvillea around every corner. Mykonos is also the jumping-off point for the archaeological site of the nearby island of Delos.

Two Days in Mykonos

Choose your beach, spread your towel and settle in for the day. Spend the late afternoon and evening exploring the bars and shops of **Little Venice**. On day two catch the first boat out to the sacred island of **Delos** (p226).

Four Days in Mykonos

Lucky you – with an extra few days you can search out some of Mykonos' further flung and less crowded beaches such as **Agios Sostis** (p234). If you prefer company then **Elia** (p234) is ideal with both gay and nude sections.

Aegean Sea

Cape Armenistis

Cape Mavros

Agios Sostis

Mersini

Mersini Bay

Panormos

Fokos

Merchias Bay

Cape Evros

Agios Stefanos

Panormos Bay

New Port

Tourlos

Lake Marathi

Old Port

Marathi

Dragonisi

Hora (Mykonos)

Vothonas

Ano Mera

Tourliani Monastery

Cape Goni

Vrissi

Mykonos Airport

Korfos

Kapari

Ornos

Agrari

Cape Kalafatis

Agios Ioannis

Psarou

Platys Gialos

Elia

Elia

Psarou

Super Paradise

Cape Mavrokefalas

Delos

Cape Alogomandra

Nea Mykonos

Platys Gialos

Paradise

Paraga

Ancient Delos

Renia

See Hora (Mykonos) Map (p232)

Arriving in Mykonos

Mykonos Airport (p234), 3km southeast of Hora, has flights year-round from Athens as well as seasonal flights from Thessaloniki.

Year-round ferries serve mainland ports Piraeus and Rafina – the latter is usually quicker if you are coming directly from Athens airport. In the high season, Mykonos is well connected with all neighbouring islands.

Where to Stay

Mykonos Town may have the greatest variety of accommodation, but hotels, apartments and domatia are scattered throughout popular locations, such as Platys Gialos and Ornos. Paraga and Paradise Beach both have party hostels. Rooms in Mykonos Town tend to be compact, due to the historic architecture of the converted homes. It is not possible to stay on Delos.

Ruins

JEKATARINKA/SHUTTERSTOCK ©

Ancient Delos

The mythical birthplace of twins Apollo and Artemis, splendid Ancient Delos was a shrine turned sacred treasury and commercial centre. This Unesco World Heritage Site is one of the most important archaeological sites in Greece. Cast your imagination wide to transform this sprawling ruin into the magnificent city it once was.

Great For...

☑ **Don't Miss**

The Terrace of the Lions, the most photographed part of the Delos site.

History

Delos was first inhabited in the 3rd millennium BC. From the 8th century BC it became a shrine to Apollo, and the oldest temples date from this era. The dominant Athenians had full control of Delos – and thus the Aegean – by the 5th century BC.

Arriving at Ancient Delos

Boats disgorge visitors at the Sacred Harbour, where long queues form for the ticket gates. Most people then head left towards the **Sanctuary of Apollo**, the spiritual heart of the complex, but it's a large site and there's no need to follow the crowds. To the right is the **Theatre Quarter**, where Delos' wealthiest inhabitants lived in houses built around peristyle

Marble grave decoration, Archaeological Museum

DAVID TOMLINSON/ALAMY STOCK PHOTO ©

ⓘ Need to Know

☏22890 22259; museum & site adult/ concession €12/6; ⊗8am-8pm Apr-Oct, to 2pm Nov-Mar

✕ Take a Break

There is no cafe operating on the island; it pays to bring water and food.

★ Top Tip

The steep path leading up **Mt Kynthos** is worth the climb for the terrific views of the encircling islands.

courtyards, with intricate, colourful mosaics. Beyond this are the Sanctuaries of the Foreign Gods and the path leading up **Mt Kynthos**. Allow the best part of an hour to visit the excellent **Archaeological Museum** (⊗8am-8pm mid-Apr–Oct) **FREE**. If there's time remaining, take the path beyond the museum to the **Stadium Quarter**.

Sanctuaries of the Foreign Gods

Delos was a place of worship for many cultures beyond the Greeks, and their temples are concentrated in the area called the **Sanctuaries of the Foreign Gods** on the slope of Mt Kynthos. The remains of a 1st-century BC synagogue have also been uncovered near the stadium.

The Kabeiroi, a mysterious group of Samothracian deities, were worshipped at **Samothrakeion**.

Built in around 150 BC, the **Sanctuary of the Syrian Gods** was dedicated to the Syrian gods Atargatis and Hadad, who were popular in the Greek world.

Deities including Serapis and Isis were honoured at the **Sanctuary of the Egyptian Gods**.

Getting There & Away

Boats for Delos leave Hora (Mykonos) at 9am, 10am, 11.30am and 5pm from May to October, returning at noon, 1.30pm, 3pm and 7.30pm. On Mondays throughout the year, and daily from November to April, only the 10am boat operates, returning at 1.30pm. The journey takes 30 minutes. Tickets are sold from the **Delos Boat Ticket Kiosk** (☏22890 28603; www.delostours. gr; adult/child return ticket €20/10), located at the foot of the jetty at the southern end of Mykonos' old harbour.

A Stroll Around Hora

This short stroll takes in Hora's key sights while introducing you to the main routes through the maze of streets.

Start Agia Anna beach

Distance 1.4km

Duration 30 minutes

Classic Photo Panagia Paraportiani

2 The landmark whitewashed church **Panagia Paraportiani** (p230) looks like it has grown organically from the rock.

3 Little Venice is a picturesque row of houses with balconies jutting over the water.

Aegean Sea

Paraportianis   Karaoli Dimitriou

Agion Anargyron

Venetias

Plateia Alefkandra

Mitropoleos

FINISH

5 Hora's famous row of seven **windmills** (p230) were built by Venetians in the 16th century.

N
0   200 m
0   0.1 miles

Port

START

Polikandrioti

Akti Kambani

Plateia Manto Mavrogenous

Agiou Ioannou

1 The golden arc of **Agia Anna** is named after little St Anne's Church near its southern end.

Take a Break...
Nice n Easy (p233) has the best brunch option with a great view of Hora's windmills.

Agiou Efthimiou

Fabrika Square (Plateia Yialos)

Agiou Ioannou

4 On Plateia Alefkandra is the 17th-century Catholic church **Our Lady of the Rosary**.

Hora

Hora (also known as Mykonos), the island's well-preserved port and capital, is a warren of narrow lanes and whitewashed buildings overlooked by the town's famous windmills. In the heart of the medieval maze – which was intentionally designed to be confusing so as to baffle raiders – tiny flower-bedecked churches jostle with glossy boutiques, and there's a cascade of bougainvillea around every corner.

This 'Greek-island village by central casting' scenario comes at a price: people. In the high season, multiple cruise ships disgorge slow-moving phalanxes of flag followers, joining the catwalk cast of wannabe Instagram influencers, celebrity spotters and gay party boys squeezing past the chic stores, cafes and bars.

◉ SIGHTS

Despite its tiny size, without question, you'll get lost in Hora. It's entertaining at first, but can become frustrating amid throngs of equally lost people and fast-moving locals. For quick-fix navigation, head to the

Windmill, Hora harbour

ALENA VEASEY/SHUTTERSTOCK ©

water and trace around the periphery of the maze before diving back in – even if there's a more direct route. It's also worth familiarising yourself with Plateia Manto Mavrogenous (Taxi Sq), and the three main streets of Matogianni, Enoplon Dynameon and Mitropoleos, which form a horseshoe through the centre.

Archaeological Museum of Mykonos   Museum

(☑22890 22325; Agiou Stefanou; adult/child €4/2; ⊙9am-4pm Sun, Mon & Wed, to 9pm Thu-Sat Apr-Oct, 9am-4pm Tue-Sun Nov-Mar) A headless, almost limbless 2nd-century BC statue of Hercules in Parian marble is the highlight of this small, well-presented collection. Otherwise it's very heavy on pottery and funerary *stelae* (carved monuments), much of it sourced from Delos and the neighbouring island of Rineia, which served as its cemetery. Periodic exhibitions incorporate contemporary art and design into the displays.

Panagia Paraportiani   Church

(Paraportianis) Built between the 15th and 17th centuries, Mykonos' most famous church comprises four small chapels – plus another on an upper storey reached by an exterior staircase. It's usually locked, but the fabulously photogenic, whitewashed, rock-like exterior is the drawcard.

Windmills   Windmill

(off Plateia Alefkandra) Constructed in the 16th century by the Venetians for the milling of wheat, seven of Mykonos' iconic windmills are picturesquely situated on a small hill overlooking the harbour.

Rarity Gallery   Gallery

(☑22890 25761; www.raritygallery.com; Kalogera 20-22; ⊙10am-11pm) **FREE** This excellent little gallery is well worth a peek for its temporary exhibitions that showcase contemporary paintings, sculpture and photography.

Aegean Maritime Museum   Museum

(☑22890 22700; www.aegean-maritime-museum.gr; Enoplon Dynameon 10; adult/student

€4/2; ⊙10.30am-1pm & 6.30-9pm Apr-Oct)
Amid the barnacle-encrusted amphorae,
ye olde nautical maps and navigation
instruments, there are numerous detailed
models of famous sailing ships and paddle
steamers. You can also learn the difference
between an Athenian trireme, a Byzantine
dromon and an ancient Egyptian seagoing
ship. There's an enormous Fresnel lighthouse lantern in the courtyard.

Mykonos Folklore Museum   Museum
(☎22890 22591; Paraportianis; by donation;
⊙10.30am-2pm & 5.30-8.30pm Mon-Sat Apr-
Oct) FREE Housed in an 18th-century sea
captain's house, this moderately interesting museum features a large collection of
furnishings and other artefacts, including a
cellar full of nautical objects.

🔒 SHOPPING

Muse   Gifts & Souvenirs
(☎22890 77370; Dilou 8; ⊙11am-3pm & 5-11pm)
Pick up a fluoro Greek god, a marble figurine modelled on the blank-faced Cycladic
originals or a replica of the classical art,
jewellery and ceramics that fill the nation's
museums.

Art & Soul   Art
(☎22890 27244; www.mykonosgallery.com;
Mavrogenous 18; ⊙10am-11pm) Run by the
Rousounelos family for over 30 years, this
gallery is for serious collectors. On display
you'll find sculpture and paintings by
renowned Greek artists, each sold with a
certificate of authenticity.

HEEL Athens Lab   Fashion, Accessories
(☎22890 77166; www.heel.gr; Panahrantou;
⊙11am-2am Apr-Oct) 🌿 Ecologically friendly
women's garments made from organic cotton and other sustainable fibres, as well as
one-of-a-kind jewellery made from recycled
materials.

✖ EATING

Taste Diaries   Crêpes €
(☎22890 29117; www.facebook.com/TheTaste
Diaries; Akti Kambani; mains €5.80-11; ⊙8am-

⚧ LGBT+ Mykonos

Mykonos is one of the most popular
beach-holiday destinations in the world
for gay men. Days are spent at glitzy Super Paradise (p235) or cruisy Elia Beach
(p234) before heading back to Hora for
a disco nap and a costume change. The
first stop of the evening is traditionally
Elysium Sunset Bar (☎22890 23952;
www.elysiumhotel.com; School of Fine Arts
District; ⊙6-10pm Apr-Oct) for views,
extortionately priced drinks and hit-
and-miss drag shows before hitting the
bars in town: **Lola** (☎22890 78391; Zanni
Pitaraki 4; ⊙8pm-3.30am; 🐾) for camp
and cocktails, or **Porta** (☎22890 27807;
www.portabar-mykonos.com; Ioanni Voinovich
5; ⊙10pm-5am) for flattering lighting and
a more blokey vibe. Everyone inevitably
ends up wiggling their hips at **JackieO'**
(☎22890 77298; www.jackieomykonos.
com; Old Harbour; ⊙sunset-sunrise) − but
don't think of arriving before 11pm −
then switching to **Babylon** (☎22890
25152; www.facebook.com/babylonmyk; Akti
Kambani; ⊙7.30pm-6am) or **@54** (☎22890
28543; www.facebook.com/at54Club; Plateia
Manto Mavrogenous; ⊙9pm-4am; 🐾) occasionally for a change of scene.

Party people should visit in late
August for XLSIOR (www.xlsiorfestival.
com), a huge gay clubbing festival that
draws some 30,000 revellers.

Super Paradise
UMUT ROSA/SHUTTERSTOCK ©

3am May, Jun, Sep & Oct, 24hr Jul & Aug; 🐾) If
you've got a craving for sweet or savoury
crêpes, waffles or creamy yoghurt – any

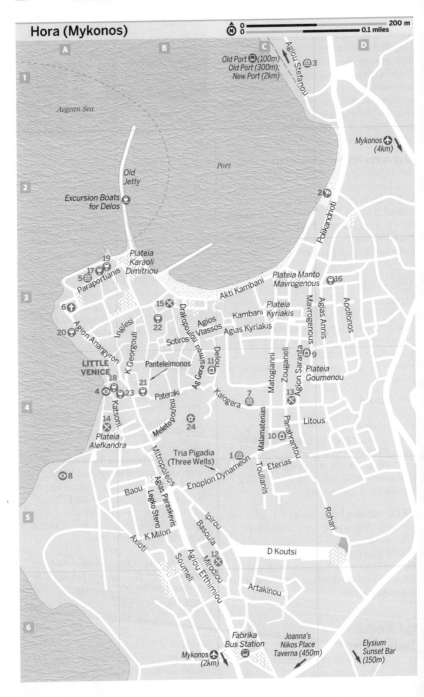

Hora (Mykonos)

200 m
0.1 miles

Aegean Sea

Old Port (100m)
Old Port (300m);
New Port (2km)

Agiou Stefanou

3

Port

Mykonos
(4km)

Old
Jetty

Excursion Boats
for Delos

2

Polikandrioti

Plateia
Karaoli
Dimitriou

19
17
5
Paraportianis

Plateia Manto
Mavrogenous

16

6

Akti Kambani

15

Drakopoulou

Ag Gerasimou

Agios
Vlassos

Kambani

Plateia
Kyriakis

Mavrogenous

Agias Annis

Apollonos

20

Agion Anargyron

Inglesi

22

Sotiros

Agias Kyriakis

9

LITTLE
VENICE

K Georgouli

Panteleimonos

18

21

Deilou

Zouganeli

Agion Saranta

Plateia
Goumenou

4
23

Pateraki

Kalogera

7

13

Katsoni

Meleto

Litous

14

24

Malamatenias

Matogianni

Panahrandou

Plateia
Alefkandra

10

8

Tria Pigadia
(Three Wells)

1

Enoplon Dynameon

Eterias

Toulianis

Mitropoleos

Baou

Agias Paraskevis

Lego Steno

Ipirou

Rohari

Axioti

K Milon

Basoula

D Koutsi

12

Agiou Efthimiou

Miradiou

Soumeli

Artakinou

Fabrika
Bus Station

Joanna's
Nikos Place
Taverna (450m)

Elysium
Sunset Bar
(150m)

Mykonos
(2km)

Hora (Mykonos)

time of the day or night in peak season – this is the place to come. It's a satisfying breakfast option, and it serves sandwiches and salads as well.

Joanna's Nikos Place Taverna €€
(☏22890 24251; Megali Ammos; mains €9-16; ⏰10am-11pm; 🐾) Run by the delightful Joanna herself and overlooking the beach just a few minutes' walk south of the windmills, this taverna focuses on Greek standards and it does them very well, particularly the zucchini fritters, Mykonian egg and fennel pie, *mousakas* and the mixed grill.

Nice n Easy Cafe €€
(☏22890 25421; www.niceneasy.gr; Plateia Alefkandra; mains €15-23, breakfasts €9-15; ⏰10am-12.30am; 🐾📶) With a great view of Mykonos' windmills from its seafront terrace, this Athenian outpost is Mykonos' best brunch option, serving hangover-assuaging eggs Benedict and healthier options such as avocado on toast, egg-white omelettes, quinoa salad and various vegan offerings. As the day progresses, burgers, sandwiches and quesadillas vie with traditional Greek fare.

Funky Kitchen European €€€
(☏22890 27272; www.funkykitchen.gr; Ignatiou Basoula 40; mains €21-26; ⏰6pm-late May-Oct; 🐾) The open kitchen of this contemporary

restaurant brings forth beautifully presented dishes marrying Mediterranean flavours with French techniques. Dishes such as octopus carpaccio with pink peppercorns, grilled fish in a *buerre blanc* sauce, and seared tuna with smoky baba ganoush might tempt you back for a repeat visit. The chocolate nirvana is heavenly.

M-Eating Mediterranean €€€
(☏22890 78550; www.m-eating.gr; Kalogera 10; mains €24-42; ⏰7pm-1am; 🐾) Attentive service, soft lighting and relaxed luxury are the hallmarks of this creative restaurant specialising in fresh Greek produce prepared with flair. Options might include the likes of Cycladic fish soup, tuna cakes served on mashed fava beans and sous vide lamb, but save room for the Mykonian honey pie.

🍸 DRINKING & NIGHTLIFE
Katerina's Bar Cocktail Bar
(☏22890 23084; www.katerinaslittlevenice mykonos.com; Agion Anargyron 8; ⏰9am-3am; 🐾) Katerina's makes no effort to be glamorous or, heaven forbid, cool – INXS is likely to be played at some point in the night – but it consequently manages to have more fun than most places in Little Venice. What is unbelievably cool is that it's owned by

the first female Greek naval captain. Plus there's an ace little balcony.

Galleraki
Cocktail Bar

(☎22890 27188; www.galleraki.com; Little Venice; ⊙10am-5am; 🛜) Choose plum waterfront seating or the upstairs balcony at this friendly cafe-bar, and order one of its fresh-fruit cocktails (like the signature 'katerinaki', made with melon) or a classic champagne concoction.

Semeli
Cocktail Bar

(☎22890 26505; www.semelithebar.gr; Little Venice; ⊙9am-late) This slick cocktail bar in the heart of Little Venice draws the bold and the beautiful with its signature cocktails and DJ sets.

⊛ ENTERTAINMENT

Cine Manto
Cinema

(☎22890 26165; www.cinemanto.gr; Meletopou-lou; adult/child €9/7; ⊙9pm & 11pm Jun-Sep) Need a break from the bars and clubs? Seek out this gorgeous open-air cinema in a garden setting. There's a cafe here, too. Movies are shown in their original language; view the program online.

ⓘ INFORMATION

Mykonos has no tourist office; visit travel agencies instead. Online, visit **Mykonos Traveller** (☎69869 93013; www.mykonostraveller.com), www.inmykonos.com and www.mykonos.gr for more information.

Delia Travel (☎22890 22322; www.facebook.com/delia.travel.mykonos; Akti Kambani; ⊙9am-9pm) Sells ferry and Delos tickets, and books accommodation and hire cars.

Hospital (☎22890 23994; Argyrena) Near the big roundabout on the road to Ano Mera.

Mykonos Trauma Care (☎22890 78549; www.mykonos-orthopedics.com; Argyrena; ⊙24hr) Private emergency-care clinic, located close to the hospital.

Sea & Sky (☎22890 28240; www.seasky.gr; Akti Kambani; ⊙8.30am-9.30pm) Information, aeroplane, ferry and Delos tickets.

ⓘ GETTING THERE & AWAY

Hora is the transport hub of the island. The Old Port Bus Station has services to the northwest and east of the island, while the **airport** (JMK; ☎22890 79000; www.mykonos-airport.com) and beaches to the southwest are served by the **Fabrika Bus Station** (Fabrika Sq).

There are various car-rental agencies around town, including **Apollon** (☎22890 24136; www.apollonrentacar.com; Periferiaki; ⊙9am-8pm) and **Anemos** (☎22890 24607; www.mykonosrentcar.com; Peri).

Excursion boats for Delos leave from the pier directly in front of the town; tickets can be purchased from a nearby kiosk (p227).

Mykonos' Beaches

Mykonos' golden-sand beaches in their formerly unspoilt state were the pride of Greece. Now most are jammed with umbrellas and backed by beach bars, but they do make for a hopping scene that draws floods of beachgoers. Moods range from the simply hectic to the outright snobby, and nudity levels vary.

Without your own wheels, catch buses from Hora or boats from Ornos and Platys Gialos to further beaches. **Mykonos Sea Transfer** (☎22890 23995; www.mykonosseatransfer.com; ⊙8am-7pm Apr-Oct) has an online timetable of its sea-taxi services.

Agios Sostis
Beach

This gorgeous, wide strip of golden sand receives far fewer visitors than the south coast. There's no shade and only limited parking but there's a popular taverna with a little sheltered cove directly below it.

Elia
Beach

This beautiful stretch of golden sand has craggy cliffs on either side and an excellent waterfront restaurant. It's backed by some large resorts and, consequently, rows of recliners line the sand. A rainbow flag down the western end (to the right facing the water) marks the gay section. Just past here is the beginning of the nude area; most of the guys head to a tiny cove a little further along the path. Buses head here, via Ano Mera, from the Old Port station.

Kapari   Beach
Scooped out of the surrounding cliffs, this very appealing sandy cove is reached via a short walk along an unpaved track from the western end of **Agios Ioannis**.

Mersini   Beach
Practically deserted sandy beach with calm waters, reachable via an unpaved road.

Panormos   Beach
A chunk of this gorgeous sandy beach is given over to a pretentious beach-bar complex, but that still leaves a large expanse of golden sand to spread out on. There's a good taverna here as well.

Paradise   Beach
Clear waters and golden sands make this one of the island's most famous beaches. It's completely lined with noisy beach bars and rows of umbrellas, but the service (particularly at Tropicana) is friendly and attentive. There's a camping resort here, a dive centre, an excellent Indian restaurant and the island's most highly rated club.

Regular buses head here from Hora's Fabrika station.

Paraga   Beach
This beautiful crescent-shaped cove became popular in the hippy era and is still known for its beach parties. There's a good selection of tavernas, plus a party hostel, a small gay section and a nudist area. Buses head here from Hora's Fabrika station.

Platys Gialos   Beach
One of Mykonos' most popular beaches, this broad stretch of white sand is lined with restaurants and has an excellent water sports centre. Buses head here from Hora's Fabrika station.

Psarou   Beach
A long stretch of white sand and teal waters, favoured by local cognoscenti. It's a short walk from Platys Gialos.

Tourliani Monastery

Located in the centre of Ano Mera, Mykonos' other main settlement, this castle-like **monastery** (€1; ⊗10am-1pm & 3.30-7pm) was founded in 1537 but rebuilt in 1767. It has a gorgeous domed church with an ornate, gilded iconostasis, and a small museum displaying vestments, historic documents and icons.

Altar and icons, Tourliani Monastery
ARMANDO BORGES/ALAMY STOCK PHOTO ©

Fokos   Beach
This little-visited sandy beach on the north coast has a good taverna, but you'll need an ATV to tackle the rutted road.

Agrari   Beach
There's lots of free sand to spread out on at this lovely sandy cove, and a beach bar to retreat to if you get parched. There are no buses but it's easily reached via a short walk from Elia Beach.

Super Paradise   Beach
Flashy, trashy and great for people-watching – Super Paradise is Mykonos' most popular gay-friendly beach. The action is split between the glitzy JackieO' Beach Club (p231) on the southern headland and the Super Paradise beach bar on the sands.

During the season, a private bus service connects the beach to Hora's Fabrika bus station.

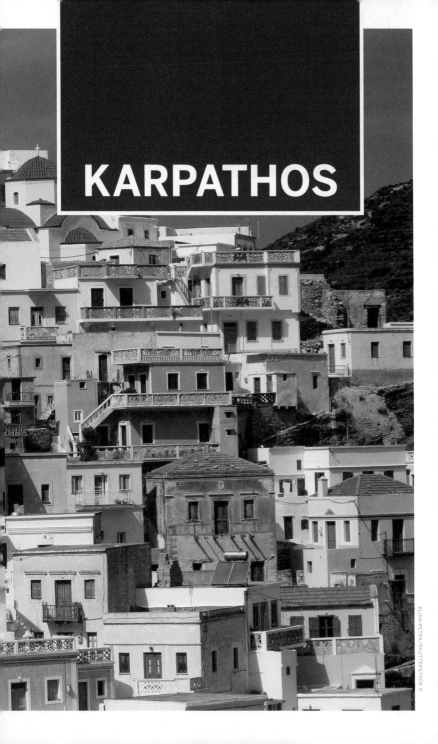

KARPATHOS

Karpathos at a Glance...

Celebrated for its wild mountains and blue coves, this long craggy island is among the least commercialised in Greece (although that is changing). Legend has it Prometheus and his Titans were born here, and with its cloud-wrapped villages and rugged beauty, there's still something undeniably primal in the air. The island's highlight is Olymbos, a time-forgotten settlement perched atop a perilous mountain ridge and where the local women still wear traditional garb. Southern Karpathos offers good beaches and is in the spotlight each summer when it hosts an international kitesurfing competition.

Two Days in Karpathos

Explore Karpathos' capital **Pigadia** (p242) or relax on **Apella Beach** (p243), 17km north of town, before setting off later in the day for the picturesque traditional village of **Olymbos** (p240) where you'll spend the night. Enjoy the spectacular sunset and jaw dropping panoramic views from this hilltop eyrie.

Four Days in Karpathos

A couple of extra days on the island can easily be swallowed up exploring the southern beach resorts of **Arkasa** (p244; near where you can learn to surf), **Finiki** (p245; good for swimming) and **Lefkos** (p245; the most beautiful crescent of sand).

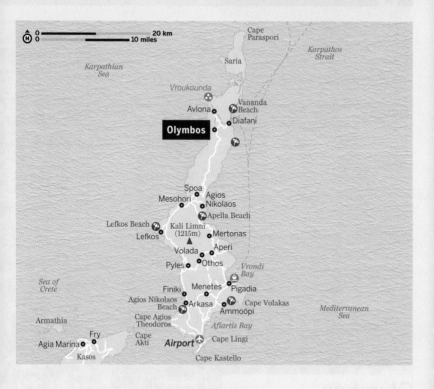

Arriving in Karpathos

The airport (p243) at the very southern tip of Karpathos is served by Olympic Air and Sky Express with connections to Athens, Rhodes and Crete.

The island's main port, Pigadia (p244), is served by Blue Star Ferries and Anek Lines (which stops at Diafani) with connections to/from Rhodes and Santorini among other places.

Where to Stay

There's plenty of choice from simple pensions, to traditional rustic rooms with platform beds. High-end options are resort style, rather than boutique.

Pigadia, Karpathos' capital and main ferry port, is a handy base, but there are more visually appealing places on the island to stay, such as Olymbos, especially if you fancy some high-mountain hiking or swimming at remote beaches.

Assumption of Virgin Mary

IZZET KERIBAR/ALAMY STOCK PHOTO ©

Olymbos

At the northern end of Karpathos, clinging to the side of Mt Profitis Elias (716m), Olymbos is one of Greece's most traditional and well-preserved villages.

Great For...

☑ **Don't Miss**

Olymbos' local ladies still wear their stunning hand-spun jackets and floral headgear.

Given its strategic remoteness high above the Aegean Sea, this tiny hamlet was isolated – and operated as a closed society – for centuries. The first residents fled there in the 7th century to avoid pirates. They tapped into spring waters, laboured at terraces for farming, and built windmills for processing their grains. Meanwhile, from their mountainous refuge, they had the perfect vantage point to spot enemies.

Eventually, a road was constructed in the 1970s (it was sealed only recently); it snakes along the spine of the island's northern mountain range with precipitous drops and jaw-dropping views. Visitors (both then and now) will find a proud village full of tiny pedestrian-only, stone alleyways. Here, elderly women still wear their traditional woven dresses and goatskin boots.

Women carrying Easter bread

❶ Need to Know

Arrive in late afternoon or early morning to have the place to yourself.

✖ Take a Break

Located next to a working windmill, **O Mylos** (☎22450 51333; mains €7-14; ⏱lunch & dinner) serves Karpathian dishes, some of which are cooked in a traditional oven.

★ Top Tip

Stay the night to witness an incredible sunset and experience the village at peace.

Some locals live in the historic houses (with the raised beds known as *soufas*) and partake in traditional celebrations and festivals, known for their colourful processions. They still sing ancient songs called *mantinades*, with on-the-spot lyrics comprising 15-syllable lines.

These days, however, tourism is the village's main source of income; considered a living museum, Olymbos juggles traditionalism with commercialism. And, it's difficult to do both, especially with the expectations of visitors who expect nothing but 'traditional'. In summer, in particular, the village has a theme-park-like atmosphere, when hordes of tourists, especially daytrippers who arrive via boat to Diafani and connecting bus – flock into the tiny alleys.

Regardless, it's a lovely spot to visit and the locals, men and women, are particularly welcoming and obliging. You can wander through the tiny lanes, and soak up the atmosphere in the **Assumption of Virgin Mary**, the 17th-century church, built in a Byzantine style, complete with a decorative wooden iconostasis. Pop into any of the *kafeneia* (traditional cafes) to enjoy a morning coffee or an evening raki. Chat to the ladies selling their handcrafts (though be realistic: there are only so many handwoven tablecloths one woman can make in winter after all; not everything will be locally spun, woven and sewn). Chat to the island's last cobbler who makes the traditional *stivania* boots worn by the women. Stop to marvel at the windmills.

Pigadia

Karpathos' capital and main ferry port, Pigadia sprawls beside a long bay in the island's southeast. Decent beaches stretch away to the north, backed by large resorts. The town lacks the photogenic good looks and geometrically pleasing whitewashed houses of other island capitals, but it makes up for this. For here, it's about the people, who are proudly, determinedly Greek. Give it a little time and wander its harbour and among waterfront bars and backstreet bakeries. Chat to the locals who frequently invite you to sit by them for a coffee. This place will grow on you.

✪ ACTIVITIES

Between May and October, excursion boats start at Pigadia harbour and call at Diafani en route. Pre-arranged buses connect Diafani with Olympos (total cost around €25). For around €10 you can be dropped off at a beach, or up to €25 for a day trip to Saria Island. Other boats may also run to Ahata, Kato Lakos, Kyra Panagia and Apella.

Tavern, Pigadia

PAWEL KAZMIERCZAK/SHUTTERSTOCK ©

✖ EATING & DRINKING

Both the quay and the pedestrian streets just behind it are lined with seafood tavernas, all-purpose brasseries, cafes and cocktail bars. Look out, too, for the Italian gelaterias on Apodimon Karpathion, parallel to the harbour.

Pretty much any one of the waterfront bars and cafes is ideal for a sunset drink or two.

Pantheon Cafe   Cafe €

(☑22450 22502; Papathanassiou; snacks €5-12; ⊙8am-late; ✳🛜) The pick of the best-of-both-worlds cafes along this pedestrian street, with a fine old wood-panelled interior decorated in *kafeneio* style of old, and a rear balcony terrace, perched high above the harbour with fabulous views. Sure, you can get a full English breakfast (€11) but it's the salads that really hit the spot. Go for the Karpathian (€9, with cucumber, olives and local bread).

Orea Karpathos   Taverna €

(☑22450 22501; Harbour; mains €7-15; ⊙noon-midnight) Smart and efficient, this quayside taverna near the ferry jetty serves authentic Karpathian specialities such as *makarounes* (homemade pasta with caramelised onions and cheese). It's known for sourcing local products where possible. Most meat mains cost under €12, and a whole grilled fish is more like €13 to €15.

To Ellenikon   Taverna €€

(☑22450 23932; Apodimon Karpathion; mains €8-20; ⊙lunch & dinner; ✳🛜✏) If you're looking for typical Karpathian food cooked the way it should be then 'the Greek' is your place. Try *saganaki* (fried cheese), meatballs, shrimp and calamari, served within the wood-accented traditional interior or outside on the narrow terrace. Also offers hefty, more 'international' dishes should you want a change. Owner, Christos, meets and greets and works the floor.

Akropolis   Brasserie €€

(☑22450 23278; Apodimon Karpathion; mains €13-28; ⊙breakfast, lunch & dinner; ✳🛜) This handsome harbourfront cafe-restaurant has a billowing ceiling arrangement and overly perfect white chairs and striped covers. And it draws in the tourists for everything from breakfast to a sunset cocktail and dinner, plus the lovely outlook to the sea beyond. The menu is strong on standard Greek faves, plus every cut of meat suitable to an American steakhouse.

Odyssey — Greek €€

(☎22450 23506; www.facebook.com/OdyseyRestaurantKarpathos; Harbour; mains €7-13.50) Owner Pascales comes from the region of Macedonia, so don't expect things to be served the same way here, despite having the same menu listings. Your culinary odyssey will include delicious dolmadhes (with lemon and oil), eggplant salad that's grilled (not boiled), and pastas and grilled meats with different herbs. Mains are served with vegetables – a welcome treat.

Caffe Karpathos — Cafe

(Angolo Italiano; ☎21022 87383; www.cafekarpathos.com; Apodimon Karpathion; ⊙7am-late; 🛜) The oldest cafe on the island was once a magnet for Italians (thus the fabulous coffee served in the original Bialetti espresso pots). These days travellers and locals alike nestle into wicker chairs, with a fabulous brew or cocktail in hand, and philosophise with Michalis, the multilingual owner. Simply relax and chat, Greek style. It's a thrill in itself.

Enplo — Cocktail Bar

(cocktails €6; ⊙8am-late; 🛜) This chilled spot on the quay offers good happy-hour cocktails (from €8). Its impressive snack menu has six vegan options.

ⓘ INFORMATION

Both the National Bank of Greece on Apodimon Karpathion, and Alpha Bank, a block higher on Dimokratias, have ATMs.

Police (☎22450 22223) Near the hospital at the western end of town.

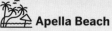
🌴 Apella Beach

However determined you may be to reach Olymbos, allow time to take the precipitous spur road that drops seawards from the east-coast highway 17km north of Pigadia. Here you'll find award-winning Apella Beach; backed by a cascading hillside of wildflowers, with towering cliffs to both the north and south, it is the finest beach in the Dodecanese. It's often described as 'sandy', though it was pebbly when we were there. Nevertheless, it's gorgeous. There's a good taverna at road's end, just above the beach.

Apella Beach
PAWEL KAZMIERCZAK/SHUTTERSTOCK ©

Possi Travel (☎22450 23342; 28 Oktovriou; ⊙8am-1pm & 5-8pm) The main travel agency for ferry and air tickets. The helpful staff speak excellent English.

Post Office (Ethnikis Andistasis) Near the hospital.

Tourist Office (www.karpathos.org; ⊙Jul & Aug) Summer-only kiosk, in the middle of the seafront.

ⓘ GETTING THERE & AROUND

The airport is 14km southwest of Pigadia. A taxi will cost around €25. From Monday to Friday there is a daily bus departure to the airport from Pigadia (€3), but don't count on getting from the airport (at the time of research it departed at 7am).

Pigadia has the island's main port, served by **Blue Star Ferries** (☎22410 22461; www.blue

Finiki port

starferries.com; Amerikis 111, New Town; ⊘9am-8pm) and **Anek Lines** (Map p258; ✆22410 35066; www.anek.gr/en; 5 Akti Sahtouri).

Pigadia's **bus station** (✆22450 22338; M Mattheou), just up from the harbour, is served by KTEL buses, which travel infrequently to various destinations across the island. You can obtain printed schedules from the station's tiny office.

There's a **taxi** (✆22450 22705; Dimokratias) stand up the hill from the harbourfront; a sign shows destinations and costs.

Given the size of the island it makes sense to rent a car. Many car-rental chains are based at the airport plus a couple of excellent in-town options will arrange pick-up. **Euromoto** (✆22450 23238, 6970130912; www.euromoto.com; scooter/car from €15/45) offers reliable rental cars; owner George knows his stuff and can help point you in the right direction, too.

Menetes

Buffeted by mountain gales, the tiny village of Menetes sits high in the cliffs just above Pigadia. Climb to the church at its highest point before exploring its narrow whitewashed streets to find the two-room **Folklore Museum** (✆6985847672; ⊘9am-1pm & 5-8pm) FREE in an ancient chapel, and the welcoming taverna **Dionysos Fiesta** (✆22450 81269 mains €6-10; ⊘breakfast, lunch & dinner; ❈🛜) run by ultra-friendly Irini.

Southern Beaches

Arkasa is one of the oldest settlements on Karpathos. The original village centre, just up from the water, is now complemented by a burgeoning beach resort below. A waterside track leads 500m to the remains of the 5th-century **Basilica of Agia Sophia**, where two chapels stand amid mosaic fragments and columns, and to an ancient acropolis on the headland beyond.

The best beach hereabouts, sandy **Agios Nikolaos Beach** is accessible from the village, but you'll need to drive there. This is the island's only surf beach; learn how to hang ten on a surfboard or a windsurfer at **Surfvival Surf School & Shop** (✆6989805037; www.surfvivalschool. com; Agios Nikolaos Beach, Arcesine; class per person from €55).

Arrayed along a neat little south-facing crescent bay, picturesque **Finiki** stands just 2km north of Arkasa. White-and-blue houses, interspersed with a peppering of tavernas, front its sleepy harbour and small grey-sand beach. The best local swimming is at **Agios Georgios Beach**, a short way south towards Arkasa. Laid back taverna **Marina Taverna** (☎22450 61100; Finiki; mains €7-16; ☺breakfast, lunch & dinner; ☎) is open all year and features an expansive terrace that surveys the gentle turquoise bay just metres from the waterfront.

The largest and most attractive of the low-key west-coast resorts, **Lefkos** is 20km north of Finiki and a 5km detour down from the main road. The curving sandy beach here is absolutely delightful. This is the kind of place where two weeks can vanish in gentle wanderings between beach and brunch.

Diafani

Diafani is an intimate, wind-blasted huddle of white houses fronted by cobalt-blue water, with a mountain backdrop. Bar the crash of the waves and old men playing backgammon, nothing else stirs. Most travellers simply pass through Diafani, so if you stay you'll likely have the beaches and trails to yourself. There's no post office or petrol station, but there is an ATM (but no bank).

✪ ACTIVITIES

Hiking trails from Diafani village are waymarked with red or blue markers or stone cairns. The most popular route heads inland, straight up the valley to Olympos. That takes around two hours – though some prefer to catch a bus uphill and walk back down. Alternatively, a 4km track (50 minutes) leads north along the coast, through the pines, to **Vananda Beach**, which has a seasonal taverna.

A more strenuous three-hour walk takes you 11km northwest to the Hellenistic site of **Vroukounda**, passing the agricultural vil-

lage of **Avlona** along the way. There are no facilities, so carry food and water with you.

Anyone planning serious walking should get hold of the 1:60,000 *Karpathos-Kasos* map, published by Terrain Maps (www.terrainmaps.gr) and available in Pigadia. Note: conditions change regularly on these paths and each season they can get a little straggly. Check with locals before you head out.

Boat excursions head north daily from Diafani to inaccessible beaches on Karpathos and the nearby island of Saria.

⊗ EATING

There are a number of decent restaurants here, most of them around the waterfront, though a couple are behind town, too.

Corali   Taverna €
(☎22450 51332; mains €7-12; ☺lunch & dinner) Run by Popi and Mihalis, this is *the* spot for fresh, tasty traditional fare. These spontaneous creatives whip up the likes of delicious *stifadho* (meat or seafood cooked with onions in a tomato puree) or eggplant. The salads are tops; vegetables are sourced locally. Service is slow but the quality of the food and *filoxenia* (hospitality) make up for it.

✪ GETTING THERE & AWAY

Anek ferries call in at Diafani's small jetty twice a week en route to/from Pigadia, Halki and Rhodes, and three times weekly en route to/from Pigadia and Kasos (€4, one hour). One of these continues to, or returns from, Crete (€19, eight hours) while two other services head to/from Santorini (€27, 15½ hours). There are also day trips by boat to Pigadia in summer, as well as assorted excursions (from €10 per person).

Tourist coaches carry day trippers from the jetty up to Olympos. Unfortunately for both locals and tourists, there's only one weekly bus to/from Pigadia, but in summer services can increase (via Olympos).

RHODES

Rhodes at a Glance...

By far the largest and historically the most important of the Dodecanese islands, Rhodes (ro-dos) abounds in beaches, wooded valleys and ancient history. Whether you arrive in search of buzzing nightlife, languid sun worshipping, diving in crystal-clear waters or to embark on a culture-vulture journey through past civilisations, it's all here. The atmospheric Old Town of Rhodes is a maze of cobbled streets that will spirit you back to the days of the Byzantine Empire and beyond. Further south is the picture-perfect town of Lindos, a soul-warming vista of sugar-cube houses spilling down to a turquoise bay.

Two Days in Rhodes

Spend day one in Lindos touring the **Acropolis** (p250) before returning to Rhodes Town (p256) and enjoying dinner at **Marco Polo Cafe** (p260). On day two navigate the cobbled alleyways of the Old Town making sure to take in the view from the ramparts. Devote a few hours to the **Archaeological Museum** (p256).

Four Days in Rhodes

With an extra few days you'll have time to properly explore Rhodes Town, taking in sights such as the **Palace of the Grand Master** (p256), **Jewish Museum of Rhodes** (p257) and the **Modern Greek Art Museum** (p257), as well as to go souvenir shopping. Spend an entertaining 20 minutes watching the **9D: Throne of Helios** (p261) movie.

Arriving in Rhodes

Diagoras Airport (p305) is near Paradisi on the west coast, 14km southwest of Rhodes Town.

Rhodes Town is the main port in the Dodecanese. Three inter-island ferry companies operate from immediately outside the walls of the Old Town. In summer, there are daily hydrofoils and catamarans to the Turkish resorts of Bodrum, Marmaris and Fethiye.

Where to Stay

The most memorable and romantic places to stay in Rhodes Town are the inns and B&Bs tucked into the Old Town's back alleys. Accommodation in Lindos is very limited, so be sure to book in advance. Also most hotels that include 'Lindos' in their names and/or addresses are located not in the village centre, but along the coast nearby.

Lindos town and the Acropolis

Acropolis of Lindos

Your first glimpse of the towering Acropolis on the cypress-silvered hill is guaranteed to steal your breath away, but at the top you'll find one of the finest views in Greece.

Great For...

ⓘ Need to Know

☎22440 31258; adult/concession/child €12/6/free; ⊙8am-7.40pm Apr-Oct, to 3pm Tue-Sun Nov-Mar

★ **Top Tip**

Visit the site early or late in the day; otherwise the crowds and the heat can be overwhelming.

The Rhodian Trireme

Towering above the pretty namesake village, the Acropolis of Lindos was first fortified in the 6th century BC. An extraordinary monument marks the foot of the final staircase up to the fortifications: the prow of a fast trireme warship, carved in vivid relief into the cliff-face. Dating from early in the 2nd century BC, it commemorates a Rhodian victory in a sea battle, and originally served as the base for a bronze statue of the triumphant admiral. An inscription identifies it as the work of Pythokritas. He is also thought to have carved the 18ft-tall statue known as the Winged Victory of Samothrace, which itself stands at the prow of a ship, and is currently held in the Louvre.

The Knights' Headquarters

The rocky crag of the Acropolis acquired its earliest defensive fortifications when the philosopher/tyrant Kleobolus ruled Lindos, during the 6th century BC. Construction of the walls that survive today, however, started 10 years after the Knights of St John captured Rhodes in 1307, though the knight initially responsible was actually a renegade Grand Master who had fallen out with the rest of his order. Known as the Knights' Headquarters, the tunnel-liked vaulted chamber through which visitors now enter the enclosure is laden with fragments of monuments and inscriptions.

Temple of Athena Lindia

The Stoa

The Hellenistic stoa that dominates the lower summit platform was erected during the 3rd century BC, to stage-manage access to the temple above. Measuring just under 90m from end to end, it consisted of two roofed but open-sided wings. Archaeologists have re-erected 26 of its original 42 columns. The broad terrace in front was added two centuries later, concealing 10 cisterns – the wellheads can still be seen – that could hold 300 cu metres of water. The now-empty bases of vanished monuments lie to all sides; many pedestals hold phantom 'footprints' where statues once stood.

> ☑ **Don't Miss**
> The summit is topped by ancient remains including a temple to Athena Lindia.

ERRECH/SHUTTERSTOCK ©

Temple of Athena Lindia

Crowning the very summit of the Acropolis, the Temple of Athena Lindia was first erected during the 9th century BC. What you see today dates from five centuries later, having replaced an earlier version that was destroyed by fire in 392 BC. Faced by these few still-standing columns, it takes considerable imagination to picture the temple in its heyday, but in this stunning setting the site still has an undeniable aura of the sacred.

The local cult of Athena may well pre-date the temple; it's thought to have originated in the vast cave of Spanayia Spiliotissa, which burrows deep into the cliff face immediately beneath this spot (and thus undercuts the temple).

With a great deal of care it's possible to hike to the cave – now home to a large number of bats – along a perilous trail that branches away from the mule path as it switchbacks up the hillside to the Acropolis. Don't try to get there from the southern side, however.

St Paul's Bay

Looking down from the southernmost tip of the Acropolis, beyond the Temple of Athena, you see what appears to be a circular lake immediately below. In fact this is the all-but-enclosed St Paul's Bay, open to the Aegean via a narrow gap in the rocks that's not visible from this vantage point. Local tradition has it that St Paul, who is mentioned in the Bible as having visited Rhodes, sought refuge here in around 57 AD, when his ship was fleeing a storm at sea.

> ✕ **Take a Break**
> The courtyard of the historic Captain's House (p264) is a lovely place for a restorative iced coffee or beer.

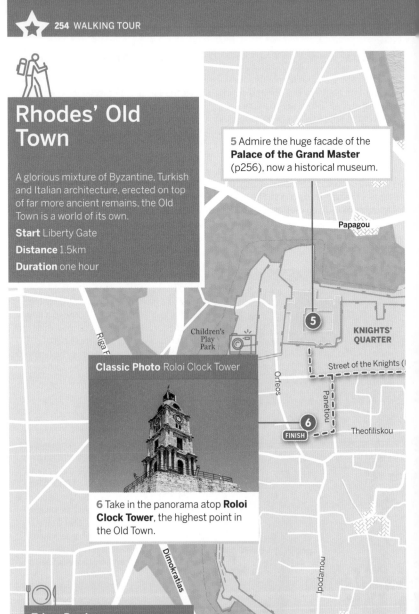

Rhodes' Old Town

A glorious mixture of Byzantine, Turkish and Italian architecture, erected on top of far more ancient remains, the Old Town is a world of its own.

Start Liberty Gate

Distance 1.5km

Duration one hour

5 Admire the huge facade of the **Palace of the Grand Master** (p256), now a historical museum.

Papagou

Children's Play Park

5

KNIGHTS' QUARTER

Street of the Knights (

Orfeos

Panetiou

Theofiliskou

Classic Photo Roloi Clock Tower

6
FINISH

6 Take in the panorama atop **Roloi Clock Tower**, the highest point in the Old Town.

Dimokratias

Ipodamou

Omirou

Take a Break...
Grab a snack at locals' favourite **Old Town Corner Bakery** (☎ 22410 38494; Omirou 88; snacks €2-6; ⏱ 7am-7pm Mon-Sat, 8am-3pm Sun).

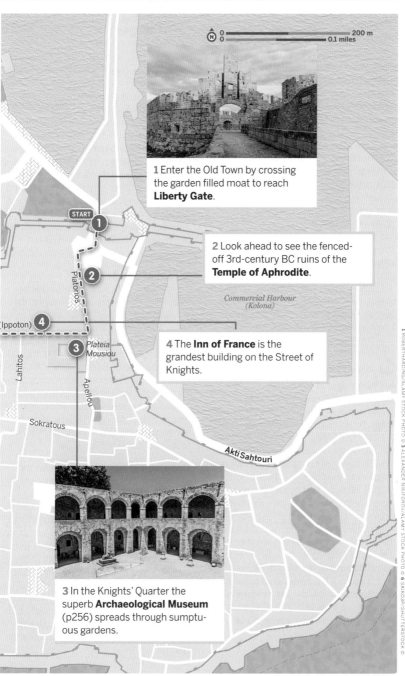

N
0   200 m
0   0.1 miles

1 Enter the Old Town by crossing the garden filled moat to reach **Liberty Gate**.

START
①

2 Look ahead to see the fenced-off 3rd-century BC ruins of the **Temple of Aphrodite**.

Platonos

②

Commercial Harbour (Kolona)

(Ippoton) ④

③ *Plateia Mousiou*

Lahitos

Apellou

Sokratous

4 The **Inn of France** is the grandest building on the Street of Knights.

Akti Sahtouri

3 In the Knights' Quarter the superb **Archaeological Museum** (p256) spreads through sumptuous gardens.

Rhodes Town

Rhodes Town is really two distinct and very different towns. The **Old Town** lies within but utterly apart from the New Town, sealed like a medieval time capsule behind a double ring of high walls and a deep moat. Few cities can boast so many layers of architectural history, with ruins and relics of the Classical, Ottoman and Italian eras entangled in a mind-boggling maze of twisting lanes.

In season, the Old Town receives a huge daily influx of day trippers and, especially, passengers from giant cruise ships. Even then, you can escape the crowds by heading away from the busy commercial streets into its hauntingly pretty cobbled alleyways. Staying a night or two, and losing yourself in the labyrinth after dark, is an experience no traveller should miss.

The **New Town**, meanwhile, is a modern Mediterranean resort, with decent beaches, upscale shops, lively nightlife and waterfront bars servicing the package crowd.

⊙ SIGHTS

Archaeological Museum   Museum
(☎22413 65257; Plateia Mousiou; adult/child €8/free, combination ticket incl Grand Master's Palace, Panagia tou Kastrou & Decorative Arts Collection €10; ⊙8am-8pm daily Apr-Oct, to 3pm Tue-Sun Nov-Mar) A weathered, sun-kissed stone lion, visible from the street, invites visitors into the magnificent 15th-century Knights' Hospital that holds Rhodes' superb archaeology museum. Exhibits range through several upstairs galleries, and across beautiful gardens to an annexe that's open shorter hours in summer (9am to 4.50pm). Highlights include the exquisite *Aphrodite Bathing* marble statue from the 1st century BC, a pavilion displaying wall-mounted mosaics, and a reconstructed burial site from 1630 BC that held a helmeted warrior alongside his horse.

Palace of the Grand Master   Historic Building
(☎22413 65270; Ippoton; adult/child €6/free, combination ticket incl Archaeological Museum, Decorative Arts Collection & Panagia tou Kastrou €10; ⊙8am-8pm Apr-Oct, to 3pm Nov-Mar) From the outside, this magnificent castle-like palace looks much as it did when erected by the 14th-century Knights Hospitaller. During the 19th century, however, it was devastated by an explosion, so the interior is now an Italian reconstruction, completed in the '18th year of the Fascist Era' (1940). Dreary chambers upstairs hold haphazard looted artworks, so the most interesting sections are the twin historical museums downstairs, one devoted to ancient Rhodes and the other to the island's medieval history.

Street of the Knights   Historic Site
(Ippoton; ⊙24hr) Austere and somewhat forbidding, the Street of the Knights (Ippoton) was home from the 14th century to the Knights Hospitaller who ruled Rhodes. The knights were divided into seven 'tongues', or languages, according to their birthplace – England, France, Germany, Italy, Aragon, Auvergne and Provence – each responsible for a specific section of the fortifications. As wall displays explain, the street holds an 'inn', or palace, for each tongue. Its modern appearance, though, owes much to Italian restorations during the 1930s.

Old Town Walls   Historic Site
(☎22413 65270; Ippoton, Palace of the Grand Master; adult/child €2/free; ⊙noon-3pm Mon-Fri) Rhodes' Old Town is rare indeed in retaining its 500-year-old fortifications all but intact. On weekdays, visitors can grasp their sheer scale by walking a broad, grassy (and largely unrailed) 1km stretch of the ramparts, from the Grand Master's palace to St John's Gate. There's no shade, but you get superb views of the domes, minarets and gardens within the Old Town; look out across the deep surrounding moat, and pass the massive, sealed-off Bastion of St George.

HERCULES MILAS/ALAMY STOCK PHOTO ©

Palace of the Grand Master

Jewish Museum of Rhodes   Museum
(☑22410 22364; www.rhodesjewishmuseum.org;
Dosiadou & Simiou; incl synagogue €4; ⊗10am-
3pm Sun-Fri Apr-Oct) The Jewish presence on
Rhodes dates back to the 2nd century BC,
while a 13th-century influx of Jewish refugees from Spain resulted in the creation of
a local 'Ladino' dialect combining Spanish
and Hebrew. This fascinating museum,
entered via the 1577 **Kahal Shalom Synagogue** (☑22410 22364; www.jewishrhodes.org;
Dosiadou & Simiou; incl museum €4; ⊗10am-
3pm Sun-Fri Apr-Oct), celebrates the history
of the community through photos and
documents, and mourns its tragic end with
mass deportations to Auschwitz in 1944.

**Acropolis
of Rhodes**   Archaeological Site
(⊗24hr) FREE Now known as the Acropolis
of Rhodes, the site of the ancient Hellenistic city of Rhodes stretches up the slopes
of Monte Smith, 1km west of the Old Town.
Only a few of the ruins have been restored,
including an elongated, tree-lined stadium
from the 2nd century BC. Steps climb from
a theatre, used for lectures by the Rhodes

School of Rhetoric (whose students included Cicero and Julius Caesar), to the stark
columns of the Temple of Pythian Apollo.

Modern Greek Art Museum   Gallery
(Nestoridio Melathro; ☑22410 43780; www.
mgamuseum.gr; Plateia Haritou, New Town;
adult/child €3/free, all four sections €8; ⊗8am-
3pm Tue-Sat) The main gallery of the four-
part Modern Greek Art Museum, near the
New Town's northern tip, holds paintings,
engravings and sculptures by some of
Greece's greatest 20th-century artists.
The real highlight is the top floor, devoted
(thanks to a bequest from his widow) to the
remarkable paintings of Valias Semertzidis
(1911–83), whose work ranged from depic-
tions of wartime struggle and hardship to
Rhodian landscapes.

🛍 SHOPPING
**Rhodes
Handmade Gallery**   Arts & Crafts
(☑22414 22242; Omirou 45; ⊗9am-9pm) Best
viewed by night, this Aladdin's cave of a
shop conjures up thoughts of the *Arabian*

Rhodes Old Town

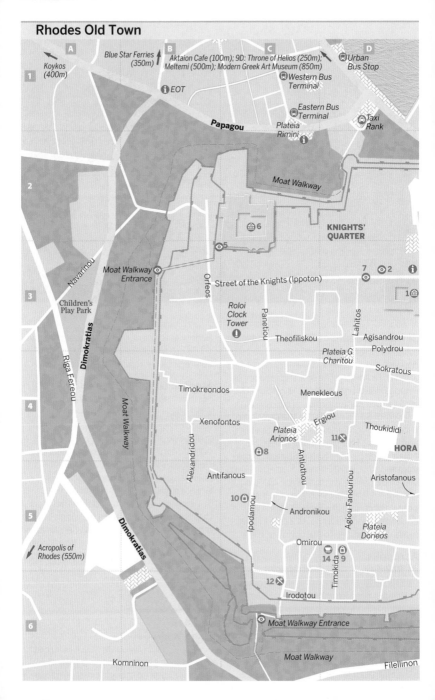

Koykos
(400m)

Blue Star Ferries
(350m)

Aktaion Cafe (100m); 9D: Throne of Helios (250m);
Meltemi (500m); Modern Greek Art Museum (850m)

Urban
Bus Stop

EOT

Western Bus
Terminal

Eastern Bus
Terminal

Taxi
Rank

Papagou

Plateia
Rimini

Moat Walkway

KNIGHTS'
QUARTER

6

5

Moat Walkway
Entrance

7 2

1

Orfeos

Navarinou

Children's
Play Park

Street of the Knights (Ippoton)

Roloi
Clock
Tower

Panetiou

Theofiliskou

Agisandrou

Lahitos

Dimokratias

Riga Fereou

Plateia G
Charitou

Polydrou

Sokratous

Timokreondos

Menekleous

Moat Walkway

Xenofontos

Alexandridou

Plateia
Arionos

Ergiou

Thoukididi

11

HORA

8

Antiothou

Antifanous

Aristofanous

10

Ipodamou

Andronikou

Agiou Fanouriou

Plateia
Dorieos

Dimokratias

Omirou

Acropolis of
Rhodes (550m)

14 9

Timokida

12

Irodotou

Moat Walkway Entrance

Komninon

Moat Walkway

Filellinon

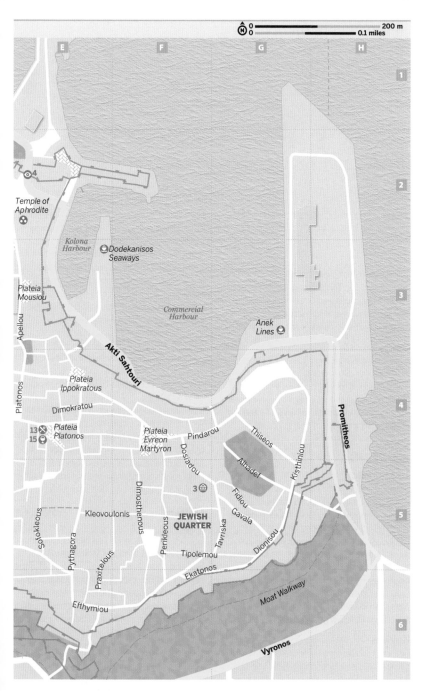

Rhodes Old Town

Nights, with its shiny brass lamps, ornate antique rings and Eastern mosaic lights glowing like clusters of fireflies.

So Greek
Food & Drinks

(☑22410 36870; https://sogreek.business.site; Ipodamou 40-42; ⊙9am-10pm Mon-Sat) ✎ The perfect pit stop for choice gifts, So Greek sells nicely packaged Greek wine, olive oil and a wide range of homemade honey, natural cosmetics and herbs and spices.

Gallery
Arts & Crafts

(☑22410 34965; Ipodamou 31, Old Town; ⊙10am-10pm) Stretching back through a maze of small rooms on this rewarding shopping lane, the unimaginatively named Gallery is a true treasure trove of carvings, crafts, paintings and all sorts of...stuff.

⊗ EATING

To Megiston
Taverna €

(☑22410 29127; Sofokleous 9; mains €6-23; ⊙10am-1.30am; ☀) Look no further for the classic Greek-holiday taverna experience: welcoming, witty waiters; retsina flowing freely; and all the classics prepared just right. People-watch al fresco, as sightseers swoon at the Ibrahim Pasha mosque opposite, and feast on the likes of *spetsofaï* (sausage stewed with chicken and peppers), lamb *kleftiko* (slow oven-baked), and succulent little Symi shrimp.

Koykos
Greek €

(☑22410 73022; www.koukosrodos.com; Mandilana 20-22, New Town; mains €3-27; ⊙24hr;

☜✎) This inviting complex of historic homes, on a pedestrian shopping street, consists of several antique-filled rooms – cuckoo clocks feature strongly – along with pavement patio seating and a bougainvillea-draped courtyard. Best known for fabulous pies (from around €2.30), it also serves classic mezedhes (small plates), plus meat and fish dishes, and a simple coffee or sandwich.

Marco Polo Cafe
Mediterranean €€

(☑22410 25562; www.marcopolomansion.gr; Agiou Fanouriou 40-42; mains €15-25; ⊙7-11pm Apr-Oct; ☜) ✎ Despite being barely visible, or even signed, from the street, this irresistible dinner-only restaurant is filled nightly, with diners savouring exquisite culinary creations like sea-bream fillets on a 'risotto' of local wheat, pork loin with figs, or octopus sous vide with cream of beetroot. Linger over a romantic meal in the delightful lemon-fragrant garden courtyard.

Meltemi
Seafood €€

(☑22410 30480; Kountourioti 8; mains €9-22.50; ⊙10am-late; ⛽☀♿) If you want to eat on the waterfront, Rhodes Town holds no better option than Meltemi, nestled into the sands of Elli Beach, just beyond Mandraki Harbour. The building itself may be drab, but the terrace views are magnificent, while the menu bursts with the tastes of the sea: octopus, jumbo prawns, lobster and calamari, all delivered with gusto.

🍸 DRINKING & NIGHTLIFE

Raxati Cafe   Bar

(📞22410 36365; Sofokleous 1-3; 🕙10am-late;
📶) This high-ceilinged, free-spirited bar
and coffeehouse, close to the attractive
Ibrahim Pasha mosque, is as pretty as
it is friendly. Inside, the stone walls are
peppered with vintage ad posters, and the
backlit bar glitters with glass spirit bottles,
while cushioned benches line recycled
Singer sewing-machine tables outside.
Snacks, cocktails, easy tunes and good
conversation.

Aktaion Cafe   Cafe

(📞22410 76856; www.aktaion-rodos.gr; Plateia
Eleftheria, New Town; 🕙8am-midnight; 📶♿)
The New Town's busy central rendezvous
sprawls across a large open-air terrace
beneath the shade of a spreading plane
tree, across the street from Mandraki Harbour. Locals and day trippers alike watch
the world go by, relaxing over drinks and
snacks, while children head straight to the
adjoining enclosed playground.

Da Luca   Cafe

(📞6974114489; Omirou 51; 🕙9am-9.59pm; 📶)
Thanks to three little tables fixed to the
ancient stonework, this tiny hole-in-the-
wall cafe provides a rare opportunity to
sit outside on one of the most charming
of the Old Town's narrow pebbled-paved
lanes, enjoying good coffee, craft beer or an
Aperol spritz, and chatting to the friendly
owners.

✪ ENTERTAINMENT

9D: Throne of Helios   Film

(📞22410 76850; www.throneofhelios.com; 25
Martiou 2, New Town; adult/child €13/9; 🕙10am-
11pm; 📶♿) This entertaining 20-minute
movie takes viewers back to the very birth
of Rhodes, its 3D effects complemented by
a further six dimensions (!) including shak-
ing chairs, falling rain, snow and bubbles.
The historic content is good, while amazing
visuals re-create the construction of the
Colossus, the creation of the medieval
citadel, and more.

Raxati Cafe

ℹ INFORMATION

You'll find plenty of ATMs throughout Rhodes Town, with useful ATM-equipped branches of Alpha Bank next door to the Old Town tourist office and on Plateia Kypriou in the New Town. The National Bank of Greece has a conveniently located office on Plateia Kyprou in the New Town, as well as a branch on Plateia Mousiou in the Old Town.

Emergencies & Ambulance (☎166)

EOT (Greek Tourist Information Office; ☎22410 44335; www.ando.gr/eot; cnr Makariou & Papagou, New Town; ☺8.30am-2.45pm Mon-Fri) National tourism information, with brochures, maps and transport details.

Main Post Office (☎22410 35560; Mandraki Harbour, New Town)

Port Police (☎22410 27634; Mandraki Harbour, New Town)

Rhodes Tourism Office – New Town (☎22410 35495; www.rhodes.gr; Plateia Rimini, New Town; ☺7.30am-3pm Mon-Fri) Conveniently poised between Mandraki Harbour and the Old Town, with public toilets alongside, this efficient office has helpful staff.

Rhodes Tourism Office – Old Town (☎22410 35945; www.rhodes.gr; cnr Platonos & Ippoton; ☺7am-3pm Mon-Fri) Rhodes Town's most useful tourist office, housed in an ancient building at the foot of the Street of the Knights, supplies excellent street maps, some good handouts on the whole island, and various commercial brochures.

Tourist Police (☎22410 27423; New Town; ☺24hr)

ℹ GETTING THERE & AWAY

AIR

Diagoras Airport (p305) is near Paradisi on the west coast, 14km southwest of Rhodes Town.

Taxis charge a set fare of €25 for trips between the airport and Rhodes Town, while buses connect the airport with Rhodes Town's Eastern Bus Terminal (25 minutes, €2.60) between 6.40am and 11.15pm daily.

BOAT

Inter-island ferry operators dock immediately outside the walls of Rhodes Old Town. Blue Star Ferries (p243) and Anek Lines (p244) use

Old Town, Rhodes Town

the Commercial Harbour, while **Dodekanisos Seaways** (22410 70590; www.12ne.gr/en) uses adjacent Kolona Harbour.

GETTING AROUND

Bicycles can be rented from **Margaritis** (22410 37420; www.margaritisrentals.gr; I Kazouli 17; 8am-9pm) in the New Town.

Excursion boats based on the quayside at Mandraki Harbour offer day trips to towns and beaches along Rhodes' east coast, including Faliraki and Lindos.

Local buses within Rhodes Town leave from the urban bus stop on Mandraki Harbour. The most useful route for visitors is bus 6, which goes to the Acropolis. Buy tickets on board.

Regular buses serve the entire island on weekdays, with fewer services on Saturday and only a few on Sunday. The **Eastern Bus Terminal** (22410 27706; www.ktelrodou.gr; Averof) and **Western Bus Terminal** (22410 26300; www.desroda.gr; Averof) at either end of the same short street in the New Town, serve half the island each. Schedules are posted beside the ticket kiosks at each terminal, and also online. All tickets cost €0.20 extra when bought from the driver as you board the bus.

Rhodes Town's main **taxi rank** (Papagou, Old Town) is on the northern edge of the Old Town, just east of Plateia Rimini; a board displays set fares for specific destinations. Meters charge slightly less for journeys in Rhodes Town than for the rest of the island. Rates double between midnight and 5am.

You can also phone for a **taxi** (in Rhodes Town 22410 69800, outside Rhodes Town 22410 69600; www.rhodes-taxi.gr).

If you're based in Rhodes Old Town, it's worth remembering that you can't drive into the Old Town, let alone park there, so it makes sense to rent a car only for the actual day(s) you're going to use it.

Drive Rent A Car (22410 68243; www.driverentacar.gr; 1st Km Tsairi-Airport; 8am-9pm) Sturdier, newer scooters and cars.

Margaritis Reliable cars, scooters and bicycles in the New Town.

Orion Rent a Car (22410 22137; www.orioncarrental.com; Leontos 38, New Town) A wide range of small and luxury cars.

Lindos

With its timeless Acropolis atop a cypress-silvered hill, and sugar-cube houses tumbling towards an aquamarine bay, your first glimpse of the ancient village of Lindos is guaranteed to steal your breath away.

Close up, things can feel very different. Lindos has become a major tourist destination, its approaches plagued by circling traffic and its narrow lanes jammed solid with sightseers. Come out of season, though, or stay the night and venture out before the daytrippers arrive, and you can still experience the old Lindos, a warren of alleyways where the mansions of long-vanished sea captains hold tavernas, bars and cool cafes. Coax your calves up to the Acropolis, and you'll encounter one of the finest views in Greece.

Two magnificent beaches line the crescent bay that curves just below it to the north. The larger, logically known as **Main Beach**, is a perfect swimming spot – sandy with shallow water – for kids. Slightly closer at hand, the smaller, taverna-fringed **Pallas Beach** is reached by a separate footpath down from the village, and connected to Main Beach by a narrow coastal path. Don't swim near the jetty here, which is home to sea urchins, but if it gets too crowded you can launch yourself from the rocks beyond.

ACTIVITIES

Lepia Dive   Diving
(6937417970; www.lepiadive.com; Pefkos;) Options with this brilliantly inclusive dive company include reef, wreck and cave dives, plus PADI courses for kids, beginners and advanced divers. The centre is adapted for wheelchairs, and offers expertly designed dives for people with additional needs, certified by Disabled Divers International. Free pickup.

Hike to the
Tomb of Kleobolus
Hiking

(🚹) An easy, enjoyable 5km (two-hour) round-trip hike escapes Lindos to reach the so-called Tomb of Kleobolus, at the tip of the bare, flat-topped promontory to the north. Starting alongside Car Park 1 above the main beach, the trail ends at a rocky hillock topped by a circular tomb actually built during the 2nd century BC, long after Kleobolus ruled Rhodes.

🅐 SHOPPING

Kori
Gifts & Souvenirs

(📱22441 14034; www.korilindos.com; Lindos Village; ⊙10am-11pm) Celebrating the work of upcoming artists and jewellers, this fabulous boutique is the best place in Lindos to buy fine gifts at affordable prices.

🅧 EATING & DRINKING

Village Cafe
Bakery €

(📱22440 31559; www.villagecafelindos.com; Lindos Village; mains €8-20; ⊙8am-6.30pm Mon-Sat, to 5.30pm Sun; 🅱🛜🚹) Near the start of the donkey path up to the Acropolis, this whitewashed bakery-cafe consists of an enticing vine-covered pebble-mosaic courtyard, shaded over to keep things cool. Drop in for hot or frozen coffee, juice or ice cream, and a mouthwatering array of breakfasts, cheesecakes, pies, salads, wraps and sandwiches. Don't miss the delectable *bougatsa* (vanilla custard pie).

Kalypso
Taverna €€

(📱22440 32135; www.kalypsolindos.com; Lindos VIllage; mains €10-24; ⊙11am-midnight; 🅱🛜) This former sea captain's residence with its beautiful stone relief is perfect for lunch or dinner on the roof terrace or inside. Sea bass, octopus, *makarounes* (homemade

pasta served with fresh onions and melted local cheese) and grilled lamb chops are but a few of the delights. Try the 'Kalypso bread' with feta and tomato.

Mythos
Taverna €€

(📱22440 31300; www.mythoslindos.com; Main Square, Lindos Village; mains €11-25; ⊙10am-1am; 🅱🛜) This popular taverna climbs from Lindos' main square through several levels and dining rooms, but most diners gravitate – or should that be levitate? – to the romantic roof terrace, against the hillside and backed by trees and colourfully spotlit flowers. Appetisers include crumbly, delicious vegetable pies; mains range from grilled fish or shrimps to lamb chops with pea puree and mustard.

Captain's House
Cafe

(📱22440 31235; Lindos Village; snacks €5; ⊙8am-midnight; 🛜) Soaked in Lyndian atmosphere, this nautically themed, 16th-century sea captain's house is perfect for a juice or coffee on your way down from the Acropolis. Grab a pew in the pebble-mosaic courtyard and admire the fabulous carved reliefs, or peer into the ground floor, restored with period furniture to display the lifestyle of its original owners.

🅘 INFORMATION

Lindos Tourist Office (📱22440 31900; Main Sq, Lindos Village; ⊙9am-3pm) Small information kiosk at the main village entrance.

🅘 GETTING THERE & AWAY

Frequent buses connect the main square with the Eastern Bus Terminal (p263) in Rhodes Town, with services every half-hour at peak times (€5.50). That journey costs €65 by taxi, while a taxi to or from the airport costs €75.

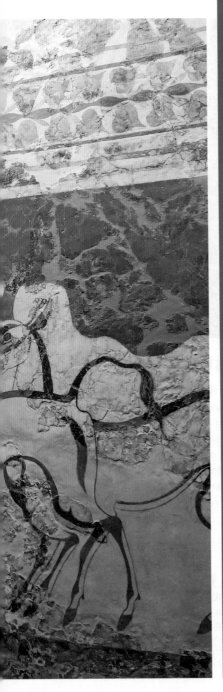

In Focus

Cycladic figurines, National Archaeological Museum (p48)

History

A doorstep between Asia Minor and Europe, Greece's history has always been tied to the rising and waning fortunes of its neighbours. For at least 2000 years various Greek civilisations flourished until the Roman Empire overwhelmed old Hellas in 86 BC. From the 15th century, the Ottomans ruled the region until 1830 when Greek Independence was formally recognised.

c 1500 BC

Santorini's volcano erupts, causing a Mediterranean-wide tsunami that may have hastened the destruction of Minoan civilisation.

1400 BC

The Mycenaeans colonise Crete, building cities such as Kydonia (Hania). Weapons manufacturing flourishes; fine arts fall into decline.

594 BC

Solon, a ruling aristocrat in Athens, introduces rules of fair play to his citizenry; seen as being the first step to real democracy.

Mycenaean Warrior Vase, National Archaeological Museum (p48)

Cycladic Civilisation

Human settlement in Greece dates back to around 700,000 years ago. By 3000 BC, settlements had developed into streets, squares and mudbrick houses. Indo-European migrants introduced the processing of bronze into Greece and from there began three remarkable civilisations: Cycladic, Minoan and Mycenaean.

The Cycladic civilisation – centred on the islands of the Cyclades – comprised a cluster of small fishing and farming communities with a sophisticated artistic temperament. Scholars divide the Cycladic civilisation into three periods: Early (3000–2000 BC), Middle (2000–1500 BC) and Late (1500–1100 BC).

The most striking legacy of this civilisation is the famous Cycladic figurines – carved statuettes from Parian marble. Other remains include bronze and obsidian tools and weapons, gold jewellery, and stone and clay vases and pots. Cycladic sculptors are also renowned for their impressive, life-sized *kouroi* (marble statues), carved during the Archaic period.

461–32 BC	336–23 BC	168 BC–AD 224
Athenian leader Pericles shifts power from Delos to Athens and orders the construction of the Parthenon.	Alexander the Great creates one of the ancient world's largest empires, stretching from Greece to northwest India.	Romans conquer mainland Greece and establish the Pax Romana, which lasts 300 years.

The Cycladic people were also accomplished sailors who developed prosperous maritime trade links with Crete, continental Greece, Asia Minor (the west of present-day Turkey), Europe and North Africa.

Minoan Civilisation

The Minoans – named after King Minos, the mythical ruler of Crete (and stepfather of the Minotaur) – built Europe's first advanced civilisation, drawing their inspiration from two great Middle Eastern civilisations: the Mesopotamian and the Egyptian.

The Minoan civilisation (3000–1100 BC) reached its peak during the Middle period; around 2000 BC the grand palace complex of Knossos was built, marking a sharp acceleration from Neolithic village life. Evidence uncovered in this palace and others indicates a sophisticated society, with splendid architecture and wonderful, detailed frescoes, highly developed agriculture and an extensive irrigation system.

The advent of bronze enabled the Minoans to build great boats, which helped them establish a powerful *thalassocracy* (sea power) and prosperous maritime trade. They used tremendous skill to produce fine pottery and metalwork of great beauty, and exported their wares throughout Greece, Asia Minor, Europe and North Africa.

Scholars are still debating the sequence of events that led to the ultimate demise of the Minoans. Scientific evidence suggests they were weakened by a massive tsunami and ash fallout attributed to the eruption of a cataclysmic volcano on Santorini (Thira) around 1500 BC. Some argue that a second powerful quake a century later decimated the society, or perhaps it was the invading force of Mycenae.

Mycenae Civilisation

The decline of the Minoan civilisation coincided with the rise of Mycenae (1600–1100 BC), which reached its peak between 1500 and 1200 BC with mainland city-states such as Corinth, Tiryns and Mycenae. Warrior kings, who measured their wealth in weapons, now ruled from heavily fortified palaces. Commercial transactions were documented on tablets in Linear B (a form of Greek language 500 years older than the Ionic Greek used by Homer). The Mycenaean's most impressive legacy is their magnificent gold masks, refined jewellery and metal ornaments, the best of which are in the National Archaeological Museum in Athens.

Geometric & Archaic Ages

The Dorians were an ancient Hellenic people who settled in the Peloponnese by the 8th century BC. In the 11th or 12th century BC, these warrior-like people fanned out to occupy much of the mainland, seizing control of the Mycenaean kingdoms and enslaving the inhabitants. The following 400-year period is often referred to as Greece's dark age;

394
Christianity is declared the official religion. All pagan worship of Greek and Roman gods is outlawed.

1453
Greece becomes a dominion of the Ottoman Turks after they seize control of Constantinople.

1460
The Venetian stronghold of Morea (Peloponnese) falls to the Turks.

however, the Dorians introduced iron and developed a new, intricate style of pottery, decorated with striking geometric designs. Significantly they were to introduce the practice of *polytheism* (the worship of many gods), paving the foundations for Zeus and his pantheon of 12 principal deities.

During the following Archaic period, about 1000–800 BC, Greek culture developed rapidly; many of the advancements in literature, sculpture, theatre, architecture and intellectual endeavour began. This revival overlapped with the Classical period (the two eras are often classified as the Hellenic period). Advances included the Greek alphabet, the verses of Homer (the 'Odyssey' was possibly the world's first epic work of literature), and the founding of the Olympic Games and central sanctuaries such as Delphi. These common bonds gave Greeks a sense of national identity and intellectual vigour.

Contest for Athens

The founding of Athens is enshrined in myth. Phoenician king Kekrops, the story goes, founded a city on a huge rock near the sea. The gods of Olympus proclaimed that it should be named for the deity who could provide the most valuable legacy for mortals. Athena (goddess of wisdom, among other things) produced an olive tree, symbol of peace and prosperity. Poseidon (god of the sea) struck a rock with his trident, creating a saltwater spring, to signify great maritime power. It was a close contest, but the gods judged that Athena's gift, which would provide food, oil and fuel, would better serve the citizens – though of course Athens today draws its wealth from Poseidon's domain as well.

Athens' Early History

The archaeological record of Athens' earliest years shows only that the hilltop site of the Acropolis, with two abundant springs, drew some of Greece's earliest Neolithic settlers.

By 1400 BC the Acropolis had become a powerful Mycenaean city. It survived a Dorian assault in 1200 BC, but didn't escape the dark age that enveloped Greece for the next 400 years. Then, in the 8th century BC, during a period of peace, Athens became the artistic centre of Greece, excelling in ceramics.

By the 6th century BC, Athens was ruled by aristocrats and generals. Labourers and peasants had no rights until Solon, the harbinger of Athenian democracy, became *arhon* (chief magistrate) in 594 BC and improved the lot of the poor by forgiving debts and establishing a process of trial by jury. Continuing unrest over the reforms created the pretext for the tyrant Peisistratos, formerly head of the military, to seize power in 560 BC.

Peisistratos built a formidable navy and extended the boundaries of Athenian influence. A patron of the arts, he inaugurated the Festival of the Great Dionysia, the precursor to Attic drama, and commissioned many splendid works, most of which were later destroyed by the Persians.

1684–87	1821	1822–29
The Venetians expel the Turks from the Peloponnese in a campaign that sees Venetian troops advance as far as Athens.	On 25 March, the War of Independence starts on the mainland. Greece celebrates this date as its national day of Independence.	Independence is declared at Epidavros on 13 January 1822, but fighting continues for another seven years before Ottomans capitulate.

Ancient Olympia

In 528 BC, Peisistratos was succeeded by his son, Hippias, no less an oppressor. With the help of Sparta in 510 BC, Athens rid itself of him.

Athens' Golden Age

The Persian Wars began in 490 BC, when King Darius, angered by Greek meddling in Persian territory, sent troops to teach a lesson. He was defeated at Marathon, but his son, Xerxes, retaliated by sacking Athens. At the battles of Salamis (480 BC) and Plataea (479 BC), the Athenians, again, with the help of Sparta, repulsed the Persians for good. From here, the city-state's power knew no bounds.

In 477 BC Athens established a confederacy on the sacred island of Delos and demanded tributes from the surrounding islands to protect them from the Persians. The treasury was moved to Athens in 461 BC and Pericles, ruler from 461 BC to 429 BC, used the money to transform the city. This period has become known as Athens' golden age – the pinnacle of the Classical era.

Most of the monuments on the Acropolis today date from this period. Drama and literature flourished due to such luminaries as Aeschylus, Sophocles and Euripides. The sculptors Pheidias and Myron and the historians Herodotus, Thucydides and Xenophon also lived during this time.

Rivalry With Sparta

Sparta did not let Athens revel in its newfound glory. Cooperation gave way to competition and the Peloponnesian Wars, which began in 431 BC and dragged on until 404 BC. Sparta gained the upper hand and Athens never returned to its former glory. But one of the fighters who survived the wars was Socrates, who went on to teach Plato, who, in turn, taught Aristotle. The 4th century BC was a high point in classical philosophy.

In 338 BC Athens was conquered by Philip II of Macedon, and his son Alexander (soon to be known as 'the Great') favoured Athens over other city-states. After Alexander's

1831	1833	1862–63
Ioannis Kapodistrias, independent Greece's first prime minister, is assassinated.	Britain, France and Russia choose 17-year-old Prince Otto of Bavaria to be the first appointed monarch in modern Greece.	King Otto is deposed in a bloodless coup. The British return the Ionian Islands (a British protectorate since 1815) to Greece.

untimely death, however, Athens passed in quick succession through the hands of his generals.

Roman & Byzantine Rule

The Romans defeated the Macedonians, and in 86 BC attacked Athens after it sided against them in a botched rebellion in Asia Minor. They destroyed the city walls and took precious sculptures to Rome. During three centuries of peace under Roman rule, known as the 'Pax Romana', Athens continued to be a major seat of learning. The Romans adopted Hellenistic culture: many wealthy young Romans attended Athens schools and anyone who was anyone in Rome spoke Greek. The Roman emperors, particularly Hadrian, graced Athens with many grand buildings.

In the late 4th century, Christianity became the official religion of Athens and worship of the 'pagan' Greek gods was outlawed. After the subdivision of the Roman Empire into east and west, Athens remained an important cultural and intellectual centre until Emperor Justinian closed its schools of philosophy in AD 529.

Athens declined and, between 1200 and 1450, was continually invaded – by the Franks, Catalans, Florentines and Venetians, all preoccupied with grabbing principalities from the crumbling Byzantine Empire.

The Hellenistic Age

The period from the death of Alexander the Great in 323 BC to around 30 BC, when the Roman Empire emerged, is known as the Hellenistic age. Contemporary arts, drama, sculpture and philosophy reflected growing awareness of a new definition of Greek identity. Hellenism would continue to prosper even under Roman rule. As the Roman province of Achaea, Greece experienced an unprecedented period of peace for almost 300 years, known as the Pax Romana. The Romans had always venerated Greek art, literature and philosophy, and aristocratic Romans sent their offspring to school in Athens. Most aspects of Hellenistic culture were adopted, from its dress to its gods, spreading its unifying traditions throughout their empire. The Romans were also the first to refer to the Hellenes as Greeks, derived from the word *graikos* – the name of a prehistoric tribe.

Ottoman Rule

On 29 May 1453, Constantinople fell under Turkish Ottoman rule (referred to by Greeks as *turkokratia*). Once more Greece became a battleground, this time fought over by the Turks and Venetians. Eventually, with the exception of the Ionian Islands (where the Venetians retained control), Greece became part of the Ottoman Empire.

Ottoman power reached its zenith under Sultan Süleyman the Magnificent, who ruled from 1520 to 1566. His successor, Selim the Sot, added Cyprus to Ottoman dominion in

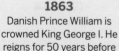

1863	**1896**	**1914**
Danish Prince William is crowned King George I. He reigns for 50 years before being assassinated in Thessaloniki in 1913.	The staging of the first modern Olympic Games in Athens marks Greece's coming of age.	Greece is initially neutral at outbreak of WWI but eventually sides with the Western Allies against Germany and Turkey.

1570. Although they captured Crete in 1669 after a 25-year campaign, the ineffectual sultans that followed in the late 16th and 17th centuries saw the empire go into steady decline.

By the end of the 18th century, pockets of Turkish officials, aristocrats and influential Greeks had emerged as self-governing cliques that ruled over the provincial Greek peasants. But there also existed an ever-increasing group of Greeks, including many intellectual expatriates, who aspired to emancipation.

Independence

In 1814 the first Greek independence party, the Filiki Eteria (Friendly Society), was founded. On 25 March 1821, the Greeks launched the War of Independence. Uprisings broke out almost simultaneously across most of Greece and the occupied islands. The fighting was savage and atrocities were committed on both sides. The campaign escalated, and within a year the Greeks had won vital ground. They proclaimed independence on 13 January 1822 at Epidavros.

Soon after, regional wrangling twice escalated into civil war, in 1824 and 1825. The Ottomans took advantage and by 1827 the Turks (with Egyptian reinforcements) had regained control. Western powers intervened and a combined Russian, French and British naval fleet sunk the Turkish-Egyptian force in the Battle of Navarino in October 1827. Despite the long odds against him, Sultan Mahmud II proclaimed a holy war, prompting Russia to send troops into the Balkans to engage the Ottoman army. Fighting continued until 1829 when, with Russian troops at the gates of Constantinople, the sultan accepted Greek independence with the Treaty of Adrianople. Independence was formally recognised in 1830.

Initially the city of Nafplio was named Greece's capital. After elected president Ioannis Kapodistrias was assassinated in 1831, Britain, France and Russia again intervened, declaring Greece a monarchy. The throne was given to 17-year-old Prince Otto of Bavaria, who transferred his court to Athens. It became the Greek capital in 1834, even though, after so many residents fled the 1827 siege, it was little more than a sleepy town of about 6000. At Otto's behest, Bavarian architects created imposing neoclassical buildings, tree-lined boulevards and squares.

In 1862 Otto was overthrown after a period of power struggles, including the British and French occupation of Piraeus, aimed at quashing the 'Great Idea' – Greece's doomed expansionist goal to assert sovereignty over its dispersed Greek populations.

The Great Idea

British influence in the Ionian Islands had begun in 1815 (following a spell of political ping-pong between the Venetians, Russians and French). The British did improve the islands' infrastructure, and many locals adopted British customs. However, Greek independence put pressure on Britain to give sovereignty to the Greek nation, and in 1864 the British left.

1924–34
Greece is proclaimed a republic and King George II leaves Greece. The Great Depression counters the nation's return to stability.

1935
King George II is reinstated. Right-wing General Ioannis Metaxas becomes prime minister.

1941–44
Germany invades and occupies Greece. Resistance groups drive out the Germans after three years.

Meanwhile, Britain eased onto the Greek throne the young Danish Prince William, crowned King George I in 1863, whose reign lasted 50 years.

In 1881, Greece acquired Thessaly and part of Epiros as a result of a Russo-Turkish war. But Greece failed miserably when it tried to attack Turkey in an effort to reach *enosis* (union) with Crete (which had persistently agitated for liberation from the Ottomans). Timely diplomatic intervention by the Great Powers prevented the Turkish army from taking Athens.

Crete was placed under international administration, but the government of the island was gradually handed over to the Greeks. In 1905 the president of the Cretan assembly, Eleftherios Venizelos (later to become prime minister), announced Crete's union with Greece (although this was not recognised by international law until 1913).

WWI & its Aftermath

During WWI, the Allies (Britain, France and Russia) put increasing pressure on neutral Greece to join forces with them against Germany and Turkey, promising concessions in Asia Minor in return. Greek troops served with distinction on the Allied side, but when the war ended in 1918 the promised land in Asia Minor was not forthcoming. Prime Minister Venizelos then led a diplomatic campaign to further the 'Great Idea' and sent troops to Smyrna (present-day İzmir) in May 1919. With a seemingly viable hold in Asia Minor, by September 1921 Greece had advanced as far as Ankara. But by this stage foreign support for Venizelos had ebbed, and Turkish forces, commanded by Mustafa Kemal (later to become Atatürk), halted the offensive. The Greek army retreated and Smyrna fell in 1922, and tens of thousands of its Greek inhabitants were killed.

The outcome of these hostilities was the Treaty of Lausanne in July 1923, whic called for a population exchange between Greece and Turkey to prevent any future disputes. Almost 1.5 million Greeks left Turkey and almost 400,000 Turks left Greece. The exchange put a tremendous strain on the Greek economy and caused great bitterness and hardship for the individuals concerned. Many Greeks had to abandon a privileged life in Asia Minor for one of extreme poverty in emerging urban shanty towns in Athens and Thessaloniki.

WWII & the Civil War

A republic was declared in 1924 amid a series of coups and counter-coups. Then in November 1935, King George II installed the right-wing General Ioannis Metaxas as prime minister. He assumed dictatorial powers and is best known for his reply of *ohi* (no) to Mussolini's ultimatum to allow Italian forces passage through Greece at the beginning of WWII. The Italians invaded anyway, but the Greeks drove them back into Albania.

Despite Allied help, when German troops invaded Greece on 6 April 1941, the whole country was rapidly overrun. The civilian population suffered appallingly during the occupation, many dying of starvation. The Germans rounded up between 60,000 and 70,000

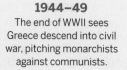

1944–49	**1967–74**	**1974**
The end of WWII sees Greece descend into civil war, pitching monarchists against communists.	Political factional bickering continues, provoking in April 1967 a right-wing military coup d'état by army generals who establish a junta.	The invasion of Cyprus by Turkish troops leads to the fall of Greece's military junta and restoration of parliamentary democracy.

Greek Jews, at least 80% of the country's Jewish population, and transported them to death camps. Numerous resistance movements sprang up, eventually polarising into royalist and communist factions that fought one another with as much venom as they fought the Germans, often with devastating results for the civilian Greek population.

The German retreat from Greece began in October 1944. Meanwhile, the resistance groups continued to fight one another. A bloody civil war resulted, lasting until 1949. The civil war left Greece in chaos. More Greeks were killed in three years of bitter civil war than in WWII, and a quarter of a million people were left homeless. The sense of despair triggered a mass exodus as almost a million Greeks left in search of a better life elsewhere, primarily to countries such as Australia, Canada and the US.

Military Coup

Georgos Papandreou came to power in February 1964. Rattled by Papandreou's tolerance of the left, a group of army colonels staged a coup on 21 April 1967 and established a military junta. Martial law was declared, political parties and trade unions banned, censorship imposed, and thousands of dissidents imprisoned, tortured and exiled.

On 17 November 1973, tanks stormed a building at the Athens Polytechnic (Technical University) to quell a student occupation calling for an uprising against the US-backed junta. More than 20 students were reportedly killed and hundreds injured. Shortly after, a disastrous political move led to the partition in Cyprus and the collapse of the junta.

Konstandinos Karamanlis, prime minister from the 1950s, was invited to return to Greece from self-imposed exile in Paris. His New Democracy (ND) party won a large majority at the November 1974 elections against the newly formed Panhellenic Socialist Union (PASOK), led by Andreas Papandreou (son of Georgos). A plebiscite voted 69% against the restoration of the monarchy, and the ban on communist parties was lifted.

Into the New Millennium

When Greece became the 10th member of the EU in 1981, it was the smallest and poorest country in the bloc. In October 1981 Andreas Papandreou's PASOK party was elected as Greece's first socialist government, ruling for almost two decades (except for 1990–3).

Athens won the competition to host the 2004 Olympics, a deadline that fast-tracked infrastructure projects such as the expansion of the metro and a new airport. At the same time, Athens was becoming more of a global destination for labour and safe harbour. In one decade, the city absorbed more than half a million migrants, a dramatic demographic shift.

The 2004 Olympics' legacy was a cleaner, greener and more efficient capital, and booming economic growth. But the optimism and fiscal good times were short-lived, as it became clear the country had overborrowed. In 2010, the Greek debt crisis set in, with strict austerity measures.

1981	2001	2004
Greece joins the EU and votes in its first elected socialist government (PASOK) under the leadership of Andreas Papandreou.	Greece adopts the euro, joining the first wave of European countries to introduce the new currency on 1 January 2002.	Athens successfully hosts the 28th Summer Olympic Games, but it costs €9 billion, double the original target.

After the Crisis

Tax hikes and drastic pension cuts – imposed as terms of a series of bailout loans from the EU and the International Monetary Foundation – have touched everyone across the country. Greece suffers some of the highest unemployment rates in Europe and the austerity measures have also widened the country's stark economic and social disparities. Homelessness, suicides, drug use and once-rare burglary and even violent crime have risen. Youth unemployment hovers around 45% and the elderly struggle to get by on pensions that have been cut by 40%.

There was brief hope in 2015, when the Syriza party came to power and promised to take a strong stand against austerity measures. But just three days after Greeks voted a resounding 'no' in a referendum on accepting bailouts, Prime Minister Alexis Tsipras capitulated to another bailout deal. People reacted with rage, mass strikes and violent clashes with the police.

In August 2018 Greece finally exited the €86 billion bailout programme that stretched back to 2010. Under Tsipras' government unemployment has fallen, consumer spending has risen and poverty is on the decline. Even so, the Greek economy has a long way to go before it reattains its precrisis level of health.

In 2019, voters, exhausted by austerity, rejected Syriza, first in the local and European Parliament elections in May, and then in the general election in July. The centre-right New Democracy party, led by Kyriakos Mitsotakis, won by a landslide, giving it an outright majority of 158 seats in the Greek parliament.

2009
Eurozone countries approve a €110-billion rescue package for the country's economic crisis, in exchange for tougher austerity laws.

2015
Greece defaults on its bailout loans and is threatened with Grexit – removal from the eurozone.

2019
Centre-right New Democracy party, led by Kyriakos Mitsotakis, wins the general election.

Reliefs at the Theatre of Dionysos, Acropolis (p38)

Ancient Greek Culture

When the Roman Empire assimilated Greece it did so with considerable respect and idealism. The Romans absorbed Greek deities, literature, myths, philosophy, fine arts and architecture. So what made the Ancient Greeks so special? From thespians to philosophers, from monster-slaying heroes to a goddess born of sea foam, the Ancient Greeks were captivating.

The Golden Age

In the 5th century BC, Athens had a cultural renaissance that has never been equalled – in fact, such was the diversity of its achievements that modern classical scholars refer to it as 'the miracle'. It's often said that Athens' 'Golden Age' is the bedrock of Western civilisation, and had the Persians won, Europe today would have been a vastly different place.

Drama

The great dramatists such as Aeschylus, Aristophanes, Euripides and Sophocles redefined theatre from religious ritual to become a compelling form of entertainment. They were to be found at the Theatre of Dionysos at the foot of the Acropolis, and their comedies and tragedies reveal a great deal about the psyche of the Ancient Greeks.

Across the country, large open-air theatres were built on the sides of hills, designed to accommodate plays with increasingly sophisticated backdrops and props, choruses and themes, and to maximise sound so that even the people in the back row might hear the actors on stage. The dominant genres of theatre were tragedy and comedy. The first known actor was a man called Thespis, from whose name we derive the word 'thespian'.

Philosophy

The greatest gift of the Athenian philosophers to modern-day thought is their spirit of rational inquiry. Posthumously considered to be Athens' greatest, most noble citizen, Socrates was forced to drink hemlock for allegedly corrupting the youth by asking probing, uncomfortable questions. However, before he died he established a school of hypothetical reductionism that is still used today.

Plato, Socrates' star student, was responsible for documenting his teacher's thoughts, and without his work in books such as the *Symposium,* they would have been lost to us. Considered an idealist, Plato wrote *The Republic* as a warning to the city-state of Athens that unless its people respected law and leadership, and educated its youth sufficiently, it would be doomed.

Plato's student Aristotle focused his gifts on astronomy, physics, zoology, ethics and politics. Aristotle was also the personal physician to Philip II, King of Macedon, and the tutor of Alexander the Great.

Sculpture

Classical sculpture began to gather pace in Greece in the 6th century BC with the renderings of nudes in marble. Most statues were created to revere a particular god or goddess and many were robed in grandiose garments. The statues of the preceding Archaic period, known as *kouroi,* had focused on symmetry and form, but in the early 5th century BC artists sought to create expression and animation. As temples demanded elaborate carvings, sculptors were called upon to create large reliefs upon them.

During the 5th century BC, the craft became yet more sophisticated, as sculptors were taught to successfully map a face and create a likeness of their subject in marble busts. Perhaps the most famous Greek sculptor was Pheidias (c 480–430 BC), whose reliefs upon the Parthenon depicting the Greek and Persian Wars – now known as the Parthenon Marbles – are celebrated as among the finest of the Golden Age.

The Heroes

Some of the greatest tales of all time – and some say the wellspring of story itself – are to be found in the Greek myths. For many of us, the fantastical adventures of Heracles and Odysseus we heard as kids still linger in our imagination, and contemporary writers continue to reinterpret these stories and characters for books and films. Standing in the ancient ruins of an acropolis and peering across the watery horizon, it's not difficult to picture the Kraken (Poseidon's pet monster) rising from the Aegean, nor to imagine that fishing boat you see heading into the sunset as Jason's *Argo* en route to Colchis for the Golden Fleece.

The average Greek is fiercely proud of their myths and will love entertaining you with a list of the gods, but they'll love it even more if you know a few of them yourself.

Socrates monument, Athens

★ Ancient Greek Philosophers

Socrates (469–399 BC)
Plato (427–347 BC)
Aristotle (384–322 BC)

Heracles (Hercules)

The most celebrated, endearing hero of ancient Greece, the son of Zeus and the mortal Alcmene. After killing his family in a fit of madness induced by the jealous Hera (sister-wife of Zeus), Heracles seeks penance by performing 12 labours set by his enemy Eurystheus, King of Mycenae. These labours included slaying the Nemean Lion and the Lernian Hydra; capturing the Ceryneian Hind and the Erymanthian Boar; cleaning the Augean Stables in one day; slaying the arrow-feathered Stymphalian Birds; capturing the Cretan Bull; stealing the man-eating Mares of Diomedes; obtaining the Girdle of Hippolyta and the oxen of Geryon; stealing the Apples of the Hesperides; and capturing Cerberus.

Theseus

The Athenian hero volunteered himself as one of seven men and maidens in the annual sacrifice to the Minotaur, the crazed half-bull, half-man offspring of King Minos of Crete. Once inside its forbidding labyrinth (from which none had returned), Theseus, aided by Princess Ariadne (who had a crush on him induced by Aphrodite's dart), loosened a spool of thread to find his way out once he'd killed the monster.

Icarus

Along with Daedalus (his father), Icarus flew off the cliffs of Crete pursued by King Minos and his troops, using wings made of feathers and wax. His father instructed him to fly away from the midday sun, but Icarus became carried away with the exhilaration of flying...the wax melted, the feathers separated and the bird-boy fell to his death.

Perseus

Perseus' impossible task was to kill the gorgon, Medusa. With her head of snakes, Medusa could turn a man to stone with a single glance. Armed with an invisibility cap and a pair of flying sandals from Hermes, Perseus used his reflective shield to avoid Medusa's stare. He cut off her head and secreted it in a bag, but it was shortly unsheathed to save Andromeda, a princess bound to a rock and about to be sacrificed to a sea monster. Medusa's head turned the sea monster to stone and Perseus got the girl.

Oedipus

Oedipus was the Ancient Greeks' gift to the Freudian school of psychology. Having been abandoned at birth, Oedipus learned from the Delphic oracle that he would one day slay his father and marry his mother. On the journey back to his birthplace, Thiva (Thebes), he killed a rude stranger and then discovered the city was plagued by a murderous Sphinx (a winged lion with a woman's head). The creature gave unsuspecting travellers and citizens a riddle: if they couldn't answer it, they were dashed on the rocks. Oedipus succeeded in solving the riddle, felled the Sphinx and so gained the queen of Thiva's hand in marriage. On discovering the stranger he'd killed was his father and that his new wife was in fact his mother, Oedipus ripped out his eyes and exiled himself.

Mythology

Ancient Greece revolved around careful worship of 12 central gods and goddesses, all of whom played a major role in the *mythos* (mythology), and none of whom can be commended for their behaviour. The ancient pantheon are (with Roman names in brackets):

○ Zeus (Jupiter) – The fire-bolt-flinging king of the gods, ruler of Mt Olympus, lord of the skies and master of disguise in pursuit of mortal maidens.

○ Hera (Juno) – Protector of women and family, the queen of heaven is both the embattled wife and sister of Zeus.

Mythical Creatures

Medusa The snake-headed one punished by the gods for her inflated vanity. Even dead, her blood is lethal.

Cyclops A one-eyed giant. Odysseus and his crew were trapped in the cave of one such cyclops, Polyphemus.

Cerberus The three-headed dog of hell, he guards the entrance to the underworld – under his watch no one gets in or out.

Minotaur This half-man, half-bull mutant leads a life of existential angst in the abysmal labyrinth, tempered only by the occasional morsel of human flesh.

Hydra Cut one of its nine heads off and another two will grow in its place. Heracles solved the problem by cauterising each stump with his burning brand.

○ Poseidon (Neptune) – God of the seas, master of the mists and younger brother of Zeus.

○ Hades (Pluto) – God of death and brother of Zeus, he ruled the underworld, bringing in the newly dead with the help of his skeletal ferryman, Charon.

○ Athena (Minerva) – Goddess of wisdom, war, science and guardian of Athens, born in full armour out of Zeus' forehead.

○ Aphrodite (Venus) – Goddess of love and beauty who was said to have been born of sea foam.

○ Apollo – God of music, the arts and fortune-telling, Apollo was also the god of light and an expert shot with a bow and arrow.

○ Artemis (Diana) – The goddess of the hunt and twin sister of Apollo was, ironically, patron saint of wild animals.

○ Ares (Mars) – God of war, bloodthirsty and lacking control. Zeus' least favourite of his progeny.

○ Hermes (Mercury) – Messenger of the gods, patron saint of travellers and the handsome one with a winged hat and sandals.

○ Hephaestus (Vulcan) – God of artisanship, metallurgy and fire, this deformed and oft-derided son of Zeus made the world's first woman of clay, Pandora, as a punishment for man.

○ Hestia (Vesta) – Virginal goddess of the hearth, she protected state fires in city halls from where citizens of Greece could light their brands.

Outdoor dining, Plaka, Athens

ALVARO GERMAN VILELA/SHUTTERSTOCK ©

The Greek Way of Life

Greeks have a famously relaxed disposition. Despite the austerity measures of recent years, their proud ways of life – which embrace family, hospitality and a rebellious, independent spirit – remain intact. Athens is bustling and it's business as usual on the Greek islands, where age-old social conventions and beliefs still hold sway.

National Psyche

Greek values and the national character came under attack during the crisis – with locals universally characterised as lazy, leisure-loving, corrupt tax-evaders recklessly bringing Europe to the brink of economic collapse. The realities are far more complex – for every 'lazy' Greek there are hard-working people juggling two jobs to provide for their families.

Greeks pride themselves on their *filotimo,* a hard-to-translate Greek concept that underpins society's cultural norms. It encompasses personal and family honour, respect and loyalty to parents and grandparents, sacrifice and help for friends and strangers alike, pride in country and heritage, and gratitude and hospitality. Though some would argue it has been eroded, the concept remains an important part of Greek identity.

The Greeks also generously extend their *filoxenia* (hospitality). The average Greek will lavish you with free drinks, fresh cake from their kitchen and the warmth they have always been famous for. Curious by nature, as well as passionate, loyal and fiery, Greeks engage in animated personal and political discussions rather than polite small talk. Nothing is off limits for conversation, and you may find yourself quizzed on highly personal matters such as why you don't have children, why you're not married and how much you earn.

Greeks can also be fervently patriotic, nationalistic and ethnocentric. Issues are debated with strong will. Greeks are unashamed about staring and blatantly observing (and commenting on) the comings and goings of people around them. They prefer spontaneity to making plans and are notoriously unpunctual (turning up on time is referred to as 'being English').

Social & Family Life

Greek life has always taken place in the public sphere, whether it's men talking politics at the local *kafeneio* (coffee house) or the elderly gathering in neighbourhood squares while their grandchildren play into the evening.

Rather than living to work, Greeks work to live. People of all ages take their afternoon *volta* (outing) along seafront promenades or town centres, dressed up and refreshed from a siesta (albeit a dying institution). On weekends they flock to the beach and seaside tavernas, and summer holidays are the highlight of the year – traditionally, the capital virtually shuts down mid-August as people take off for the islands, beach towns or their ancestral villages. A peculiarly Greek social talking point is how many swims you've had that summer.

Greek society remains dominated by the family, and while many men may appear soaked with machismo, the matriarchal domestic model is still very much commonplace, with women subtly pulling the strings in the background. These strong family ties and kinship are helping Greeks survive testing times. Greece's weak welfare system means Greeks rely on families and social groups for support. Most Greek businesses are small, family-run operations and parents strive to provide homes for their children when they get married. Greeks rarely move out of home before they marry, unless they go to university or work in another city. While this was changing among professionals and people marrying later, low wages and rising unemployment have forced many young people to stay – or return – home.

Greeks retain strong regional identities and ties to their ancestral villages. Even the country's most remote villages are bustling during holidays. Greece's large diaspora plays a significant role in the life of many islands and villages, returning each summer in droves.

Sporting Passions

If the streets are quiet, you can't get a taxi or you hear a mighty roar coming from nearby cafes, chances are there's a football (soccer) game underway. Greece's most popular spectator sport inspires local passions and often unedifying fan hooliganism.

Greece's Super League is dominated by big football clubs: Olympiakos of Piraeus and arch-rivals Panathinaikos of Athens, along with AEK Athens and Thessaloniki's PAOK.

Greece is one of the power-houses of European basketball. Panathinaikos has won six Euroleague championships, while Olympiakos claimed its third title in 2013. Nigerian-born Greek basketballer Giannis Antetokounmpo became the poster boy for Greece's immigrants in 2013 when he was picked for the Milwaukee Bucks in the NBA draft (having had his Greek citizenship fast-tracked).

★ **Best Religious Festivals**

Festival of Agios Georgios (St George), April

Orthodox Easter, April or May

Feast of St John the Baptist, June

Feast of the Dormition, August

Orthodox Easter procession, Corfu

The State

Personal freedom and the right to protest and protect their democratic rights are sacrosanct to Greeks. Trade-union activism, mass demonstrations and crippling general strikes are a routine part of life in Athens and other major cities, with police and property normally bearing the brunt of antiestablishment sentiment. This rebellious spirit came to the fore during antiausterity protests, as Greeks resisted economic reforms crucial to help curb Greece's soaring national debt.

The nation's capacity to overcome its economic woes has been stifled by systemic problems with Greece's political and civil life, aspects of society that Greeks have long criticised and perpetuated. A residual mistrust of the state and its institutions is a legacy of years of foreign occupation, while political instability fostered a weak civil society based on tax evasion, political patronage and nepotism, and a black-market economy. Merit has long taken second place to political interests when allocating coveted public-sector jobs or EU funds. Making headway with Greece's bloated and inefficient bureaucracy required *meson* (the help of someone working in the system). The infamous *fakelaki* (envelope of cash) became a common way to cut red tape. At its worst, the system fed corruption and profiteering.

Aversion to the perceived over-regulated approach of Western nations is also part of the national psyche. An undercurrent of civil disobedience extends to lax attitudes to road rules (you will see motorcyclists carrying their helmets while they ride as they chat on their mobile phones) or parking restrictions.

Faith & Identity

While most Greeks aren't devout, Orthodox Christianity – the official religion of Greece – remains an important part of their identity and culture. Families flock to church for lively Easter celebrations, weddings, baptisms and annual festivals, but it's largely women and the elderly who attend church services regularly.

Religious rituals are part of daily life. You will notice taxi drivers, motorcyclists and people on public transport make the sign of the cross when they pass a church; compliments to babies and adults are followed by the *'ftou ftou'* (spitting) gesture to ward off the evil eye; and people light church candles in memory of loved ones. Hundreds of privately built small chapels dot the countryside, while the tiny roadside *iconostases* (chapels) are either shrines to road-accident victims or dedications to saints.

During consecutive foreign occupations the Church was the principal upholder of Greek culture, language and traditions, and it still exerts significant social, political and economic influence, though ongoing financial and sexual scandals have taken their toll.

Byzantine church frescoes

MARK READ/LONELY PLANET©

The Arts

*Greece is revered for its artistic and cultural legacy,
and the arts remain a vibrant and evolving element
of Greek culture, identity and self-expression.
Despite, or because of, Greece's recent economic
woes, it has seen a palpable burst of artistic activity
and creativity, fuelling an alternative cultural scene
of low-budget films, artist collectives, and small
underground theatres and galleries.*

Visual Arts

Byzantine & Renaissance Art

Until the start of the 19th century, the primary art form in Greece was Byzantine religious painting. There was little secular artistic output under Ottoman rule, during which Greece essentially missed the Renaissance.

Byzantine church frescoes and icons depicted scenes from the life of Christ and figures of the saints. The 'Cretan school' of icon painting, influenced by the Italian Renaissance and artists fleeing to Crete after the fall of Constantinople, combined technical brilliance and dramatic richness. The most famous Cretan-born Renaissance painter is El Greco

Benaki Museum at 138 Pireos St

★ **Best Art Galleries**

Basil & Elise Goulandris Foundation (p63)

Modern Greek Art Museum (p257)

Benaki Museum at 138 Pireos St (p55)

('The Greek' in Spanish), née Dominikos Theotokopoulos (1541–1614). He got his grounding in the tradition of late-Byzantine fresco painting before moving to Spain in 1577, where he lived and worked until his death.

Modern Art

Modern Greek art evolved after Independence, when painting became more secular, focusing on portraits, nautical themes and the War of Independence. Major 19th-century painters included Dionysios Tsokos, Theodoros Vryzakis, Nikiforos Lytras and Nicholas Gyzis, a leading artist of the Munich School (where many Greek artists of the day studied).

During the 20th century Greek creatives drew inspiration from worldwide movements and developments in the art world, such as the expressionist George Bouzianis, the cubist Nikos Hatzikyriakos-Ghikas and surrealist and poet Nikos Engonopoulos. Other notable Greek 20th-century artists include Konstantinos Parthenis, Fotis Kontoglou, Yiannis Tsarouhis, Panayiotis Tetsis, Yannis Moralis, Dimitris Mytaras and Yiannis Kounellis, a pioneer of the Arte Povera movement.

Contemporary Art

Contemporary Greek art has been gaining exposure in Greece and abroad, with a growing number of Greek artists participating in international art events. The Greek arts scene has become more vibrant, less isolated and more experimental, and Athens' street art is gaining recognition.

Many Greek artists have studied and made their homes and reputations abroad, but a new wave is returning or staying put, contributing to a fresh artistic energy. Watch for work by street artists, Cacao Rocks and INO, the collages of Chryssa Romanos, painter Lucas Samaras, kinetic artist Takis, and sculptor Stephen Antonakos, whose works often incorporate neon.

Modern Greek Literature

Greek literature virtually ceased under Ottoman rule, and was then stifled by conflict over language – Ancient Greek versus the vernacular *dimotiki* (colloquial language). The compromise was *katharevousa*, a conservative form of ancient Greek. (*Dimotiki* was made the country's official language in 1976.)

One of the most important works of early Greek literature is the 17th-century 10,012-line epic poem 'Erotokritos', by Crete's Vitsenzos Kornaros. Its 15-syllable rhyming verses are still recited in Crete's famous *mantinadhes* (rhyming couplets) and put to music.

Greece's most celebrated (and translated) 20th-century novelist is Nikos Kazantzakis (1883–1957), whose novels are full of drama and larger-than-life characters, such as the magnificent title character in his 1946 work *Life and Times of Alexis Zorbas* (better known as *Zorba the Greek*). Another great novelist of the time, Stratis Myrivilis (1890–1969), wrote the classics *Vasilis Arvanitis* and *The Mermaid Madonna*.

Eminent 20th-century Greek poets include Egypt-born Constantine Cavafy (1863–1933) and Nobel-prize laureates George Seferis (1900–71) and Odysseus Elytis (1911–96), awarded in 1963 and 1979 respectively.

Other local literary giants of the 20th century include Iakovos Kambanellis (1921–2011), Kostis Palamas (1859–1943), a poet who wrote the words to the *Olympic Hymn,* and poet-playwright Angelos Sikelianos (1884–1951).

Contemporary Writers

Greece has a prolific publishing industry but scant fiction is translated into English. Contemporary Greek writers who have made small inroads into foreign markets include Apostolos Doxiadis with his international bestseller *Uncle Petros and Goldbach's Conjecture* (2000) and award-winning children's writer Eugene Trivizas.

Greek publisher Kedros' modern-literature translation series includes Dido Sotiriou's *Farewell Anatolia* (1996), Maro Douka's *Fool's Gold* (1991) and Kostas Mourselas' bestselling *Red-Dyed Hair* (1996), which was made into a popular TV series.

The quirky, Rebus-like Inspector Haritos in Petros Markaris' popular crime series provides an enjoyable insight into crime and corruption in Athens. *Che Committed Suicide* (2010), *Basic Shareholder* (2009), *The Late Night News* (2005) and *Zone Defence* (2007) have been translated into English.

Carving a name for himself as the pre-eminent literary voice of contemporary Greece is Christos Ikonomou. In both his 2016 collection of short stories, *Something Will Happen, You'll See* (focusing on the lives of poor Athenians) and *Good Will Come from the Sea* (2019; four loosely connected tales set on an unnamed Greek island), the country's economic crisis provides the grim background.

Bypassing the translation issue and writing in English are Panos Karnezis whose books include *The Maze* (2004), *The Birthday Party* (2007) and *The Fugitives* (2015); and Soti Triantafyllou, author of *Poor Margo* (2001) *and Rare Earths* (2013). Other notable contemporary authors available in translation include Alexis Stamatis, who penned *Bar Flaubert* (2000) and *The Book of Rain* (2015), and Vangelis Hatziyannidis, writer of *Four Walls* (2006) and *Stolen Time* (2007).

Plays by Yiorgos Skourtis (b 1940) and Pavlos Matessis (1933–2013) have been translated and performed abroad.

Cinema

Greek movies have racked up multiple Academy Award nominations over the years, as well as two Palme d'Ors at Cannes for *Missing* (1982) and *Eternity and a Day* (1998) – the latter directed by Theo Angelopoulos (1935–2012), one of Greece's most critically acclaimed filmmakers.

The best known films about the country remain the 1964 Oscar-winner *Zorba the Greek* and *Never on a Sunday* (1960) for which Melina Mercouri won a Cannes festival award. Another classic is Nikos Koundouros' 1956 noir thriller *O Drakos* (*The Fiend of Athens*), regularly voted top Greek film of all time by the Hellenic Film Critics' Association.

In recent years, a new generation of filmmakers has been gaining international attention for what some critics have dubbed the 'weird wave' of Greek cinema. Examples include the award-winning films of Yorgos Lanthimos, some of which are in English *(Alps; The Lobster; The Killing of a Sacred Deer)* and Athina Rachel Tsangari *(Attenburg; Chevalier).*

Ektoras Kygizos' extraordinary *Boy Eating Bird Food* (2012) is an allegory for Greece's recent economic plight, and emblematic of the small, creative collaborations largely produced in the absence of state or industry funding.

Music

For most people, Greek music and dance evoke images of spirited, high-kicking laps around the dance floor to the tune of the bouzouki (a musical instrument in the lute family). Greece's strong and enduring music tradition, however, is a rich mosaic of musical influences and styles.

While many leading performers draw on traditional folk, *laïka* (popular urban folk) and *rembetika* (blues), Greece's vibrant music scene is also pumping out its share of pop, club dance music, jazz, rock, rap and hip-hop.

Traditional Folk Music

Traditional folk music was shunned by the Greek bourgeoisie after Independence, when they looked to Europe – and classical music and opera – rather than their Eastern or 'peasant' roots.

Greece's regional folk music is generally divided into *nisiotika* (the lighter, upbeat music of the islands) and the more grounded *dimotika* of the mainland – where the *klarino* (clarinet) is prominent and lyrics refer to hard times, war and rural life. The spirited music of Crete, dominated by the Cretan *lyra* (a pear-shaped, three-string, bowed instrument) and lute, remains a dynamic musical tradition, with regular performances and recordings by new-generation exponents.

Rembetika, Laïka & Entehna

The Greek 'blues' *rembetika* has two styles. *Smyrneika* (or *cafe aman*) music emerged in the mid- to late 19th century in the thriving port cities of Smyrna and Constantinople, which had large Greek populations, and in Thessaloniki and Athens. With a rich vocal style, haunting *amanedhes* (vocal improvisations) and occasional Turkish lyrics, its sound had more Eastern influence. The second style, dominated by the six-stringed bouzouki, evolved in Piraeus. *Rembetika* ensembles perform seated in a row and traditionally play acoustically.

Laïka (popular or urban folk music) is a mainstream offshoot of *rembetika*, which emerged in the late 1950s and '60s, when clubs in Athens became bigger and glitzier, and the music more commercial. The bouzouki went electric and the sentimental tunes about love, loss, pain and emigration came to embody the nation's spirit. The late Stelios Kazantzidis was the big voice of this era, along with Grigoris Bithikotsis.

Classically trained composers Mikis Theodorakis and Manos Hatzidakis led a new style known as *entehni mousiki* ('artistic' music) also known as *entehna*. They drew on *rembetika* and used instruments such as the bouzouki in more symphonic arrangements, and created popular hits from the poetry of Seferis, Elytis, Ritsos and Kavadias.

Composer Yiannis Markopoulos later introduced rural folk music and traditional string instruments such as the *lyra, santouri* and *kanonaki* into the mainstream, and brought folk performers such as Crete's legendary Nikos Xylouris to the fore.

During the junta years the music of Theodorakis and Markopoulos became a form of political expression (Theodorakis' music was banned and the composer jailed). Today, headline *laïka* performers include Yiannis Ploutarhos, Antonis Remos and Thanos Petrelis.

Contemporary & Pop Music

While few Greek performers have made it big internationally – 1970s singers Nana Mouskouri and Demis Roussos remain the best known – Greece has a strong local music scene, from traditional and pop music to Greek rock, heavy metal, rap and electronic dance.

Some of the most interesting music emerging from Greece fuses elements of folk with Western influences. One of the most whimsical examples was Greece's tongue-in-cheek 2013 Eurovision contender, in which *rembetika* (blues) veteran Agathonas Iakovidis teamed up with the ska-Balkan rhythms of Thessaloniki's kilt-wearing Koza Mostra.

Big names in popular Greek music include Dionysis Savopoulos, dubbed the Bob Dylan of Greece, and seasoned performers George Dalaras and Haris Alexiou.

Standout contemporary performers include Cypriot-born Alkinoos Ioannides, folk singer Eleftheria Arvanitakiis, ethnic-jazz-fusion artists Kristi Stasinopoulou and the Cretan-inspired folk group Haïnides. Also check out Imam Baildi (www.imambaildi.com), a band who give old Greek music a modern makeover.

Greek Gig Guide

In summer Greece's leading acts perform in outdoor concerts around the country. In winter they perform in clubs in Athens and large regional towns.

Authentic folk music is harder to find. The best bet is at regional *panigyria* (open-air festivals) during summer. Look for posters, often around telephone and power poles, or ask around.

Athens' live-music scene includes intimate *rembetika* (blues) clubs and glitzy, expensive, cabaret-style venues known as *bouzoukia*. Second-rate *bouzoukia* clubs are referred to as *skyladhika* (doghouses) – apparently because the crooning singers resemble whining dogs. *Bouzoukia* are the venues for flower-throwing (plate-smashing is rare these days), wanton (and expensive) displays of exuberance, excess and *kefi* (good spirits or mojo).

Greek Dance

Greeks have danced since the dawn of Hellenism. Some folk dances derive from the ritual dances performed in ancient temples – ancient vases depict a version of the well-known *syrtos* folk dance. Dancing was later part of military education; in times of occupation it became an act of defiance and a covert way to keep fit.

Regional dances, like musical styles, vary across Greece. The slow and dignified *tsamikos* reflects the often cold and insular nature of mountain life, while the brighter islands gave rise to light, springy dances such as the *ballos* and the *syrtos*. The Pontian Greeks' vigorous and warlike dances such as the *kotsari* reflect years of altercations with their Turkish neighbours. Crete has its graceful *syrtos,* the fast and triumphant *maleviziotiko* and the dynamic *pentozali,* with its agility-testing high kicks and leaps. The so-called 'Zorba dance' *(syrtaki)* is a stylised dance for two or three dancers with arms linked on each other's shoulders, though the modern variation is danced in a long circle with an ever-quickening beat. Women and men traditionally danced separately and had their own dances, except in courtship dances such as the *sousta*.

Contemporary dance is gaining prominence, with leading local troupes taking their place among the international line-up at the Athens International Dance Festival.

Porch of the Caryatids, Acropolis (p38)

Architecture

For those with an eye to the past, part of the allure of Greece is the sheer volume of its well-preserved buildings. Stand in the ruins of the Parthenon and with a little imagination it's easy to transport yourself back to classical 5th-century Greece. The Renaissance was inspired by the ancient style, as was the neoclassical movement and the British Greek Revival.

Minoan Magnificence

Most of our knowledge of Greek architecture proper begins at around 2000 BC with the Minoans, who were based in Crete but whose influence spread throughout the Aegean to include the Cyclades. Minoan architects are famous for having constructed technologically advanced, labyrinthine palace complexes. The famous site at Knossos is one of the largest. Usually characterised as 'palaces', these sites were in fact multifunctional settlements that were the primary residences of royalty and priests, but housed some plebs too. Large Minoan villages, such as those of Gournia and Palekastro in Crete, also included internal networks of paved roads that extended throughout the countryside to link the settlements with the palaces. More Minoan palace-era sophistication exists in Crete at Phaestos, Malia and Ancient Zakros, and at the Minoan outpost of Ancient Akrotiri on the south of Santorini.

Several gigantic volcanic eruptions rocked the region in the mid-15th century BC, causing geological ripple effects that at the very least caused big chunks of palace to fall to the ground. The Minoans resolutely rebuilt on an even grander scale, only to have more natural disasters wipe the palaces out again. The latter effected an architectural chasm that was filled by the emerging Mycenaean rivals on mainland Greece.

Grandeur of Knossos

According to myth, the man tasked with designing a maze to withhold the dreaded Minotaur was famous Athenian inventor Daedalus, father of Icarus. He also designed the Palace of Knossos for King Minos.

First discovered by a Cretan, Milos Kalokirinos, in 1878, it wasn't until 1900 that the ruins of Knossos were unearthed by Englishman Sir Arthur Evans. The elaborate palace complex at Knossos was originally formed largely as an administrative settlement surrounding the main palace, which comprised the main buildings arranged around a large central courtyard (1250 sq metres). Over time the entire settlement was rebuilt and extended. Long, raised causeways formed main corridors; narrow labyrinthine chambers flanked the palace walls (this meandering floor plan, together with the graphic ritual importance of bulls, inspired the myth of the labyrinth and the Minotaur). The compound featured strategically placed interior light wells, sophisticated ventilation systems, aqueducts, freshwater irrigation wells and bathrooms with extensive plumbing and drainage systems. The ground levels consisted mostly of workshops, cylindrical grain silos and storage magazines.

Thanks to its restoration, today's Knossos is one of the easiest ruins for your imagination to take hold of.

Mycenaean Engineering

The Mycenaeans had a fierce reputation as builders of massive masonry. These war-mongering people roamed southern mainland Greece, picking off the choice vantage points for their austere palaces, fenced within formidable citadels. The citadels' fortified Cyclopean-stone walls were on average an unbreachable 3m to 7m thick. The immense royal beehive tomb of the Treasury of Atreus (aka Tomb of Agamemnon) at Mycenae was constructed using tapered limestone blocks weighing up to 120 tonnes. The palace at Tiryns has stupendous corbel-vaulted galleries and is riddled with secret passageways; the incredibly well-preserved Nestor's Palace, near modern Pylos, also illustrates the Mycenaeans' structural expertise.

Classic Compositions

The Classical age (5th to 4th centuries BC) is when most Greek architectural clichés converge. This is when temples became characterised by the famous orders of columns, particularly the Doric, Ionic and Corinthian.

In the meantime, the Greek colonies of the Asia Minor coast were creating their own Ionic order, designing a column base in several tiers and adding more flutes. This more graceful order's capital (the head) received an ornamented necking, and Iktinos fused elements of its design in the Parthenon. This order is used on the Acropolis' Temple of Athena Nike and the Erechtheion, where the famous Caryatids sculptures regally stand.

Towards the tail end of the Classical period, the Corinthian column was in vogue. Featuring a single or double row of ornate leafy scrolls (usually the very sculptural acanthus), the order was subsequently adopted by the Romans and used only on Corinthian temples in Athens. The Temple of Olympian Zeus, completed during Emperor Hadrian's reign, is

Stavros Niarchos Foundation Cultural Center

★ Best Contemporary Architecture

Acropolis Museum (p44)

Stavros Niarchos Foundation Cultural Center (p52)

Onassis Cultural Centre (p74)

a grand, imposing structure. Another temple design, the graceful, circular temple *tholos* (dome) style, was used for the great Sanctuary of Athena Pronea at Delphi.

The Greek theatre design is a hallmark of the Classical period (an example is the 6th-century-BC Theatre of Dionysos on the south slope of the Acropolis) and had a round stage, radiating a semicircle of steeply banked stone benches that seated many thousands. Cleverly engineered acoustics meant every spectator could monitor every syllable uttered on the stage below. Many ancient Greek theatres are still used for summer festivals, music concerts and plays.

Hellenistic Citizens

In the twilight years of the Classical age (from about the late 4th century BC), cosmopolitan folks started to weary of temples, casting their gaze towards a more decadent urban style. The Hellenistic architect was in hot demand for private homes and palace makeovers as wealthy citizens, dignitaries and political heavyweights lavishly remodelled their abodes in marble, and striking mosaics were displayed as status symbols. The best Hellenistic ancient-home displays are the grand houses at Delos.

Byzantine Zeal

Church-building was particularly expressive during the time of the Byzantine Empire in Greece (from around AD 700 to the early 13th century). The original Greek Byzantine model features a distinctive cross shape – essentially a central dome supported by four arches on piers and flanked by vaults, with smaller domes at the four corners and three apses to the east. Theologian architects opted for spectacular devotional mosaics and frescoes instead of carvings for the stylistic religious interiors.

In Athens, the very appealing 12th-century Church of Agios Eleftherios incorporates fragments of a classical frieze in Pentelic marble; the charming 11th-century Church of Kapnikarea sits stranded, smack-bang in the middle of downtown Athens – its interior flooring is of coloured marble, and the external brickwork, which alternates with stone, is set in patterns. Thessaloniki's 8th-century Church of Agia Sofia, with its 30m-high dome, is a humble version of its namesake in İstanbul.

Frankish, Venetian & Ottoman Offerings

After the sacking of Constantinople by the Crusaders in 1204, much of Greece became the fiefdoms of Western aristocrats. The Villehardouin family punctuated the Peloponnesian landscape with Frankish castles, such as at Kalamata and at Mystras, where they also built a palace that ended up as a court of the Byzantine imperial family for two centuries. When the Venetians dropped by to seize a few coastal enclaves, they built the impenetrable 16th-century Koules fortress in Iraklio, the very sturdy fortress at Methoni and the imposing 18th-century Palamidi fortress at Nafplio.

Remarkably few monuments are left to catalogue after four centuries of Ottoman Turkish rule (16th to 19th centuries). Though many mosques and their minarets have sadly crumbled or are in serious disrepair, some terrific Ottoman-Turkish examples still survive. These include the prominent pink-domed Mosque of Süleyman in Rhodes Old Town. The Fethiye Mosque and Turkish Baths are two of Athens' few surviving Ottoman reminders.

Neoclassical Splendour

Regarded by experts as the most beautiful neoclassical building worldwide, the 1885 Athens Academy reflects Greece's post-Independence yearnings for grand and geometric forms, and Hellenistic detail. Renowned Danish architect Theophile Hansen drew inspiration from the Erechtheion to design the Academy's Ionic-style column entrance (guarded over by Apollo and Athena); the great interior oblong hall is lined with marble seating, and Austrian painter Christian Griepenkerl was commissioned to decorate its elaborate ceiling and wall paintings. In a similar vein, the Doric columns of the Temple of Hephaestus influenced Theophile's solid-marble National Library, while Christian Hansen (Theophile's brother) was responsible for the handsome but more sedate Athens University, with its clean lines.

Meticulously restored neoclassical mansions house notable museums such as the acclaimed Benaki Museum in Athens.

Many provincial towns also display beautiful domestic adaptations of neoclassicism.

Know Your Columns

Doric The most simple of the three styles. The shaft (the main part of the column) is plain and has 20 sides, while the capital (the head) is formed in a simple circle. Also there's no base. An obvious example of this is the Parthenon.

Ionic Look out for the ridged flutes carved into the column from top to bottom. The capital is also distinctive for its scrolls, while the base looks like a stack of rings.

Corinthian The most decorative and popular of all three orders. The column is ridged; however, the distinctive feature is the capital's flowers and leaves, beneath a small scroll. The base is like that of the Ionic.

Modern & Contemporary Ideas

Recently, Athens has embraced a sophisticated, look-both-ways architectural aesthetic to showcase its vast collection of antiquities and archaeological heritage (witness the Acropolis Museum), and to beautify landscapes for pedestrian zones to improve the urban environment. Examples include the well-designed facelift of the historic centre, including its spectacular floodlighting (designed by the renowned Pierre Bideau) of the ancient promenade, and the cutting-edge spaces emerging from once-drab and derelict industrial zones, such as the Technopolis gasworks arts complex in Gazi.

Built for the 2004 Olympics, the Athens Olympic Complex was designed by Spanish architect Santiago Calatrata. It has a striking, ultramodern glass-and-steel roof, which is suspended by cables from large arches. The laminated glass, in the shape of two giant leaves, is capable of reflecting 90% of the sunlight.

Even more impressive is Renzo Piano's Stavros Niarchos Foundation Cultural Center (SNFCC), which generates 100% of its energy needs in summer from the 5400 photovoltaic panels on its roof.

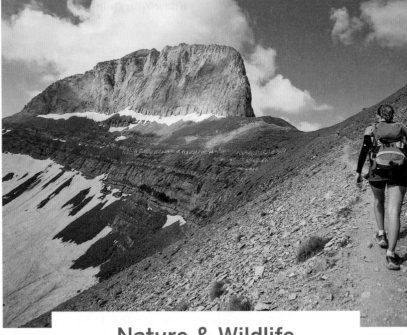

Mount Olympus National Park

HEMIS/ALAMY STOCK PHOTO ©

Nature & Wildlife

Greece is an ideal location for getting up close to nature. Hike through valleys and mountains covered with wildflowers, come eye to eye with a loggerhead turtle or simply stretch out on a beach. Environmental awareness is beginning to seep into the fabric of Greek society, leading to slow but positive change. However, problems such as deforestation and soil erosion date back thousands of years.

Geography & Geology

No matter where you go in Greece, it's impossible to be much more than 100km from the sea. Rugged mountains and seemingly innumerable islands dominate the landscape, which was shaped by submerging seas, volcanic explosions and mineral-rich terrain. The mainland covers 131,944 sq km, with an indented coastline stretching for 15,020km. Mountains rise over 2000m and occasionally tumble down into plains. The Aegean and Ionian Seas link together the country's 1400 islands, with just 169 of them inhabited. These islands fill 400,000 sq km of territorial waters.

Volcanic activity regularly hits Greece. In 1999 a 5.9-magnitude earthquake near Athens killed nearly 150 people and left thousands homeless. Since 2006, the country has had seven quakes ranging from 6.4 to 6.9 in magnitude. None caused major damage.

Greece is short on rivers, with none that are navigable, although they've become popular locations for white-water rafting. The long plains of the river valleys, and those between the mountains and the coast, form Greece's only lowlands. The mountainous terrain, dry climate and poor soil leave farmers at a loss, and less than 25% of the land is cultivated. Greece is, however, rich in minerals, with reserves of oil, manganese, bauxite and lignite.

Wildflowers & Herbs

Greece is endowed with a variety of flora unrivalled in Europe. The wildflowers are spectacular, with more than 6000 species, including more than 200 varieties of orchid. They continue to thrive because most of the land is inadequate for intensive agriculture and has therefore escaped the ravages of chemical fertilisers.

The regions with the most wildflowers are the Lefka Ori (White Mountains) in Crete and the Mani area of the Peloponnese. Trees begin to blossom as early as the end of February in warmer areas and the wildflowers start to appear in March. During spring, hillsides are carpeted with flowers, which seem to sprout even from the rocks. By summer the flowers have disappeared from everywhere but the northern mountainous regions. Autumn brings a new period of blossoming.

Herbs grow wild throughout much of Greece and you'll see locals out picking fresh herbs for their kitchen. Locally grown herbs are also increasingly sold as souvenirs and are generally organic.

Forests

The lush forests that once covered ancient Greece are increasingly rare. Having been decimated by thousands of years of clearing for grazing, boatbuilding and housing, they've more recently suffered from severe forest fires. Northern Greece is the only region that has retained significant areas of native forest – there are mountainsides covered with dense thickets of hop hornbeam *(Ostrya carpinifolia)*, noted for its lavish display of white-clustered flowers. Another common species is the Cyprus plane *(Platanus orientalis insularis)*, which thrives wherever there's ample water.

National Parks

National parks were first established in Greece in 1938 with the creation of Mount Olympus National Park. There are now 10 national parks and two marine parks, which aim to protect Greece's unique flora and fauna.

Facilities for visitors are often basic, abundant walking trails are not always maintained, and the clutch of refuges is very simple. To most, the facilities matter little when compared to nature's magnificent backdrop. It's well worth experiencing the wild side of Greece in one of these settings.

Ainos National Park

CEPHAS PICTURE LIBRARY/ALAMY STOCK PHOTO ©

Watching for Wildlife

On the Ground

In areas widely inhabited by humans, you're unlikely to spot any wild animals other than the odd fox, weasel, hare or rabbit. The more remote mountains of northern Greece continue to support a wide range of wildlife, including wild dogs and shepherds' dogs, which often roam higher pastures on grazing mountains and should be given a wide berth.

Greece has an active snake population and in spring and summer you will inevitably spot them on roads and pathways around the country. Fortunately the majority are harmless, though the viper and the coral snake can cause fatalities. Lizards are in abundance too.

In the Air

Birdwatchers hit the jackpot in Greece as much of the country is on north–south migratory paths. Storks are visible visitors, arriving in early spring from Africa and returning to the same nests year after year. These are built on electricity poles, chimney tops and church towers, and can weigh up to 50kg. Keep an eye out for them in northern Greece, especially in Thrace in Macedonia. Thrace has the richest colony of fish-eating birds in Europe, including species such as egrets, herons, cormorants and ibises, as well as the rare Dalmatian pelican.

In the Seas

One of Europe's most endangered marine mammals, the Mediterranean monk seal (*Monachus monachus*) ekes out an extremely precarious existence in Greece. Approximately 200 to 250 monk seals, about 50% of the world's population, are found in both the Ionian and Aegean Seas. Small colonies also live on the island of Alonnisos and there have been reported sightings on Tilos.

There is still the chance that you will spot dolphins from a ferry deck, though a number of the species, including common dolphins (*Delphinus delphis*) and Risso's dolphins (*Grampus griseus*) are now considered endangered. The main threats to dolphins are a diminished food supply and entanglement in fishing nets.

Environmental Issues

Illegal development of mainly coastal areas, and building in forested or protected areas, has gained momentum in Greece since the 1970s. Despite attempts at introducing laws, and protests by locals and environmental groups, corruption and the lack of an infrastructure to enforce the laws means little is done to abate the land grab. The issue is complicated by population growth and increased urban sprawl. Developments often put a severe strain on water supplies and endangered wildlife. While a few developments have been torn down, in more cases illegal buildings are legalised as they offer much-needed, affordable housing.

The lifting of the diesel ban in Athens and Thessaloniki in 2012 decreased air quality as people opted for cheaper transport. As heating oil tripled in price, people turned to burning wood, often treated, as well as garbage to keep warm. Wintertime particle pollution increased by 30% on some evenings, with lead and arsenic particles found in the air. Smog is a particular problem in Athens as the greater metropolitan area hosts over half of the country's industry, not to mention the lion's share of Greece's population. Athens has subsequently pledged to ban all diesel vehicles from its city centre by 2025.

Each year, forest fires rage across Greece, destroying many thousands of hectares, often in some of the country's most picturesque areas. During the summer of 2018 a series of wildfires across coastal areas of Attica, not far from Athens, claimed 102 lives. This was the country's worst natural disaster since wildfires destroyed large tracts of Mt Parnitha and the Peloponnese in 2007 when 63 people died.

The increasing scale of recent fires is blamed on rising Mediterranean temperatures and high winds. Many locals argue that the government is ill-prepared and that its attempts to address the annual fires are slow. Fearing they won't receive help, many locals refuse to leave areas being evacuated, preferring to take the risk and attempting to fight the flames themselves.

Loggerhead Turtles

Endangered loggerhead turtles (*Caretta caretta*) swim in the seas surrounding Greece with nests in the Peloponnese and on Kefallonia and Crete. Greece's turtles have many hazards to dodge: entanglement in fishing nets and boat propellers, consumption of floating rubbish, and the destruction of their nesting beaches by sunloungers and beach umbrellas, which threaten their eggs. It doesn't help that the turtles' nesting time coincides with the European summer-holiday season.

Loggerhead-turtle hatchlings use the journey from the nest to the sea to build up their strength. Helping the baby turtles to the sea can actually lower their chances of survival.

Survival Guide

Directory A–Z

Accessible Travel

Access for travellers with disabilities has improved somewhat in recent years, though mostly in Athens where there are more accessible sights, hotels and restaurants. Much of the rest of Greece, with its abundance of stones, marble, slippery cobbles and stepped alleys, remains inaccessible or difficult for wheelchair users. People who have visual or hearing impairments are also rarely catered to.

Careful planning before you go can make a world of difference.

Travel Guide to Greece (www. greecetravel.com/handicapped) Links to local articles, resorts and tour groups catering to tourists with physical disabilities.

DR Yachting (www.disabled sailingholidays.com) Two-day

to two-week sailing trips around the Greek islands in fully accessible yachts.

Sirens Resort (www.disable ds-resort.gr) Located 81km west of Athens in Loutraki, this family-friendly resort has accessible apartments, tours and ramps into the sea.

Download Lonely Planet's free Accessible Travel guides from http://lptravel.to/AccessibleTravel.

Accommodation

Greece's plethora of accommodation means that, whatever your taste or budget, there is somewhere to suit your needs. All places to stay are subject to strict price controls set by the tourist police. It's difficult to generalise accommodation prices in Greece as rates depend entirely on the season and location. Don't expect to pay the same price for a double room on one of the islands as you would in central Greece or Athens.

When considering hotel prices, take note of the following points.

○ Prices include community tax and VAT (value-added tax).

○ An Overnight Stay Tax of between €0.50 and €4 depending on the star rating of your accommodation will also be added per night.

○ A mandatory charge of 20% is levied for an additional bed (although this is often waived if the bed is for a child).

○ During July and August accommodation owners will charge the maximum price, which can be as much as double the low-season price. In spring and autumn prices can drop by 20%.

○ Also during high season there may be a two- or three-night minimum reservation policy, particularly at accommodation in the most popular islands and resorts.

○ Rip-offs are rare; if you suspect that you have been exploited, make a report to the tourist police or the regular police, and they will act swiftly.

Customs Regulations

There are no duty-free restrictions within the EU. Upon entering Greece from

Food Price Ranges

The following price ranges refer to the average cost of a main course (not including service charges).

€ less than €10
€€ €10–20
€€€ more than €20

outside the EU, customs inspection is usually cursory for foreign tourists and a verbal declaration is generally all that is required. Random searches are still occasionally made for drugs. Import regulations for medicines are strict; if you are taking medication, make sure you get a statement from your doctor before you leave home. It is illegal, for instance, to take codeine into Greece without an accompanying doctor's certificate.

It is strictly forbidden in Greece to acquire and export antiquities without special permits issued by the Hellenic Ministry of Culture/General Directorate of Antiquities and Cultural Heritage (gda@culture.gr). Severe smuggling penalties might be incurred. It is an offence to remove even the smallest article from an archaeological site.

Electricity

Type C
220V/50Hz

Climate

Athens

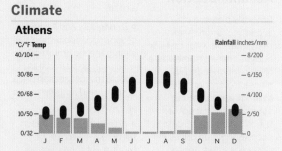

Thessaloniki

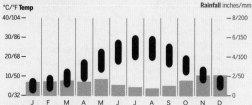

Crete (Iraklio)

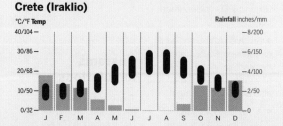

Type F
230V/50Hz

Discount Cards

Camping Card International (CCI; www.campingcardinter national.com) Gives up to 25% savings in camping fees and third-party liability insurance while in the campground. Valid in over 2500 campsites across Europe.

European Youth Card (www. eyca.org) Available for anyone up to the age of 26 or 31, depending on the country. You don't have to be a resident of Europe. It provides discounts of up to 20% at sights, shops and for some transport. Available from the website or travel agencies in Athens and Thessaloniki for €14.

International Student Identity Card (ISIC; www.isic.org) Entitles the holder to half-price admission to museums and ancient sites, and discounts at some budget hotels and hostels. Available from travel agencies in Athens. Applicants require documents proving their student status, a passport photo and €15. Available to students aged 12 to 30.

Seniors cards Card-carrying EU pensioners can claim a range of benefits such as reduced admission to ancient sites and museums, and discounts on bus and train fares.

LGBT+ Travellers

Same sex unions (but not marriages) were legally recognised in Greece in 2015 and attitudes to the LGBT+ community have grown more liberal across the country. However, the Orthodox Church plays a prominent role in shaping society's views on issues such as sexuality, so you may find your sexuality being frowned upon by some locals – especially outside major cities.

Rest assured, Greece is an extremely popular destination for LGBT+ travellers for a reason. Athens has a busy scene, but most LGBT+ travellers head for the islands. Mykonos has long been famous for its bars, beaches and general hedonism.

The Beloved Republic (http://thebelovedrepublic. com) is a company specialising in organising same-sex unions in Greece. For more info on LGBT+ Greece see https://queerintheworld. com/gay-greece.

Health

Although medical training is of a high standard in Greece, the public health service is badly underfunded. Hospitals can be overcrowded, hygiene is not always what it should be, and relatives are expected to bring in food for the patient – which can be a problem for a solo traveller. Conditions and treatment are much better in private hospitals, which are expensive. All this means that a good health-insurance policy is essential.

○ If you need an ambulance in Greece call 166 or 112.

○ There is at least one doctor on every island, and larger islands have hospitals.

○ Pharmacies can dispense medicines that are available only on prescription in most European countries.

○ Consult a pharmacist for minor ailments.

○ If you're an EU citizen, a European Health Insurance Card (EHIC) covers you for most medical care but not emergency repatriation or nonemergencies. Citizens from other countries should find out if there is a reciprocal arrangement for free medical care between their country and Greece.

Internet Access

Free wi-fi is available in most hotels, many cafes and some restaurants. A number of cities have free wi-fi zones in shopping and eating areas and plazas. Internet cafes have virtually disappeared – instead buy a local SIM with data to insert in your unlocked device. Some, but not all, hotels offer computers for guests to use.

Practicalities

Weights & Measures The metric system is used.

Newspapers Greek current affairs are covered in the daily English-language edition of *Kathimerini* (www.ekathimerini.com) within the *New York Times International Edition*.

Magazines *Greece Is* (www.greece-is.com) is a free bi-annual magazine available in many good hotels with an excellent website packed with features on tourist aspects of the country. *2Board* (www.aia.gr), Athens airport's official magazine, is also worth a browse for listings and features on the capital and surrounds.

DVDs Greece is region code 2 for DVDs.

Money

Debit and credit cards are accepted in cities, but elsewhere it's handy to have cash. Most towns have ATMs, but they may be out of order.

ATMs

ATMs are found in every town large enough to support a bank and in almost all the tourist areas. If you have MasterCard or Visa, there are plenty of places to withdraw money. Cirrus and Maestro users can make withdrawals in all major towns and tourist areas.

Note that in small tourist villages, the only option may be a Euronet ATM (yellow and blue). These charge a €3.95 fee (compared to €2 to €3 at bank ATMs), and offer significantly worse exchange rates.

Be aware that many ATMs on the islands can lose their connection for a day or two at a time, making it impossible for anyone (locals included) to withdraw money. It's useful to have a backup source of money.

Automated foreign-exchange machines are common in major tourist areas. They take all major European currencies, Australian and US dollars and Japanese yen, and are useful in an emergency, although they charge a hefty commission.

Be warned that many card companies can put an automatic block on your card after your first withdrawal abroad, as an antifraud mechanism. To avoid this happening, inform your bank of your travel plans.

Cash

Nothing beats cash for convenience – or for risk. If you lose cash, it's gone for good. It's best to carry no more cash than you need for the next few days. It's also a good idea to set aside a small amount, say €100, as an emergency stash.

Note that Greek shopkeepers and small-business owners sometimes don't have small change. When buying small items it is better to tender coins or small-denomination notes.

Credit Cards

Credit cards are an accepted part of the commercial scene in Greece. In fact, since 2018 (as part of the 'management' of the financial crisis) Greeks aged below 65 and earning an income have been required by law to have a credit card. As a result, hotels and commercial ventures must be able to process them.

The main credit cards are MasterCard and Visa, both of which are widely accepted. They can also be used as cash cards to draw cash from the ATMs of affiliated Greek banks. Daily withdrawal limits are set by the issuing bank and are given in local currency only (though you may be given the opportunity to accept or decline a fixed exchange rate of your home currency).

Tipping

Restaurants Tipping is not traditionally the culture in Greece, though it is appreciated. Locals tend to leave a few coins. Depending on where you are, you can round it up or leave around 10%.

Taxis Round up the fare. There's a small fee for handling bags;

this is an official charge, not a tip.

Bellhops Bellhops in hotels appreciate a small gratuity of around €1.

Opening Hours

Opening hours vary throughout the year. The following are high-season hours; hours decrease significantly for shoulder and low seasons, and some places close completely. In tourist locations, some shops stay open longer year round.

Banks 8.30am to 2.30pm Monday to Thursday, 8am to 2pm Friday

Restaurants 11am to 11pm

Cafes 10am to midnight

Bars 8pm to late

Clubs 10pm to 4am

Post Offices 7.30am to 2pm Monday to Friday (rural); 7.30am to 8pm Monday to Friday, 7.30am to 2pm Saturday (urban)

Shops 8am to 2pm Monday, Wednesday and Saturday; 8am to 2pm and 5pm to 9pm Tuesday, Thursday and Friday

Photography

○ Digital memory cards are readily available from camera stores.

○ Never photograph a military installation; some are less than obvious and near to wildlife-viewing areas.

○ Flash photography is not allowed inside churches and it's considered taboo to photograph the main altar.

○ Greeks usually love having their photos taken, but always ask permission first.

○ At archaeological sites you will be stopped from using a tripod as it marks you as a 'professional'.

Public Holidays

New Year's Day 1 January

Epiphany 6 January

First Sunday in Lent February

Greek Independence Day 25 March

Good Friday 17 April 2020, 30 April 2021, 22 April 2022

Orthodox Easter Sunday 19 April 2020, 2 May 2021, 24 April 2022

May Day (Protomagia) 1 May

Whit Monday (Agiou Pnevmatos) 8 June 2020, 21 June 2021, 13 June 2022

Feast of the Dormition 15 August

Ohi Day 28 October

Christmas Day 25 December

St Stephen's Day 26 December

Safe Travel

If you take the usual precautions, Greece is a safe place to travel and you're more likely to suffer from heat exhaustion or sunburn than from any kind of crime.

○ Pickpocketing is an issue; always be vigilant in busy bus stations, markets or on crowded streets.

○ Watch out for adulterated drinks made from cheap illegal imports, and drink spiking, especially at party resorts.

○ If you need to report something, go first to the *touristikí astynomía* (tourist police) in cities and popular tourist destinations; at least one staff member will speak English.

Telephone

The Greek telephone service is maintained by the public corporation OTE (pronounced o-*teh;* Organismos Tilepikoinonion Ellados). You may still find some public phones in central locations (eg near plazas) in both cities and villages, though as most people now use mobile (cell) phones, these are becoming rarities.

Note that in Greece the area code must always be dialled when making a call (ie all Greek phone numbers are 10-digit).

Mobile Phones

There are several mobile service providers in Greece, among which Cosmote (www.cosmote.gr), Vodafone (www.vodafone.gr) and Wind (www.wind.gr) are the

Important Phone Numbers

In Greece, the area code must be dialled for ordinary numbers, meaning you always dial the full 10-digit telephone number. Emergency numbers are shorter, as detailed in the table below.

Country code	☎30
International access code	☎00
Ambulance	☎166
Police	☎100
Tourist police	☎1571

best known. Of these three, Cosmote tends to have the best coverage in remote areas. All offer 4G connectivity and pay-as-you-talk services for which you can buy a rechargeable SIM card and have your own Greek mobile number. If you're buying a package, be sure to triple-check the fine print. There are restrictions on deals such as 'free minutes' only being available to phones using the same provider.

The use of a mobile phone while driving in Greece is prohibited, but the use of a Bluetooth headset is allowed.

Phonecards & Public Phones

Public phones use OTE phonecards, known as *telekarta*, not coins. These cards are available at *periptera* (street kiosks), and some corner shops and tourist shops. Public phones are easy to operate. The 'i' at the top left of the push-button dialling panel brings up the operating instructions in English.

It's also possible to use payphones with discount-card schemes. This involves dialling an access code and then punching in your card number. The OTE version of this card is known as 'Chronokarta'. The cards come with instructions in Greek and English, and the talk time is good compared with the standard phone-card rates.

Time

Greece is two hours ahead of GMT/UTC and three hours ahead on daylight-saving time – which begins on the last Sunday in March, when clocks are put forward one hour. Daylight saving ends on the last Sunday in October.

Toilets

● Nearly all places in Greece have Western-style toilets, including hotels and restaurants. Public toilets at transport terminals (bus and train) sometimes have Ottoman/Turkish squat-style toilets.

● Public toilets tend to be limited to airports and bus and train stations, with the very occasional one in tourist-heavy town centres. Cafes are the best option if you get caught short, but in tourist-heavy places, it's polite to buy something for the privilege.

● The Greek plumbing system can't handle toilet paper; apparently the pipes are too narrow and anything larger than a postage stamp seems to cause a problem. Toilet paper etc must be placed in the small bin provided next to every toilet.

Tourist Information

The Greek National Tourist Organisation (www. visitgreece.gr) is known as GNTO abroad and EOT within Greece. The quality of service from office to office varies dramatically; in some you'll get information aplenty and in others you'll be hard-pressed to find anyone behind the desk. EOT offices can be found in major tourist locations. In some regions tourist offices are run by the local government/municipality.

Visas

The list of countries whose nationals can stay in Greece for up to 90 days without a visa includes Australia, Canada, all EU countries, Iceland, Israel, Japan, New Zealand, Norway, Switzerland and the USA. Other countries included are the European principalities of Monaco and San Marino, and most South American countries. The list changes though – contact Greek embassies for the latest. The Greek Ministry of Foreign Affairs publishes an updated list of countries requiring visas (www.mfa.gr/en/visas).

If you wish to stay in Greece for longer than three months within a six-month period, you will probably require a national visa (type D) from the Greek embassy in your country of residence. You are unable to apply for this in Greece.

Women Travellers

Many women travel alone in Greece. The crime rate remains relatively low and solo travel is probably safer than in most European countries. This does not mean that you should be lulled into complacency; bag snatching and sexual assault do occur, particularly at party resorts on the islands.

The majority of Greek men treat foreign women with respect. However, you may still come across smooth-talking guys who aren't in the least bashful about approaching women in the street. They can be very persistent, but they are usually a hassle rather than a threat.

Transport

Getting There & Away

Greece is easy to reach by air or sea – particularly in summer when it opens its arms (and schedules) wide. Getting to or from Greece overland takes more planning but isn't impossible. Flights, cars and tours can be booked online at lonelyplanet.com/bookings.

Air

Greece has four main international airports that take chartered and scheduled flights. Other international airports across the country include Santorini (Thira), Karpathos and Kefallonia; these are most often used for charter flights from the UK, Germany and Scandinavia.

Eleftherios Venizelos International Airport (ATH; ☏210 353 0000; www.aia.gr) Athens' international airport is near Sparta, 27km east of the capital. It has all the modern conveniences, including 24-hour luggage storage and a children's play area.

Nikos Kazantzakis International Airport (HER; ☏2810 397800; www.ypa.gr/en/our-airports/kratikos-aerolimenas-hrakleioy-n-kazantzakhs) About 5km east of Iraklio (Crete). Has an ATM, duty-free shop and cafe-bar.

Diagoras Airport (RHO; ☏22410 88700; www.rho-airport.gr) On the island of Rhodes.

Makedonia International Airport (SKG; ☏2310 985 000; www.thessalonikiairport.com) About 15km southeast of Thessaloniki.

Aegean Airlines (A3; ☏801 112 0000; https://en.aegeanair.com) and its subsidiary, **Olympic Air** (☏801 801 0101, 21035 50500; www.olympicair.com), have flights between Athens and destinations throughout Europe, as well as to Cairo, İstanbul, Tel Aviv and Toronto. They also operate flights throughout Greece, many of which transfer in Athens. Both

Border Crossings

Make sure you have all of your visas sorted out before attempting to cross land borders into or out of Greece. Before travelling, also check the status of borders with the relevant embassies.

airlines have exemplary safety records.

Land

International train travel, in particular, has become much more feasible in recent years, with speedier trains and better connections. You can now travel from London to Athens by train and ferry in less than two days. By choosing to travel on the ground instead of the air, you'll also be reducing your carbon footprint.

Sea

Ferries can get very crowded in summer. If you want to take a vehicle across, it's wise to make a reservation beforehand. Port tax for departures to Turkey is around €10.

Another way to visit Greece by sea is to join one of the many cruises that ply the Aegean.

Getting Around

Air

The vast majority of domestic mainland flights are handled by the country's national carrier **Aegean Airlines** (A3; ☏801 112 0000; https://en.aegeanair.com) and its subsidiary, **Olympic Air** (☏801 801 0101, 21035 50500; www.olympicair.com). You'll find offices wherever there are flights, as well as in other major towns. There are also a number of smaller Greek carriers, including Thessaloniki-based **Astra Airlines** (☏23104 89391; www.astra-airlines.gr) and **Sky Express** (☏21521 56510; www.skyexpress.gr).

There are discounts for return tickets for travel between Monday and Thursday, and bigger discounts for trips that include a Saturday night away. Find full details and timetables on airline websites. Viva.gr (https://travel.viva.gr) is a good website for finding cheap domestic flights as well as other travel and entertainment tickets.

The baggage allowance on domestic flights varies according to the airline and the category of ticket you've purchased, and can be scrutinised carefully at check-in. It's usually 20kg if the domestic flight is part of an international journey.

Bicycle

Cycling is not popular among Greeks – but it's gaining popularity, plus kudos with tourists. You'll need strong leg muscles to tackle the mountains; or you can stick to some of the flatter coastal routes. Bike lanes are rare to nonexistent; helmets are not compulsory. The main dangers are the cars on the roads – locals and tourists alike.

- You can hire bicycles in most tourist places, but they are not as widely available as cars and motorcycles. Prices range from €10 to €15 per day, depending on the type and age of the bike.

- Bicycles are carried free on ferries but cannot be taken on the fast ferries (catamarans and the like; there simply isn't room to store them).

- You can buy decent mountain or touring bikes in Greece's major towns, though you may have a

---

Climate Change & Travel

Every form of transport that relies on carbon-based fuel generates CO_2, the main cause of human-induced climate change. Modern travel is dependent on aeroplanes, which might use less fuel per kilometre per person than most cars but travel much greater distances. The altitude at which aircraft emit gases (including CO_2) and particles also contributes to their climate change impact. Many websites offer 'carbon calculators' that allow people to estimate the carbon emissions generated by their journey and, for those who wish to do so, to offset the impact of the greenhouse gases emitted with contributions to portfolios of climate-friendly initiatives throughout the world. Lonely Planet offsets the carbon footprint of all staff and author travel.

problem finding a ready buyer if you wish to on-sell it. Bike prices are much the same as across the rest of Europe: anywhere from €300 to €2000.

Boat

Greece has an extensive network of ferries – the only means of reaching many of the islands. Schedules are often subject to delays due to poor weather (note: this is a safety precaution) plus the occasional industrial action, and prices fluctuate regularly. Timetables are not announced until just prior to the season due to competition for route licences. In summer, ferries run regular services between all but the most out-of-the-way destinations; however, services seriously slow down in winter (and in some cases stop completely).

Ferry companies have local offices on many of the islands. The big companies compete for routes annually (and seem to merge and demerge regularly). A useful website to check is **Greek Ferries** (☑ 281 052 9000; www.greekferries.gr), which is also available as an app.

Bus

The bus network is comprehensive. All long-distance buses, on the mainland and the islands, are operated by regional collectives known as KTEL (www.ktelbus. com). Within towns and cities, different companies run inter urban services.

The fares are fixed by the government; bus travel is reasonably priced. All have good safety records.

○ It is important to note that big cities like Athens, Iraklio and Thessaloniki may have more than one bus station, each serving different regions. Make sure you find the correct station for your destination.

○ There is no central source of bus information, and each KTEL company runs its own website, with varying amounts of info. Thessaloniki's (KTEL Makedonia) is the best, and it falls off rapidly from there. Frustratingly, KTEL bus timetables only give the end destination – check when you buy tickets at stations about intermediate town stops on a given route.

○ In remote areas, the timetable may be in Greek only, but most booking offices have timetables in both Greek and Roman script.

○ It's best to turn up at least 20 minutes before departure – buses have been known to leave a few minutes before their scheduled departure.

○ When you buy a ticket you may be allotted a seat number, printed on the ticket. (In some cases locals ignore these.)

○ You can board a bus without a ticket and pay on board, but on a popular route or during high season, you may have to stand.

○ The KTEL buses are safe, modern and air-conditioned. In more remote, rural areas they may be older and less comfortable. Note that buses often have toilets on board that are not used; instead, on longer journeys, they must stop every 2½ hours.

○ Smoking is prohibited on all buses in Greece.

Car & Motorcycle

In the past, Greece had a terrible reputation for road safety. In recent years, however, roads and highways have improved dramatically and European Commission statistics (2010–18) report a drop of 45% in fatalities. However, no one who has travelled on Greece's roads will be surprised to hear that the road toll of 69 deaths for every million inhabitants is still a lot higher than the EU average of 49. Overtaking is listed as the greatest cause, along with speed. Accidents can occur on single-lane roads when slower vehicles pull to the right on both sides and are overtaken at the same time, leading to head-on collisions.

Heart-stopping moments aside, your own car is a great way to explore off the beaten track. The road network has improved enormously in recent years, with a similar increase in tourist traffic, especially on the islands. This brings its own problems such as parking and congestion in island towns. There are regular (if costly) car-ferry services to almost all islands.

Motorcycle Warning

If you plan to hire a motorcycle or moped, you require a motorcycle licence. Expect gravel roads, particularly on the islands; scooters are particularly prone to sliding on gravelly bends. If you plan to use a motorcycle or moped, check that your travel insurance covers you; many insurance companies don't cover motorcycle accidents.

Practicalities

Automobile Associations Nationwide roadside assistance is provided by **ELPA** (Elliniki Leschi Aftokinitou kai Periigiseon; 24hr roadside assistance 10400).

Entry EU-registered vehicles enter free for up to six months without road taxes being due. A green card (international third-party insurance) is required, along with proof of date of entry (ferry ticket or your passport stamp). Non-EU-registered vehicles may be logged in your passport.

Driving licences EU driving licences are valid in Greece. Rental agencies require the corresponding driving licence for every vehicle class (eg motorcycle/moped licence for motorbikes or mopeds). Greek law requires drivers from outside the EU to have an International Driving Permit (IDP). Rental agencies will request it, as may local authorities if you're stopped. IDPs can only be obtained in person and in the country where your driving

licence was issued. Carry this alongside your regular licence.

Fuel Available widely throughout the country, though service stations may be closed on weekends and public holidays. On the islands, there may be only one petrol station; check where it is before you head out. Self-service and credit-card pumps are not the norm in Greece. Petrol in Greece is among the most expensive in Europe. Petrol types include *amolyvdi* (unleaded) and *petreleo kinisis* (diesel).

Hire

Car

○ All the big multinational companies are represented in Athens; most have branches in major towns and popular tourist destinations. The majority of islands have at least one outlet.

○ By Greek law, rental cars have to be replaced every 10 years. However, very often a car is quite scratched up when you get it. Be sure to take photos of all the damage.

○ The minimum driving age in Greece is 18 years, but most car-hire firms require you to be at least 21 (or 23 for larger vehicles). In some cases, you pay extra if you're a younger driver.

○ High-season weekly rates with unlimited mileage start at about €280 for the smallest models (eg a Fiat Seicento), dropping to about €150 per week in winter.

○ You can often find great deals at local companies. Their advertised rates can be up to 50% cheaper than the multinationals and they are normally open to negotiation, especially if business is slow.

○ On the islands, you can rent a car for the day for around €35 to €60, including all insurance and taxes.

○ Always check what the insurance includes; there are often rough roads or dangerous routes that you can only tackle by renting a 4WD.

○ It is not possible to take a car hired in Greece into another country.

○ Unless you pay with a credit card, most hire companies will require a minimum deposit of €120 per day.

○ Some of the international car-rental agencies have a policy that if you rent for a longer term (eg three or more days), you must prepay for a tank of gas. If you return the car with the tank full, you're entitled to a refund, but you absolutely must ask for it – there's no guarantee the prepayment will be automatically refunded.

The major car-hire companies in Greece include the following:

Avis (www.avis.gr)

Budget (www.budget.gr)

Europcar (www.europcar -greece.gr)

Motorcycle

o Mopeds, motorcycles, scooters and quad bikes (ATVs) are available for hire wherever there are tourists to rent them. Most machines are newish and in good condition. Nonetheless, check the brakes at the earliest opportunity.

o You must produce a licence that shows proficiency to ride the category of bike you wish to rent; this applies to everything from 50cc up. British citizens must obtain a Category A1 licence from the Driver & Vehicle Licensing Agency (www.dft.gov.uk/dvla) in the UK (in most other EU countries separate licences are automatically issued).

o Rates start from about €20 per day for a moped or 50cc motorcycle, ranging to €35 per day for a 250cc motorcycle. Out of season these prices drop considerably, so use your bargaining skills.

o Most motorcycle hirers include third-party insurance in the price, but it's wise to check this. This insurance will not include medical expenses.

o Helmets are compulsory and rental agencies are obliged to offer one as part of the hire deal.

Road Conditions

o Main highways in Greece have been improving steadily over the years and are now all excellent.

o The old highways are now quite empty of big trucks, and much nicer for driving.

o Some main roads retain a two-lane/hard-shoulder format, which can be confusing and even downright dangerous.

o Roadworks can take years and years in Greece – especially on the islands, where funding often only trickles in. In other cases, excellent new tarmac roads may have appeared that are not on any local maps.

o Many island roads aren't paved, which doesn't always show up clearly on GPS or online maps – take care not to get stuck down dirt tracks that aren't meant to be driven on.

Road Hazards

o Slow drivers – many of them unsure and hesitant tourists who stop suddenly on corners and other inappropriate places – can cause serious traffic events on Greece's roads.

o Road surfaces can change rapidly when a section of road has succumbed to subsidence or weathering. Snow and ice can be a serious challenge in winter, and drivers are advised to carry snow chains. In rural areas, keep a close eye out for animals wandering on to roads.

o Roads passing through mountainous areas are often littered with fallen rocks, which can cause extensive damage to a vehicle's underside or throw a motorbike rider.

o When driving on a single carriageway, slower vehicles, including older trucks, tend to pull over to the right into the 'safety' lane, allowing impatient drivers to pass around them. The issue is, this happens from both sides, so as a car pulls out to pass in the free space (which locals seem to wrongly consider a 'lane'), fatal head-on collisions are common.

Road Rules

o In Greece, as throughout continental Europe, you drive on the right and overtake on the left.

o Outside built-up areas, unless signed otherwise, traffic on a main road has right of way at intersections. In towns, vehicles coming from the right have right of way. This includes roundabouts – even if you're in the roundabout, you must give way to drivers coming on to the roundabout to your right.

o Seatbelts must be worn in front seats, and in back seats if the car is fitted with them.

o Children under 12 years of age are not allowed in the front seat.

o It is compulsory to carry a first-aid kit, fire extinguisher and warning triangle, and it is forbidden to carry cans of petrol.

○ Helmets are compulsory for motorcyclists. Police will book you if you're caught without a helmet.

○ Outside residential areas the speed limit is 120km/h on highways, 90km/h on other roads and 50km/h in built-up areas. The speed limit for motorcycles is the same as cars. Drivers exceeding the speed limit by 20% are liable to receive a fine of €40 to €120; exceeding it by 30% costs €350 plus your licence will be suspended for 60 days.

○ A blood-alcohol content of 0.05% can incur a fine, while over 0.08% is a criminal offence.

○ It is illegal to use a mobile phone while driving. If caught, you may be charged between €100 and €300 and have your licence suspended for 30 days.

○ If you are involved in an accident and no one is hurt, the police are not required to write a report, but it is advisable to go to a nearby police station and explain what happened. You may need a police report for insurance purposes. If an accident involves injury, a driver who does not stop and does not inform the police may face a prison sentence.

Local Transport

○ All the major towns have local buses.

○ Athens has a good underground system, and Thessaloniki is in the process of constructing one, too (expected to open at the end of 2020). Note that only Greek student cards are valid for a student ticket on the metro.

○ Taxis are widely available and are reasonably priced by European standards.

○ Some taxi drivers in Athens have been known to overcharge unwary travellers. If you have a complaint about a taxi driver, take the cab number and report your complaint to the tourist police.

○ Useful taxi apps include Beat (www.thebeat.co/gr) and Taxiplon (www.taxiplon.gr).

○ Trains are operated by **OSE** (Organismos Sidirodromon Ellados; 14511; www.trainose.gr). The railway network is extremely limited with lines closed in recent years in areas such as the Peloponnese. OSE's northern line is the most substantial.

Language

The Greek language is believed to be one of the oldest European languages, with an oral tradition of 4000 years and a written tradition of approximately 3000 years.

If you read the pronunciation guides given with each phrase in this chapter as if they were English, you'll be understood. Note that **dh** is pronounced as 'th' in 'there'; **gh** is a softer, slightly throaty version of 'g'; and **kh** is a throaty sound like the 'ch' in the Scottish 'loch'. All Greek words of two or more syllables have an acute accent (´), which indicates where the stress falls. In our pronunciation guides, stressed syllables are in italics.

To enhance your trip with a phrasebook, visit **lonelyplanet.com**. Lonely Planet iPhone phrasebooks are available through the Apple App store.

Basics

Hello.	Γειά σας.	ya·sas (polite)
	Γειά σου.	ya·su (informal)
Goodbye.	Αντίο.	an·di·o
Yes./No.	Ναι./Οχι.	ne/o·hi
Please.	Παρακαλώ.	pa·ra·ka·lo
Thank you.	Ευχαριστώ.	ef·ha·ri·sto
You're welcome	Παρακαλώ.	pa·ra·ka·lo
Excuse me.	Με συγχωρείτε.	me sing·kho·ri·te
Sorry.	Συγγνώμη.	sigh·no·mi

What's your name?

| Πώς σας λένε; | pos sas le·ne |

My name is ...

| Με λένε ... | me le·ne ... |

Do you speak English?

| Μιλάτε αγγλικά; | mi·la·te an·gli·ka |

I don't understand.

| Δεν καταλαβαίνω. | dhen ka·ta·la·ve·no |

Accommodation

campsite	χώρος για	kho·ros yia
	κάμπινγκ	kam·ping
hotel	ξενοδοχείο	kse·no·dho·khi·o
youth hostel	γιουθ χόστελ	yuth kho·stel

How much	Πόσο	po·so
is it ...?	κάνει ...;	ka·ni ...
per night	τη βραδυά	ti·vra·dhya
per person	το άτομο	to a·to·mo

Eating & Drinking

That was delicious.

| Ήταν νοστιμότατο! | i·tan no·sti·mo·ta·to |

Please bring the bill.

| Το λογαριασμό, | to lo·ghar·ya·zmo |
| παρακαλώ. | pa·ra·ka·lo |

I don't eat ...	Δεν τρώγω ...	dhen tro·gho ...
fish	ψάρι	psa·ri
(red) meat	(κόκκινο)	(ko·ki·no)
	κρέας	kre·as
peanuts	φυστίκια	fi·sti·kia
poultry	πουλερικά	pu·le·ri·ka

Emergencies

Help!	Βοήθεια!	vo·i·thya
Go away!	Φύγε!	fi·ye
I'm lost.	Έχω χαθεί.	e·kho kha·thi
Where's the	Πού είναι η	pu i·ne i
toilet?	τουαλέτα;	tu·a·le·ta
Call ...!	Φωνάξτε ...!	fo·nak·ste ...
a doctor	ένα γιατρό	e·na yi·a·tro
the police	την	tin
	αστυνομία	a·sti·no·mi·a
I'm ill.	Είμαι άρρωστος.	i·me a·ro·stos

Directions

Where is ...?

| Πού είναι ...; | pu i·ne ... |

What's the address?

| Ποια είναι η διεύθυνση; | pia i·ne i dhi·ef·thin·si |

Can you show me (on the map)?

| Μπορείς να μου δείξεις | bo·ris na mu dhik·sis |
| (στο χάρτη); | (sto khar·ti) |

Turn left.

| Στρίψτε αριστερά. | strips·te a·ri·ste·ra |

Turn right.

| Στρίψτε δεξιά. | strips·te dhe·ksia |

at the next corner

| στην επόμενη γωνία | stin e·po·me·ni gho·ni·a |

at the traffic lights

| στα φώτα | sta fo·ta |

Behind the Scenes

Acknowledgements

Climate map data adapted from Peel MC, Finlayson BL & McMahon TA (2007) 'Updated World Map of the Köppen-Geiger Climate Classification', *Hydrology and Earth System Sciences*, 11, 1633–44.

Illustrations pp42–3 and pp180–1 by Javier Zarracina; pp110–11 by Michael Weldon.

Cover photograph: Fira, Santorini, Vladimir_Timofeev/Getty Images ©

This Book

This 1st edition of Lonely Planet's *Best of Greece & the Greek Islands* guidebook was researched and written by Simon Richmond, Kate Armstrong, Stuart Butler, Peter Dragicevich, Anna Kaminski, Hugh McNaughtan, Kate Morgan, Kevin Raub, Andy Symington and Greg Ward. This guidebook was produced by the following:

Destination Editor Brana Vladisavljevic

Senior Product Editors Elizabeth Jones, Kathryn Rowan

Regional Senior Cartographer Anthony Phelan

Product Editor Kate James

Book Designers Michael Weldon, Mazzy Prinsep

Assisting Editors Sarah Bailey, James Bainbridge, Judith Bamber, Samantha Cook, Melanie Dankel, Jennifer Hattam, Rosie Nicholson, Monique Perrin, Christopher Pitts, Tamara Sheward

Cover Researcher Naomi Parker

Thanks to Imogen Bannister, Nigel Chin, Charlotte Orr

Send Us Your Feedback

We love to hear from travellers – your comments keep us on our toes and help make our books better. Our well-travelled team reads every word on what you loved or loathed about this book. Although we cannot reply individually to postal submissions, we always guarantee that your feedback goes straight to the appropriate authors, in time for the next edition. Each person who sends us information is thanked in the next edition, the most useful submissions are rewarded with a selection of digital PDF chapters.

Visit lonelyplanet.com/contact to submit your updates and suggestions or to ask for help. Our award-winning website also features inspirational travel stories, news and discussions.

Note: We may edit, reproduce and incorporate your comments in Lonely Planet products such as guidebooks, websites and digital products, so let us know if you don't want your comments reproduced or your name acknowledged. For a copy of our privacy policy visit lonelyplanet.com/privacy.

Index

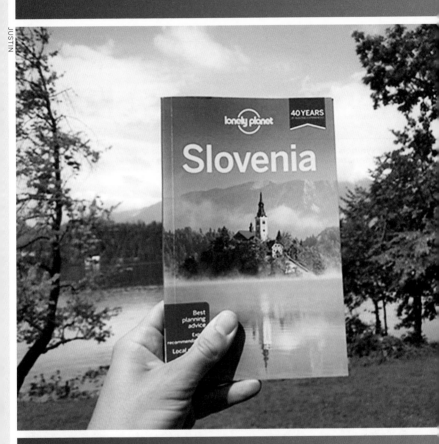

Symbols & Map Key

Look for these symbols to quickly identify listings:

- ◉ Sights
- ✪ Activities
- ✪ Courses
- ✪ Tours
- ✪ Festivals & Events
- ✪ Eating
- ✪ Drinking
- ✪ Entertainment
- ✪ Shopping
- ✪ Information & Transport

These symbols and abbreviations give vital information for each listing:

🍃 Sustainable or green recommendation

FREE No payment required

- ☎ Telephone number
- ☺ Opening hours
- ℗ Parking
- ⊘ Nonsmoking
- ✳ Air-conditioning
- @ Internet access
- 🛜 Wi-fi access
- 🏊 Swimming pool
- 🚌 Bus
- ⛴ Ferry
- 🚊 Tram
- 🚆 Train
- 🍴 English-language menu
- 🌱 Vegetarian selection
- 👪 Family-friendly

Find your best experiences with these Great For... icons.

- Art & Culture
- Beaches
- Budget
- Cafe/Coffee
- Cycling
- Detour
- Drinking
- Entertainment
- Events
- Family Travel
- Food & Drink
- History
- Local Life
- Nature & Wildlife
- Photo Op
- Scenery
- Shopping
- Short Trip
- Sport
- Walking
- Winter Travel

Sights
- Beach
- Bird Sanctuary
- Buddhist
- Castle/Palace
- Christian
- Confucian
- Hindu
- Islamic
- Jain
- Jewish
- Monument
- Museum/Gallery/ Historic Building
- Ruin
- Shinto
- Sikh
- Taoist
- Winery/Vineyard
- Zoo/Wildlife Sanctuary
- Other Sight

Points of Interest
- Bodysurfing
- Camping
- Cafe
- Canoeing/Kayaking
- Course/Tour
- Diving
- Drinking & Nightlife
- Eating
- Entertainment
- Sento Hot Baths/ Onsen
- Shopping
- Skiing
- Sleeping
- Snorkelling
- Surfing
- Swimming/Pool
- Walking
- Windsurfing
- Other Activity

Information
- Bank
- Embassy/Consulate
- Hospital/Medical
- Internet
- Police
- Post Office
- Telephone
- Toilet
- Tourist Information
- Other Information

Geographic
- Beach
- Gate
- Hut/Shelter
- Lighthouse
- Lookout
- Mountain/Volcano
- Oasis
- Park
- Pass
- Picnic Area
- Waterfall

Transport
- Airport
- BART station
- Border crossing
- Boston T station
- Bus
- Cable car/Funicular
- Cycling
- Ferry
- Metro/MRT station
- Monorail
- Parking
- Petrol station
- Subway/S-Bahn/ Skytrain station
- Taxi
- Train station/Railway
- Tram
- Underground/ U-Bahn station
- Other Transport

Peter Dragicevich

After a successful career in niche newspaper and magazine publishing, both in his native New Zealand and in Australia, Peter finally gave in to Kiwi wanderlust, giving up staff jobs to chase his diverse roots around much of Europe. Over the last decade he's written literally dozens of guidebooks for Lonely Planet on an oddly disparate collection of countries, all of which he's come to love. He once again calls Auckland, New Zealand his home – although his current nomadic existence means he's often elsewhere.

Anna Kaminski

Originally from the Soviet Union, Anna grew up in Cambridge, UK. She graduated from the University of Warwick with a degree in Comparative American Studies, a background in the history, culture and literature of the Americas and the Caribbean, and an enduring love of Latin America. Her restless wanderings led her to settle briefly in Oaxaca and Bangkok and her flirtation with criminal law saw her volunteering as a lawyer's assistant in the courts, ghettos and prisons of Kingston, Jamaica. Anna has contributed to almost 30 Lonely Planet titles.

Hugh McNaughtan

A former English lecturer, Hugh swapped grant applications for visa applications, and turned his love of travel into a full-time thing. Having done a bit of restaurant reviewing in his home town (Melbourne), he's now eaten his way across four continents. He's never happier than when on the road with his two daughters. Except perhaps on the cricket field.

Kate Morgan

Having worked for Lonely Planet for over a decade now, Kate has been fortunate enough to cover plenty of ground working as a travel writer on destinations such as Shanghai, Japan, India, Russia, Zimbabwe, the Philippines and Phuket. She has done stints living in London, Paris and Osaka but these days is based in one of her favourite regions in the world – Victoria, Australia. In between travelling the world and writing about it, Kate enjoys spending time at home working as a freelance editor.

Kevin Raub

Atlanta native Kevin started his career as a music journalist in New York, working for *Men's Journal* and *Rolling Stone* magazines. He ditched the rock 'n' roll lifestyle for travel writing and has written more than 95 Lonely Planet guides, focused mainly on Brazil, Chile, Colombia, the USA, India, Italy and Portugal. Raub also contributes to a variety of travel magazines in both the USA and UK. Along the way, the self-confessed hophead is in constant search of wildly high IBUs in local beers. Find him at www.kevinraub.net or follow him on Twitter and Instagram (@RaubOnTheRoad).

Andy Symington

Andy has written or worked on more than a hundred books and other updates for Lonely Planet (especially in Europe and Latin America) and other publishing companies, and has published articles on numerous subjects for a variety of newspapers, magazines and websites. He part-owns and operates a rock bar, has written a novel and is currently working on several fiction and nonfiction writing projects. Andy, from Australia, moved to northern Spain many years ago. When he's not off with a backpack in some far-flung corner of the world, he can probably be found watching the tragically poor local football side or tasting local wines after a long walk in the nearby mountains.

Greg Ward

Since his youthful adventures on the hippy trail to India, and living in northern Spain, Greg has written guides to destinations all over the world. As well as covering the USA from the Southwest to Hawaii, he has ranged on recent assignments from Corsica to the Cotswolds, and Dallas to Delphi. Visit his website, www.gregward.info, to see his favourite photos and memories.

Our Story

A beat-up old car, a few dollars in the pocket and a sense of adventure. In 1972 that's all Tony and Maureen Wheeler needed for the trip of a lifetime – across Europe and Asia overland to Australia. It took several months, and at the end – broke but inspired – they sat at their kitchen table writing and stapling together their first travel guide, *Across Asia on the Cheap*. Within a week they'd sold 1500 copies. Lonely Planet was born.

Today, Lonely Planet has offices in Franklin, London, Melbourne, Oakland, Dublin, Beijing, and Delhi, with more than 600 staff and writers. We share Tony's belief that 'a great guidebook should do three things: inform, educate and amuse'.

Our Writers

Simon Richmond

Journalist and photographer Simon Richmond has specialised as a travel writer since the early 1990s and first worked for Lonely Planet in 1999 on their *Central Asia* guide. He's long since stopped counting the number of guidebooks he's researched and written for the company, but countries covered include Australia, China, Greece, India, Indonesia, Iran, Japan, Malaysia, Mongolia, Myanmar (Burma), Poland, Russia, Singapore, South Africa, South Korea, Turkey and the USA. For Lonely Planet's website he's written features on topics from the world's best swimming pools to the joys of Urban Sketching – follow him on Instagram (@simonrichmond) to see some of his photos and sketches.

Kate Armstrong

Kate Armstrong has spent much of her adult life travelling and living around the world. A full-time freelance travel journalist, she has contributed to more than 50 Lonely Planet guides and trade publications and is regularly published in Australian and worldwide publications. She is the author of several books and children's educational titles.

Stuart Butler

Stuart has been writing for Lonely Planet for a decade and during this time he's come eye to eye with gorillas in the Congolese jungles, met a man with horns on his head who could lie in fire, huffed and puffed over snowbound Himalayan mountain passes, interviewed a king who could turn into a tree, and had his fortune told by a parrot. Oh, and he's met more than his fair share of self-proclaimed gods. When not on the road for Lonely Planet he lives on the beautiful beaches of southwest France with his wife and two young children.

More Writers

STAY IN TOUCH LONELYPLANET.COM/CONTACT

AUSTRALIA The Malt Store, Level 3, 551 Swanston St, Carlton, Victoria 3053
☎03 8379 8000,
fax 03 8379 8111

IRELAND Digital Depot, Roe Lane (off Thomas St), Digital Hub, Dublin 8, D08 TCV4, Ireland

USA 155 Filbert St, Ste 208, Oakland, CA 94607
☎510 250 6400,
toll free 800 275 8555,
fax 510 893 8572

UK 240 Blackfriars Road, London SE1 8NW
☎020 3771 5100,
fax 020 3771 5101

 twitter.com/lonelyplanet   facebook.com/lonelyplanet   instagram.com/lonelyplanet   youtube.com/lonelyplanet   lonelyplanet.com/newsletter